Voice Actor's Guide to Recording at Home and on the Road

Voice Actor's Guide to Recording at Home and on the Road

Harlan Hogan
Jeffrey P. Fisher

Course Technology PTR
A part of Cengage Learning

Australia • Brazil • Japan • Korea • Mexico • Singapore • Spain • United Kingdom • United States

COURSE TECHNOLOGY
CENGAGE Learning™

Voice Actor's Guide to Recording at Home and on the Road
Harlan Hogan
Jeffrey P. Fisher

Publisher and General Manager, Course Technology PTR: Stacy L. Hiquet

Associate Director of Marketing: Sarah Panella

Manager of Editorial Services: Heather Talbot

Marketing Manager: Mark Hughes

Acquisitions Editor: Orren Merton

Project/Copy Editor: Karen A. Gill

Technical Reviewer: Eldad Guetta

PTR Editorial Services Coordinator: Jen Blaney

Interior Layout Tech: ICC Macmillan Inc.

Cover Designer: Lon Czarnecki

Indexer: Sharon Shock

Proofreader: Brad Crawford

© 2009 Course Technology, a part of Cengage Learning.

ALL RIGHTS RESERVED. No part of this work covered by the copyright herein may be reproduced, transmitted, stored, or used in any form or by any means graphic, electronic, or mechanical, including but not limited to photocopying, recording, scanning, digitizing, taping, Web distribution, information networks, or information storage and retrieval systems, except as permitted under Section 107 or 108 of the 1976 United States Copyright Act, without the prior written permission of the publisher.

For product information and technology assistance, contact us at
Cengage Learning Customer & Sales Support, 1-800-354-9706

For permission to use material from this text or product,
submit all requests online at **www.cengage.com/permissions**
Further permissions questions can be e-mailed to
permissionrequest@cengage.com

Porta-Booth is a registered trademark of Wordsworth, Inc. All other trademarks are the property of their respective owners.

Library of Congress Control Number: 2007938250

ISBN-13: 978-1-59863-433-4

ISBN-10: 1-59863-433-X

Course Technology
25 Thomson Place
Boston, MA 02210
USA

Cengage Learning is a leading provider of customized learning solutions with office locations around the globe, including Singapore, the United Kingdom, Australia, Mexico, Brazil, and Japan. Locate your local office at: **international.cengage.com/region**

Cengage Learning products are represented in Canada by Nelson Education, Ltd.

For your lifelong learning solutions, visit **courseptr.com**

Visit our corporate Web site at **cengage.com**

Printed in the United States of America
1 2 3 4 5 6 7 11 10 09

For Steve Schatzberg:
S2, you always make me laugh,
always ask the great questions,
and always define the
true meaning of friendship.

—H2

For Brian Holmsten once again,
for his wonderful friendship
that I've continued to cherish
for all these years.
Thanks!

—JPF

Acknowledgments

Harlan and Jeffrey would like to thank Orren Merton and Mark Hughes of Cengage Learning for asking us to write an updated and expanded second go-round of *Voice Actor's Guide to Recording at Home and on the Road.* Also, our sincerest gratitude goes to our wonderful editors, Karen Gill and the acerbic, though imaginary, Prunella Sykes. They had the oft-Herculean task of changing our ramblings into grammatically correct and semicoherent phrases—a task made even more difficult by the plethora of lame jokes and silly definitions we found ourselves amused by. We were blessed to have the ever-creative, ever-patient Lon Czarnecki of Headcake Media shoot our crazy on-the-road recording photos and design the book's inventive front and back covers. And we'd be remiss not to acknowledge the constant support and patience of our families—not just when we're writing, but especially when we write. (Who do you think we try the lame jokes out on?)

Jeffrey would also like to thank Harlan, the best writing partner a person could ever have. It was even more fun writing the second edition than the first! Harlan claims he wrote some really nice stuff about Jeffrey, too, but both Karen and Prunella deleted them citing, "Redundant!" to which Harlan replied, "Ditto."

About the Authors

Harlan Hogan has more than 30 years' experience as a voice-over actor and is known for the scores of classic and contemporary ad slogans that have reached your ears through his voice, from "It's the cereal even Mikey likes" and "When you care enough to send the very best" to his daily thanks to "viewers like you for your generous contribution to your PBS station." He coauthored with Jeffrey Fisher the first edition of *The Voice Actor's Guide to Home Recording*. Harlan's book *VO: Tales and Techniques of a Voice-Over Actor* is a perennial best-seller. In addition to writing scores of commercials, he is the author of an award-winning video series for kids called *An Almost Painless Guide to Government*, a full-length play called *Bury the Show*, and both narrator and writer of Mythic Pictures' 17-part video documentary *America in the Twentieth Century*. He lives in the suburbs of Chicago and telecommutes everywhere via his home and on-the-road studio.

Jeffrey P. Fisher is an award-winning and in-demand sound designer who provides audio, video, music, writing, training, consulting, and media production services. He's also an award-winning instructor of audio and video production and post-production at the College of DuPage in Glen Ellyn, Illinois, and has taught at DePaul University in Chicago, Illinois. He writes extensively about music, sound, and video for print and the Web and has authored 11 books, including *Instant Sound Forge; Cash Tracks: Compose, Produce, and Sell Your Original Soundtrack Music and Jingles; Moneymaking Music; Ruthless Self-Promotion in the Music Industry*; and *Profiting from Your Music and Sound Project Studio.* He spends a lot of time in a dark room hunched over a computer working his magic on audio soundtracks for clients and independent films and documentaries, including the award-winning *The Craving Heart* and *So You Want Michael Madsen?*

Contents

Chapter 3 Choosing the Right Computer for Recording at Home and on the Road 23

Chapter 4 Assembling Your Home Studio—Hardware 45

Chapter 7
Home Recording—Away from Home 111

Chapter 8
Basic Production Techniques 125

Chapter 9
Teleportation—Long-Distance Direction 159

Chapter 10
Profitable Promotion 175

Chapter 11
Working the World Wide Web 187

Chapter 12
Advanced Production Techniques 207

Introduction

Hi. This is Harlan Hogan. As I prepared to write this opening treatise—you know, staring at the computer screen waiting for beads of blood to trickle down my forehead—I found myself reminiscing. Actually, I was just procrastinating, but let's call it nostalgia instead of laziness. It was April 17, 2004 …

> I'm seated at a long, long, table onstage at the Beverly Garland hotel in Hollywood. There are over 300 attendees, and I'm flattered to be in the company of some of the brightest voice-over performers and authors on the planet.
>
> The occasion is the *Voice Over Resource Guide's* "Meet the Authors" seminar—an opportunity for voice performers to hear from voice-over authors, including Elaine Clark (*There's Money Where Your Mouth Is*), Nancy Cartwright (of *Simpsons* fame and *My Life as a Ten-Year-Old Boy*), Alan Barzman (*Hearing Voices*), and many others. There were many stories, much laughter, and loads of questions.
>
> I was invited because my first book, *VO: Tales and Techniques of a Voice-Over Actor*, had just recently been published. Someone in the crowd asked me about the home studio section in my book, and I replied that, even while writing it, I realized that there could and should be a whole book on the subject just for voice performers. As I replied, "What we need is a nontechnical guide to home recording," I realized that subject would be my next book. Discussion and debate about home recording then began in earnest, and LA voice actor Steve Schatzberg asked me to show the crowd the on-the-road gear I had used just that morning to record a political spot from my hotel room.
>
> Joe Bevilacqua (*Scenes for Actors & Voices*, by Daws Butler) joined in and demonstrated his portable setup as I compulsively went into my 2004 standard song and dance that, in my opinion, home studio recording was where our business was inevitably moving.
>
> Now, those of you who have seen any of my standard songs and dances know they're not a pretty sight and, despite my enthusiasm, not everyone that day agreed with Joe and me. Some actors, studio owners, casting directors, and agents frankly didn't want to hear anything about recording from home, high-quality, inexpensive microphones, waveforms, or MP3 delivery.
>
> But burying your head in the sand doesn't make technology go away.

I've been a voice talent long enough to remember when many producers were outraged as voice and singing demos started being distributed on cassettes—after all, reel-to-reel tapes had much better fidelity. That's true, but cassettes and later CDs were so much easier to handle and play. Of course, today most demos exist only in cyberspace, where both convenience and quality are instantaneous.

As it turned out, a quantum shift in *where* and *how* we work *was* inevitable, fueled by affordable equipment and ever-easier-to-use software, coupled with an Internet-connected global marketplace for voice-over work. I was fortunate enough to meet Jeffrey Fisher, experienced audio engineer, musician, and author. He is one of those oh-so-rare experts who can make very complicated things seem simple. We decided to coauthor the first edition of *The Voice Actor's Guide to Home Recording.*

But so much has changed in a couple of years, and that's why you now hold a fresh copy of the completely revised and greatly expanded second edition with a slightly modified title!

The advances in home studio equipment and the ever-decreasing cost and complexity of recording at home (and on the road) have been dramatic, since our first edition came out in 2004 and the majority of voice performers are regularly auditioning and performing their sessions from home studios now.

It's important to always keep in mind that we voice actors are not trying to compete with commercial recording studios—we *are* competing, however, with other voice actors around the globe who have already embraced the wonders of ISDN and the Internet. Every voice actor I know loves to go to a professional studio and relish the luxury of having an engineer handle all the "techie" stuff. But reality is reality, and much of the time we are performing the engineering tasks ourselves, so we have to get good at it or we'll simply no longer be competitive with *our* competition.

Most talent agents and many casting directors, too, now embrace the MP3 audition delivery system, especially now that practically everything is auditioned—oftentimes nationwide. Our agents no longer have to spend long days in the audio booth recording actors. Internet delivery of auditions allows them to once again be agents, not engineers, but without a talent pool equipped with home studios, this scenario would be a dream.

Like everything in life, there is a downside to "instant" auditions. The time frame from the moment an agent gets a script to the time the producer wants it back gets shorter and shorter. In fact, just a few moments ago, I got a call from Joan Sparks at Stewart Talent asking if I could audition a script and have it to the potential client by Sunday morning. Not a problem. I'm happy to be asked, and it will just take a few minutes in my booth. The amazing part is that right now it's 7:30 on a Friday evening, and without a home studio, I couldn't deliver. It also confirms what an amazingly boring nightlife I have.

Being capable of recording yourself at home (or on location) means you won't miss auditions and sessions just because you're on a shoot, on vacation, or unwilling to arm wrestle your way through bumper-to-bumper traffic, spend 25 bucks to park, and then cool your heels in a waiting room rereading last November's *Hollywood Reporter* just to read a 30-second audition when you finally get your turn in the sound booth. With in-house facilities, you'll read it and e-mail it. It's that simple. So setting up a reasonably priced, personal recording studio and learning how to use it is what this book is all about.

Well, that's my take on it from a voice-actor's perspective. Now let's get Jeffrey's view as a recording professional.

Thanks, Harlan.

You know, some people might think I'm "putting myself out of work" by helping voice-overs set up and operate their own studios, but nothing could be further from the truth.

I'm Jeffrey Fisher, and when it comes to commercial work—radio, TV, films, documentary, corporate presentations, games, the Internet, and so on—time was and always will be money, no matter how the paradigm might change. When you spend less time making quality audio productions, you will also spend less money. Now, I know that keen insight is no great revelation, but more than ever, the need for speed permeates today's creative endeavors. It's all about shortened production and post-production schedules. Who can do the best work the fastest? That's the battle cry of purse-string-holding producers everywhere.

Simultaneously, these same producers and directors have become more technologically savvy. Although they might not know RAM from ... uh ... a ram, they do know that computers and other high-tech gear means things get done faster and better. And faster is cheaper. Of course, let's not forget that better is always good, too.

Time compression and gee-whiz technology—both basic and advanced—are real boons for the smart voice actor. How, you say? Simple. By taking over some of these time-consuming and burdensome chores, you make the work of an overloaded and deadline-conscious production team easier. When you can record yourself at home and e-mail back an audition almost instantly, you have shown your ability to be mindful and supportive of the speed-demon world of modern production. Better still, if you can record a broadcast-quality session, clean up your performance, and deliver the completed voice track fast, you will save the producer a lot of time and money. Best yet, when you can connect directly with the creatives via ISDN or Internet-based air-quality delivery programs like *Source-Connect*, *Audio TX*, and *Sound Streak* that deliver your performance in real time, you are a world-class competitor in the voice-over market.

The by-product of all this is that you will save yourself time and money, too! After an initial—albeit humble—investment in some basic audio production gear, your payback will be fast ... probably in only a few jobs. Also, the wear and tear on your body, mind, and vehicle produced by running to auditions and sessions all over the place will be significantly reduced. And while that kind of reward is often intangible, there is often a more tangible reward to taking this path, and that frequently involves cold hard cash.

Frankly, without taking advantage of the technology and approaches that we will delve into in these pages, you simply won't have a voice-over career. I hate to be harsh, but I'm not interested in hiring a VO who doesn't have his own studio and recording skills. I have better, more pressing things to do than record and edit performances that more often than not can be handled quite well indeed by a well-equipped and skilled VO.

This book is about harnessing recording technology to your personal advantage, which can be both good and bad. It's good in that you can use a recording setup to accomplish many of the tasks required by a voice-over career. It's bad because you might be a technophobe, uncomfortable with all those knobs, switches, and cables. Oh, those cables. Geek spaghetti. I can hear you saying to yourself, "If this book is anything like my (*insert electronic device that hates you here*) instructions, I'm putting it back on the shelf."

Stop. Wait a minute. Whoa. Don't close the cover just yet. We can promise you that this book will help you dip your toes into the recording waters in a simple, no-nonsense way. And if you stick with us, you'll be swimming the recording ocean painlessly.

The truth is, you *can* and *will* set up and run your own personal recording studio. More importantly, you will cross the chasm gleefully after you've devoured and applied the concepts in this book!

To be honest, it is a terrific time to be alive from a technological standpoint. The hardware and software available today is nothing short of amazing, and it's getting better all the time. Also, the usability factor has greatly improved. Devices continue to become simpler to use without sacrificing quality or features. You just need to look at an iPhone to see how far we've come both with the gadgets and our ability to actually use them. In fact, Apple's iPhone allows you to customize ring tones using an audio editor—a mini version of exactly what you'll be using to record and edit your auditions and sessions.

I've had the good fortune to work alongside novices and pros alike. I've also had the opportunity to train novices and pros. What I've discovered is that those who aren't afraid of technology—those who are willing to take some chances and explore the possibilities—are far more successful. People whose usually unfounded phobias paralyze them rarely seize the best opportunities. They get frustrated and ultimately fail. That's not you, right?

As one Neanderthal said millions of years ago, "Technology good, no be scared of new paradigm." Don't you be afraid, either. Technology and computers can make your life easier. They can frustrate you, but only if you let them. Technology is good when it works for you. And so it's part of your job to grab the new paradigm by its fluffy little ears and make it work for you. Don't be afraid of the computer or its peripherals. (Geek alert: peripherals = stuff you connect to the computer.) Treat your computer like the idiot savant it is and make it do what you ask. It will happily deliver (give or take a hiccup or two now and again).

And if we still can't convince you, then you will never fully realize the potential you have using your voice, your acting skills, a microphone, and a computer-based recorder. I promise the knobs will be few, the cables minimal, and the geek factor minimized to a few asides for the truly needy.

However, this is the second edition of the book.

And if one thing has been apparent in the intervening years between editions, it is this: most up-and-coming and established VOs no longer need to be convinced that having a studio is important. They now know that recording, editing, and delivery skills are required to have any modicum of success. Without a studio, all you have is your talent—and that's not enough to make it these days. Recording gear is simply a tool that enables you to create your product. It's no different from a carpenter's hammer—both are inexplicably linked and inseparable.

But that's not news to you. That's why you picked up this book and have agreed to take the journey. And for those of you who joined us previously, you can be sure that there will be far more new concepts to take your skills to the next level. We will cover the basics, dig into some advanced considerations, provide choices for all career levels and aspirations, present some strong opinions on what to do and what not to do, and provide the sound advice, specific instructions, and marching orders you need to be successful recording at home or on the road.

Here we go.

1 The New Paradigm—A Home Studio Is a Required Tool of the Trade

"Well, of course we talk. Don't everybody?"

—Jean Hagen as silent film star Lina Lamont (with a voice to peel paint . . .) in *Singin' in the Rain,* 1952, MGM

It's no secret that technology has fundamentally changed the way and the where that voice actors audition and perform. Actors have had to adapt to technological change and new opportunities long before the computer era. Radio, for example, required performers to act without being seen, and silent motion pictures were the opposite. Today, computer-based recording, the Internet, MP3s, ISDN, and inexpensive but professional-sounding recording gear represent a revolution in our business not unlike the invention of "the talkie." A 1930 edition of *Fortune Magazine* claimed, "The advent of American talking movies is beyond comparison the fastest and most amazing revolution in the whole history of industrial revolutions." Overwrought hyperbole aside, home studio and remote recording are amazing revolutions. More importantly, they have become a necessary and *expected* tool of our trade—if we hope to compete in today's voice-over world. Of course, you know that. That's why you bought this book.

If the thought of setting up your studio and suddenly becoming a recording engineer intimidates you, you're not alone. Relax. We'll show you the basic skills you need to survive and succeed in this new paradigm and as much as humanly possible do it in a nontechnical way. How? We've already helped hundreds of other actors in the first edition of this book. Jeffrey and I have received countless letters and e-mails thanking us for demystifying the whole home recording process. Most rewarding is hearing how many performers now find the recording and editing process actually fun.

More than likely, you will too.

Home recording lets you work on your technique in a stress-free environment and really hone your voice-over craft. Keep in mind that your new audio production skills will be just as important to you—a twenty-first century actor pursuing voice work—as is your training in movement, makeup, improvisation, and speech.

Nothing stands still in the creative world, and those who refuse to learn new skills generally get left behind, like our celluloid friend Lina Lamont when her voice had to be dubbed for her talking picture debut, much to her career-ending chagrin.

We'll be assuming throughout this book that you have some basic computer skills—you don't need to be an expert, but at least have an understanding of the fundamentals of opening and saving files, navigating, using the mouse, and accessing the Internet. If you've ever used a word processing program and are comfortable selecting, copying, cutting, and pasting text, you'll find audio editing familiar. It's like word processing only with sound. Instead of manipulating words, you'll select, copy, cut, and paste waveforms on your computer monitor (see Figure 1.1). The basic skills are really that simple.

The Business of Getting Business—Auditions

Performing and making money doing voice-overs starts with the biggest challenge an actor faces—getting the work. Even the most established and successful voice-over actors audition. A lot. But auditioning is costly in both time and money.

All across the country and around the world, auditioning voice scripts from home-based studios is now the norm. Recording final scripts is almost as common. The Internet and MP3 files have made it all so easy. If you don't know, MP3s are audio files that are a

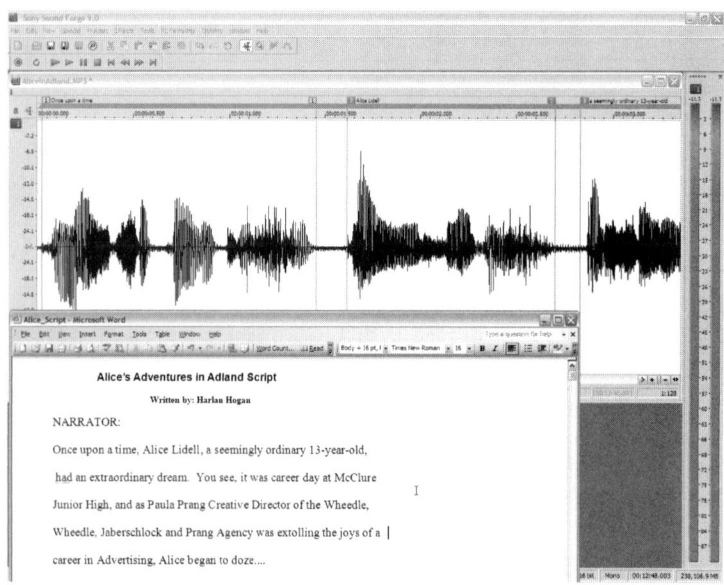

Figure 1.1 Word processing with sound.

more manageable file size, which makes them easier to e-mail. They don't sound quite as good as a CD recording, but for most voice work—especially auditions—they are perfectly acceptable.

In some instances, you will need to send a better quality file to those clients who demand it. (One of them has a last name that rhymes with *isher*.) These files are usually way too large to e-mail (see Figure 1.2), so you may need to implement FTP or use a file sending service (more on these later, of course).

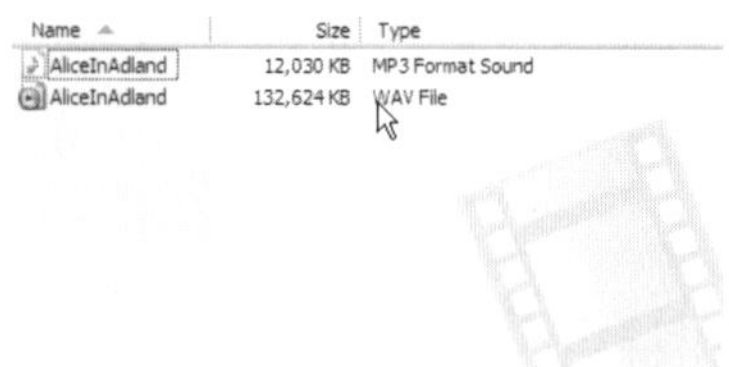

Figure 1.2 WAV file size/MP3 comparison.

Auditioning and recording sessions using home studios is truly a win-win proposition for everyone involved—actors, casting agents, talent agents, and producers. Aside from the obvious convenience, it means you no longer have to miss out on important auditions or sessions because you are out of town on vacation or hopefully on-location shooting a major motion picture. We'll show you how the same skills and much of the same equipment that you'll use in your home studio can be taken on the road so you can send voice recordings to anyone from anywhere.

The Business of Getting Business—Sessions

For actual sessions (and some auditions), you'll usually need to get direction from a producer/director, so you'll use the good old-fashioned telephone for a "phone patch" or a high-tech digital ISDN "phone," or Internet-based software solution. However, regular phone lines (called POTS lines, which sounds more sophisticated than "Plain Old Telephone Service") don't have enough bandwidth to deliver air-quality audio. Therefore, after the session, you'll send the files to the client via the Internet. On the other hand, the digital phone lines used with an ISDN codec (coder/decoder) *can* send broadcast-ready audio in real time. In the past few years, new software programs like *Source-Connect* (see Figure 1.3) and *Audio TX* have been developed that use the Internet to send and receive air-quality audio in real time. Just like ISDN, when the session is over, you're done. Well, except for filling out the paperwork.

Today, a great many producers simply expect voice talent to have professional-quality home studios, and your access to one often plays a key role in who gets the job. Producers want to cast without worrying about where that talent is located and without the

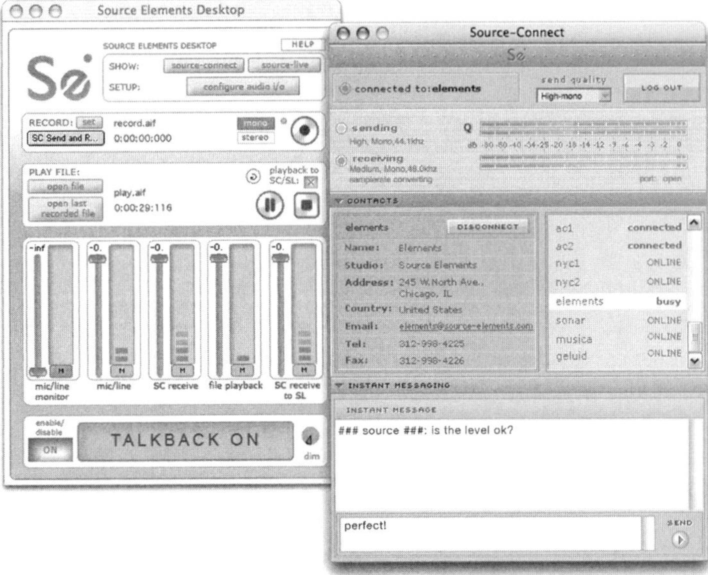

Figure 1.3 *Source-Connect.*

hassle and considerable costs of booking two separate recording studios. Some clients—the ones we all love—are actually willing to pay you an additional fee for the use of your own studio!

The Business of Getting Business—Voice Demos

In the voice-over world, you need a top-notch voice demo. And you must keep that demo up to date. But the cost of producing and constantly revising a voice demo seems to escalate as fast as the price of a barrel of oil.

The most expensive part of producing voice demos is that daunting "What-if?" phase. You assemble all the audio clips from your recent work, or you pay studio time to record "created" commercials, narrations, and promos and assemble them into 1- or 2-minute masterpieces of dynamite audio. After paying a hefty studio bill, you play your new creations for your agent or a producer or two and—guess what? It's back to the studio to "cut and paste"—moving this spot there, rerecording that documentary, lowering the sound effects on the movie trailer, and eliminating the middle spot that your agent said, as pleasantly as possible, "Just sucks." *(Now there's a term you two have no doubt heard from editors who preceded me! —Prunella Skykes, your editor)*

This ongoing tweaking makes the bills stack up and the money come out of your pocket, because that "perfect" demo hasn't created any income—yet.

Finally, you're finished! Some CD copies are ordered, and your demos go up on your Web site and your agent's. Then you land a major network commercial, one that you and your agent agree you must have on your demo. So it's back to the studio, to do it all—and pay for it all—over again.

This is where your home-based recording studio can save you thousands of dollars, while keeping you competitive. You can record "created" spots to your heart's content, working for the perfect take. You can assemble the first draft—what many engineers call the rough cut—to test with your agent. Then you can recut and remix it over and over with nary a bill in the mailbox from your favorite studio.

When you are happy—okay, let's face it, you will never be 100 percent content with your demo; no actor ever is—you should take your audio files to a professional recording engineer to "sweeten" them and make the final version for duplication and Web posting. Don't skip this step; the little that you'll pay for the engineer's professional expertise is invaluable at this stage. Also, it's good business, because many audio engineers recommend actors for jobs. So the studio fees you pay often pay off as a networking investment.

You just might find that you have an affinity for the demo assembly process. It may be so interesting that you'll want to begin producing and recording demos for other actors—for a modest fee, of course. That's a nice return on your recording equipment investment, don't you think?

The Business of Getting Business—The Internet

The Internet is not only our electronic post office for sending our voices coast to coast and worldwide. The Web is an even better way to showcase our voice talent than traditional media, like CDs. As any voice-over from newbie to old pro knows, the expense of designing, duplicating, and distributing our voice-demos on disc can be astronomical. Postage costs alone are staggering, not to mention the packing envelopes, cases, labels, and cover art. Much like the cassette of yesteryear (see Figure 1.4), the days of shipping shiny plastic discs are thankfully over!

Your Web site offers a much better, more cost-effective way to make your demos available to prospective employers (see Figure 1.5). The expense of maintaining a basic Web site is marginal compared to traditional hard copy distribution. With your home recording studio, you can change, update, and customize your voice demos as often as you want and simply "post" them on your personal Web page, as well as to your agent's and other Web-based voice-over sites.

Figure 1.4 What is this?

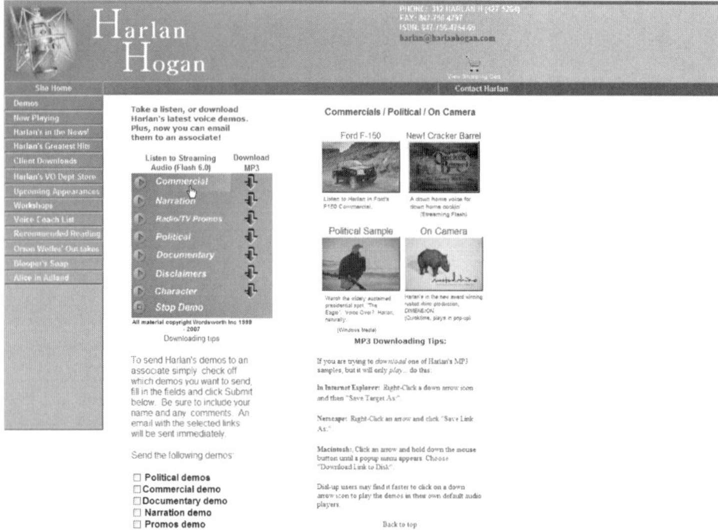

Figure 1.5 Web site demo player.

The Business of Getting Business—Making Money Recording at Home

Your little recording rig coupled with your soon-to-be-acquired audio engineering skills—and your acting talent—can even earn you some extra money. You may get confident enough to take on audio production for projects including TV/radio spots, on-hold messages, audio books, and even video soundtracks.

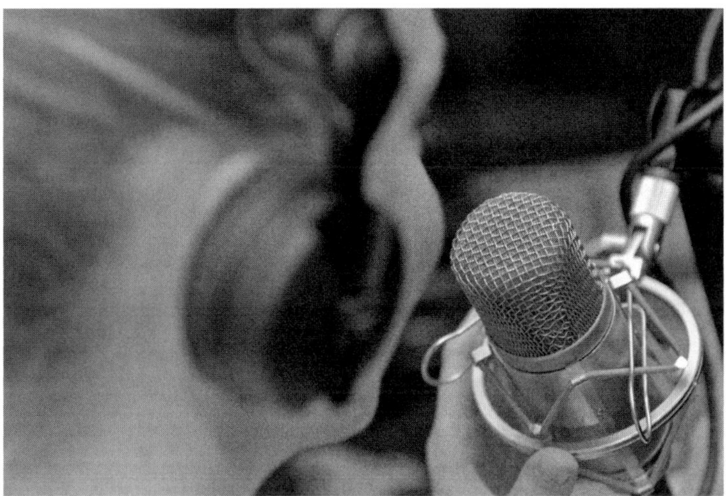

The Business of Getting Business—Studio Speak

If you've ever taken up a new hobby or sport, you know the hardest part is learning all the terminology so you can "talk the talk." You can learn the basics of sailing in an hour or so but spend years figuring out the lingo: halyards, vangs, upper and lower shrouds are pretty incomprehensible terms to most landlubbers. Did you know that sailboats don't have ropes? Nope, that there long stringy thing is a line, matey. Course, those lines that control the sails are called sheets, sailor.

While actors can often wax poetic on the subtle nuances taught by Stanislavski, Meisner, and Strasberg in "actor-speak," they find themselves flummoxed by the seemingly arcane phrases tossed around in the recording studio. From compression ratios, "Would you prefer a soft or hard knee, sir?" to decibels and waveforms (the nonsailing kind), we promise to demystify the nomenclature enough for you to "talk the talk." And we'll do all this with an eye—and ear—to get you started on the fun parts of recording, editing, mixing, and delivering your own audio.

The Business of Getting Business—Global Agents

Technology has fundamentally changed the way agents *and* clients cast, interact, and work with voice talent, too. At face value, that may sound like an overstatement, but it's not. *(Funny you boys would talk about face value. Judging this book by its cover—and I do—face value isn't your collective strength. —Prunella)*

Casting

Producers seeking voice talent used to hold auditions at their place of business, at an agent's office, or at a casting director's. Now this occurs less and less. Most producers simply e-mail script copy complete with talent direction and deadlines to an agent, casting director, or one of the Internet-based casting services like Voice Bank. A short time later, MP3 auditions flow in from around the country for convenient stay-at-work casting.

Now the agent/actor relationship is a supply-chain partnership, with the agent filtering the right scripts to the appropriate talent in the agency's stable and those performers promptly zipping auditions back to the agent to be sent to the potential employer.

Interaction

Technology has allowed many actors to have multiple agents around the country and the globe, expanding their opportunities. Agents, in turn, can expand their roster of talented professionals without geographic boundaries.

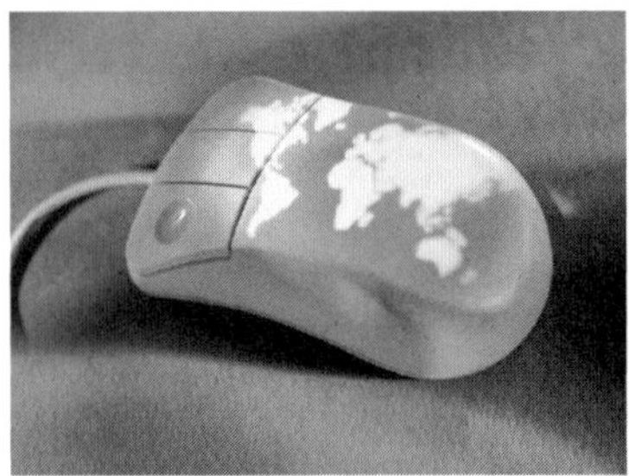

There are downsides to this, of course. The personal, day-to-day and face-to-face relationship is quickly disappearing. Those who enjoyed the social side of this business may find it difficult to accept this new reality. But the fact is, even local talent send in their MP3 auditions and avoid a costly commute and even costlier parking. Agents are finally spared the task of sitting in "the booth" recording actor after actor. Now they can spend that time doing the real work of booking and negotiating.

Sessions

For our employers, recording and directing performers over the phone, Internet, and ISDN is now so common that many producers rarely step foot in a studio. When they do—more often than not—there is no live performer in the booth. (Of course, we've both had sessions where the talent appeared to be dead, and their performance supported that assumption. Here we're actually talking about the booth being empty.)

Producers have a worldwide choice of talent, and since so many performers have pro-quality home studios, it doesn't add to the cost. Sessions from home frequently occur even when the voice talent lives in the same town, just up the street. The fact is this: it's easier and quicker to just "dial 'em up."

Naturally, the human dynamic changes when we can't see each other (the reverse of the silent picture) and talent and directors have to verbally communicate very clearly as they work together to fine-tune the performance.

The Business of Getting Business—Audition Web Sites

Technology has also created new casting venues via the Web. In essence, these auditioning sites bypass traditional agents altogether. Most charge the performer rather than the producer a fee—a quantum shift from the traditional commissions paid to an agent. These sites vary widely in the quality and quantity of the material to be auditioned. Some encourage a bidding war between talent, while other sites accept only legitimate work at fair performer fees. Some sites will add anyone willing to pay the freight, and others are very selective, taking only a limited number of top-level voice actors. The bottom line is that with Internet voice casting sites, it is both buyer *and* seller beware. Still, these new venues offer another source of opportunity for voice actors thanks again to technology and . . . the home studio revolution!

A Note to Podcasters When we wrote the first edition of this book, few people had ever heard of a podcast. Shortly after the book's publication, podcasts, like blogs, iTunes, and YouTube, exploded. Personal broadcasting became a reality, and many podcasters embraced our book as a no-nonsense, nontechnical resource.

Thanks for your support of the previous book, and welcome to this new edition.

As a matter of fact, many voice actors who we've trained in home recording have discovered podcasting as a great way to promote their work. Actors, like our good friend Jeff Hoyt, regularly produce original podcasts from their home studio, like Jeff's often-hysterical *Hoytus Interruptus*.

So, even though we named this book *Voice Actor's Guide* . . . , feel free to get out a Sharpie and scribble in *podcaster* everywhere we reference *actor*.

2 Recording from the Comfort of Home—Seven Easy Steps to Get Started

"Don't worry. As long as you hit that wire with the connecting hook at precisely 88 mph the instant lightning strikes the tower, everything will be fine."

—Christopher Lloyd as Dr. Emmet Brown, *Back to the Future,* 1985, Amblin Entertainment

Well, heck, Michael J. Fox had it easy. It took only a lousy three steps to get him back to the future. You, on the other hand, have seven-plus things to accomplish to get you to your voice-over future.

So what do you need to get "on the air" fast? Here's a get-started-now primer that outlines the basics of recording at home in a no-nonsense, nontechnical way. You'll find the real detail in subsequent chapters. Think of this chapter as the overview of what you're really getting into. (And you *do* want to get into it.) This chapter forms the foundation upon which the rest of the book builds.

If you're somewhat further along with your technical skills, you may want to skip this chapter but, of course, you'd miss some clever repartee. (*Ed. Note: That remains to be seen. —Prunella*) We'd like to begin our mutual journey by taking a quick look at the seven basics of home recording and delivery.

(1) Computer

We can't stress enough how today's voice actor—actually any actor—needs access to a computer to compete.

Period.

So, first and foremost, let's start with a decent computer. A laptop or desktop will do. Laptops are generally more expensive, but they do double-duty if you're a road warrior—working with you on location or on vacation. Today's desktops and laptops are equally powerful, so that point is moot. Mac or PC, silver, white, or pink-polka dots with leopard print trim—it really doesn't matter what you choose as long as it appeals to not only your sense of style, but your pocketbook. Choose a computer that feels right—intuitively—to your working style.

Thankfully, the demands of audio production for basic, quality voice recording do *not* require you to have the latest, greatest hardware. You can really get by with a rather basic setup for 97.3 percent of your voice work.

All right, maybe it's only 96.9 percent.

Okay, we just made up a percent—because we know that damn near anything you're likely to record will be just fine on any computer that was made within the past five years.

However, if your computer still requires an ink ribbon and Wite-Out, it's time to invest in something a bit more modern. Rest assured—we'll discuss the many options currently available in excruciatingly greater detail in Chapter 3, "Choosing the Right Computer for Recording at Home and on the Road."

An up-to-date computer gives you four distinct advantages:

- It lets you record your voice.
- It lets you edit your recordings and present your voice in the best light.
- It lets you deliver your voice performance to anyone, anywhere via the Web.
- It lets you operate and promote your voice-over career.

You might expect one more bullet on this list: "It lets you record better sound." But you would be... wrong! You see, computers don't really have a sound (other than annoying fan noise, keyboard clicking, and "You've got mail!" nonsense). The *quality* of sound recordings in your computer comes from several other components that we'll discuss in a moment.

Your shiny new computer won't do all the things we want it to right out of the box; you have to add a few more pieces to complete the puzzle.

(1a) High-Speed Internet Access

Do we even have to mention the need for high-speed Internet access? Sound files are large to send and receive, so speed is of the essence. The voice-over world evolves quickly, and you need Web access at fast speeds to compete. Also, you need a Web site to promote your abilities. Since having a computer without high-speed Internet access is akin to having a Ferrari without wheels, we've included this little tidbit here instead of separating it out as its own step.

(2) Microphone

Your voice comes from the vocal cords in your throat vibrating in ways that make people actually willing to pay you money to speak. Unfortunately, your computer doesn't recognize your dulcet tones on their own; it needs some friends—like the microphone.

A microphone actually captures the energy from your speech and turns it into another form of energy. Surely, you fondly remember—as do we—this axiom from graduation requirement 107-C: Fundamentals of Physics: "Energy cannot be created or destroyed, only transformed from one kind of energy into another." In a mic's case, your voice gets transformed first into mechanical energy and then into electrical energy.

Okay, in the event that you didn't excel in physics class like one of us (*and I can guess which one—Prunella*), perhaps this explanation will suffice: "In a land of orcs, wizards, and ogres, a mysterious force exists where human speech turns into a magical flow of sparkly fairy dust by a stick-shaped magical wand. This dust carries the whispering voice along a strand of gossamer copper filament into a shiny, whirring magical box where it is transformed into a beautiful soundtrack of life, captured and preserved for eternity."

Either way, the quality of the microphone (stick-shaped magic wand, if you insist . . .) is important.

Cheap mics sound cheap. Expensive mics cost a lot of money but, surprisingly, not all expensive mics sound that good.

The built-in mic—the cheapie that shipped with your computer—is useless for anything other than dictation or a call on Skype. But there is good news: quality, very good- to great-sounding mics abound today, most manufactured in China and former Soviet geographies, and they sound almost as good as the fabled German-made gems of the past.

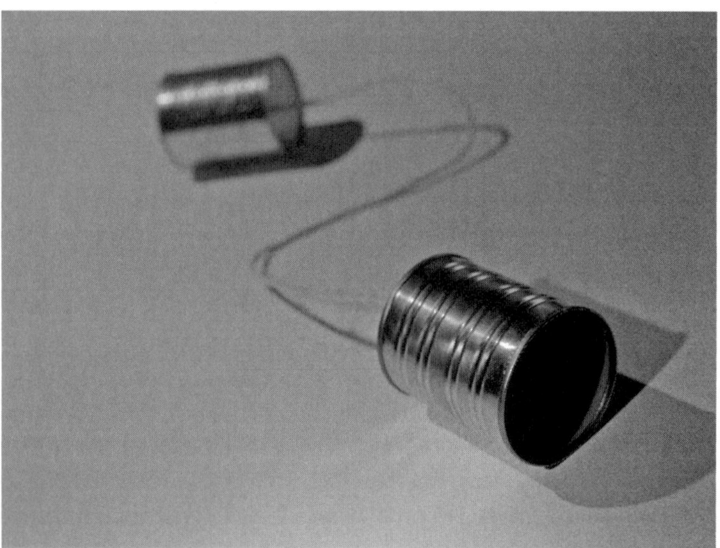

Finding the right microphone, one that complements *your* voice, is the journey you need to be willing to take. All mics sound different—sometimes subtly and other times amazingly dissimilar. What works for Harlan may not work for you. At all. Find the right mic for your voice, and invest in it. Your recordings will shine.

We can hear some of you screaming, "Just tell me the right mic to buy, and shut up already." Some of you may be nicer than that rude reader, of course. We really do understand your pain. The problem is, we don't really know what the best mic is for you. There's a reason why there are dozens and dozens of mics to choose from. There's a reason we continue to test new mics all the time—often with surprising and pleasant results. We're still searching for that elusive Holy Grail microphone, too.

Meanwhile, we need to be content with some tried and true examples. Without going into too much detail (that's what Chapter 3 is about), consider a large-diaphragm condenser mic. Generally, this mic works the best for spoken word voice-overs. You can spend from $59 to $10,000 on such a mic. And, of course, you'll need some hardware to go with it, because hand holding a mic gets old, exhausting, and noisy fast. You'll need a suitable stand to hold the mic, plus an audio cable and a pop filter.

But even with a solid mic choice, it is still only one part of the chain.

(3) Microphone Preamplifier

We told you that mics put out electricity (fairy dust to some of you), but it is really just a tiny trickle. It's not enough energy for the computer to munch on at all. Therefore, you need a device that boosts the output of the microphone to a suitable level. This is called a microphone preamplifier, or preamp for short.

Much like the mic itself, the quality of the preamp imparts its distinctive tone on your recordings. Typically, the stock preamp included with computers is inferior. The makers probably spent 50 cents on the device at best, and just like anything else in today's world, you don't get much for your four bits.

Oh, it'll work in a pinch, but it'll probably sound thin, muffled, and ______________. (*Insert derogatory adjective here.*) The computer's built-in preamp won't win you the praises of agents, casting directors, or others who want to hear you at your best.

But wait... there's "bad" news. All large-diaphragm condenser mics need additional power to work. This power usually comes through the preamp in the form of what's known as phantom power.

SFX: Scary music...

Phantom power is what gives those monsters that live under the bed the ability to subsist on cracker crumbs and mismatched socks until one day, when you least expect it—they leap forth to terrorize children of all ages.

SFX: Needle scratches across vinyl record...

Actually, phantom power is no big deal—power is sent to mics that need it using the same microphone cable. Typical mic inputs on computers, however, do *not* supply the necessary power, so professional-level mics won't work directly with the computer.

So what do you do?

(4) Audio Interface

Getting pro-level sound in and out of a computer requires an audio interface—sometimes known as a sound card or an A to D converter (analog to digital, A/D, or ADC). This is just another piece of hardware that's attached to the little wheel where the hamster runs inside your computer—or not. Most computers ship with a low-quality sound card. Laptops, in particular, are notorious for their lo-fi sound capabilities. Those cheapie internal sound cards work fine for games, Web surfing, Internet phone calls, video conferencing, and so forth, but for professional-sounding voice-overs, they just don't cut the mustard, the cheese, flimsy Formica look-alike countertops, or even acoustic foam!

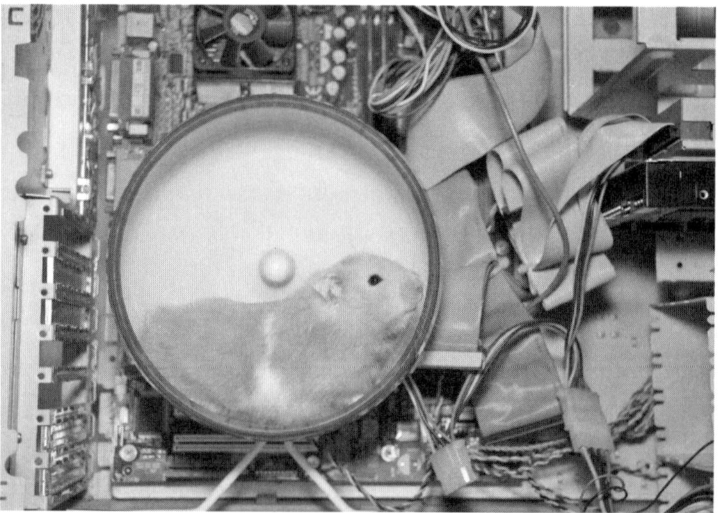

The audio interface/sound card has a critical function. It turns the electricity that the mic pumps out into a digital stream that the hamster... er, computer... recognizes. While it doesn't have a sound, *per se,* this digital conversion is important, as that's what you really record, edit, and eventually send out. Amazingly, your voice will be reduced by this device to a string of 0s and 1s. (And you thought the magic wand thing was far-fetched.)

You need to invest in a pro-level audio interface that replaces the one that shipped with your computer. This must have a high-quality microphone preamp that supplies phantom power to your professional microphone.

There is a myriad of choices, including USB and FireWire-based designs. We'll explore those in greater detail in Chapter 3.

(4a) USB Microphones

What if you could have a mic, preamp, phantom power, and digital converter all in one? Enter the USB-based microphone that simply plugs into your computer's USB port, gets power from it, and quickly delivers those 0s and 1s to your recording software. They're plug and play all the way—but with a few drawbacks.

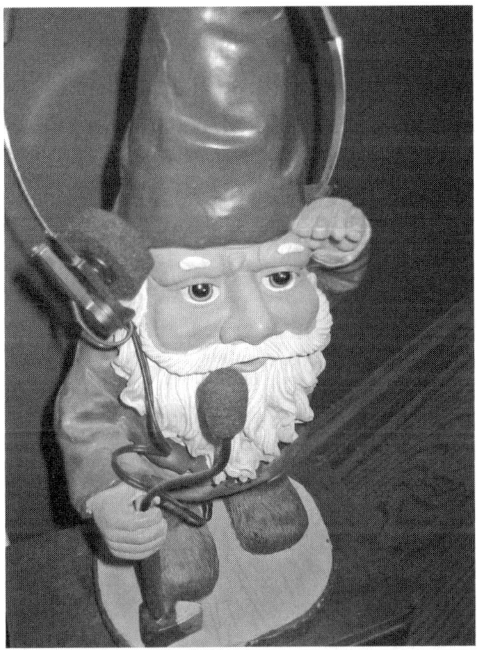

Many people love the obvious simplicity of USB microphones, and they work pretty well overall. Our only complaint is that most of the USB mics today don't sound all that great. Good, not *great*. We're also concerned that if you—like most of us—have a limited budget, buying only a USB mic limits its use in other situations. You can't plug it into a mixing board, for example, or use it onstage.

Another potential negative is that cord length for USB devices is limited to a maximum of 15 feet, so you may not be able to get far enough away from your computer to avoid picking up fan noise, hamster wheel squeaks, and the like. If you have set up a recording booth (and you can bet there will be lots of detail on that in Chapter 7, "Home Recording—Away from Home."

Finally, many USB mics do not let you hear yourself in your headphones as you record. You have to play back what you record to hear how good (or how bad) your performance was and determine whether there was any extraneous noise being recorded that you didn't notice because you were too busy talking. Most VOs prefer to hear themselves on headphones as they record, but many of these mics don't make that possible. Recently, several USB microphones were developed that include a tiny headphone jack on the mic itself to address the monitoring problem.

However, we have a better solution up our sleeves. Forget everything we just told you and go out right now and buy [*censored*], two [*censored*], and a [*censored*]. (*You have to wait until the next chapter to learn what those things are. —Prunella*) [*Expletive deleted.*]

(5) Recording Software

Computers do the tasks we ask of them because of software programs, so you'll need a program that's dedicated to recording audio. There are some who say you must have a fancy recording tool to turn in quality work. That is, of course, utter bunk but promoted through clever marketing by companies with very deep pockets who'd love to take your hard-earned cash. Some of the most popular programs are—in fact—wretched overkill for our purposes.

Since the mic, preamp, and sound card are what *really* give you your "sound," the software that records that sound matters very little. Features aside, it's still just zeros and ones as far as the software is concerned. A great many Mac users find the included iLife program works just fine for their voice recordings. Although PC users don't have a similar standard program included with their computer, there are several inexpensive (some free!) programs that work exceptionally on that platform and are a download away.

In all cases, the software you choose must let you record, edit, fix mistakes, compile the best bits, and save both a high-quality file and an MP3. There are many other things you can do with more sophisticated software, but for most of us, those features are "nice-to have," not "need-to-have."

(6) Speakers and Headphones

We bet you know what we're going to say next. The built-in/typical computer speakers aren't good enough for professional voice-over work. You also know by now that we won't recommend those earbuds that shipped with your MP3 player as a high-quality alternative to a good set of headphones—"cans" in studio vernacular.

While you don't need audiophile-level speakers or headphones, you do need *good* quality ones that tell you the truth about your recording. If your speakers/headphones lie, you may make misinformed decisions and send inferior quality recordings out the proverbial door.

(7) A Room of Your Own

To record a clear, intimate voice track, you need to keep noise out of your finished recording. If you live near a noisy part of town, say an airport, we have a simple solution—move.

Seriously, there are some uncomplicated precautions you can take to ensure your recordings don't sound like they were recorded in the subway tunnel at rush hour.

Obviously, locate your recording area away from noisy equipment, like computer fans and heating/air conditioning air ducts. The farther you can locate your microphone away from noise sources, the better.

You can dramatically improve the sound of your recordings by simply getting closer to the mic. The farther away you are from it, the more you pick up the room around you. Your voice starts to sound thin and distant, like a home video, and the listener hears a hollow and boomy "box," instead of the tight "studio sound" we are all accustomed to hearing on radio and TV.

That's it. Those are seven critical first steps to get you started. Now that you've been suitably prepared, it's time to make the smart buying decisions that make sense for your career and budget.

To paraphrase Bette Davis as Margo Channing in *All About Eve,* "Get out your check-books. It's going to be a bumpy night!"

3 Choosing the Right Computer for Recording at Home and on the Road

"No 9000 computer has ever made a mistake or distorted information. We are all, by any practical definition of the words, foolproof and incapable of error."

—Douglas Rain voice-over as The HAL 9000 computer, *2001: A Space Odyssey*, 1968, MGM

So we all know the digital age has dawned. But what does that mean to voice actors? A lot! Digital refers to the computer technology we use in our daily personal and business lives. This includes cell phones, MP3 players, and yes, actual, physical computers—those lumps of plastic you see gathering dust on desks and sliding through airport X-ray machines in dingy gray containers.

Today, you need to get your voice into the digital world, and only one tool can take you there efficiently and effectively—your computer.

An investment in a suitable computer system will become your central technological hub, around which your home/portable studio—indeed, your entire voice-acting career—revolves.

You'll use it as a recorder capturing your spoken word performances. Even better, your computer software will help you tweak those recordings and put your best work forward. The computer will also allow you to save your work in files that you can send digitally, anywhere in the world.

Cassettes are long gone—now just a blip on the Smithsonian's radar. Even shiny compact discs are trending downward toward extinction. Now you can simply e-mail your voice. And a computer is how that happens.

Your computer can do more than just record your voice and send your files, though. It can help you promote your career and handle your business matters: Web surfing, e-mailing, writing, promoting, bookkeeping, and so much more. Having your own computer is the only way to effectively compete in the VO world, and choosing the right one is what this chapter is all about.

Plain and simple: you need to get your voice "digitized" and into the computer for the following reasons:

- **Quality.** Digital recordings are far superior to almost any other format available today. When it comes to audio recording, they are low noise and faithfully reproduce the sounds you record. Pound for pound (which is really dollar for dollar), you can put together a high-quality recording studio in your home or build a portable rig for fractions of pennies of what it cost less than a decade ago to build an analog or analog/digital counterpart.
- **Speed.** Working in the digital domain is fast and efficient. You can edit your sound recordings just like you edit a document in a word processor, making your performances perfectly timed and perfectly delivered.
- **Ease.** Most recording software today is fairly easy to set up and use. It works much like a familiar cassette deck, but with far more powerful features. And it sounds infinitely better than any cassette ever did!
- **Flexibility.** You can deliver your finished recordings via e-mail to an agency or client.

Now, some of you might wonder if a standalone recording device of some kind might work just as well. There are recorders available today (see Figure 3.1) that are all-in-one boxes that include the built-in mics, external microphone inputs, preamps, digital recorder, and more. These devices work fine, *but* they lack the Internet connectivity of a computer/recorder.

Figure 3.1 Standalone recorder.

If you already have a computer, then use this chapter to make sure it's suitable for professional voice recording. (Chances are, it's fine.) If you're shopping for a new system, then the information here will be invaluable.

PC or Mac?

When it comes to computers, there are, of course, two choices. Do you buy a Mac or a PC? There is actually a third choice—computers that run the Linux operating system. However, since Linux is for those who already possess their degrees from Geekdom University (and if that's you, why did you buy this book?), we'll stick to the two most popular operating systems here.

> Macs are better than PCs.
>
> My PC can beat up your dad's Mac.

Arrgh! We're confident that the debate over which is better will continue forever. Both platforms work well. Both hang and crash. Both make a loud noise when they hit the ground after being tossed from a third-floor window. Both are easy to learn and hard to understand at times. Both have secret tricks that only your 12-year-old nephew knows. And both are equal when it comes to condescending and confounding stupidity—neither has the corner on that! Most importantly, since audio is our primary purpose here, one platform doesn't sound better than the other, because it's what you plug into the computer that gives you a particular sound.

Therefore, it really doesn't matter which platform you choose; it comes down to software. And the software you need to record your voice is readily available for both PC and Mac environments. Today's Macs can even run the Windows operating system side by side with their own (using a software add-in such as Boot Camp). That means that even if you find a PC software solution you really love, you can go ahead and run it on a Mac.

Although we'll primarily feature PC-based software in this book's illustrations, the basic concepts you learn will be completely applicable to any Mac-based software as well.

The only real decision you need to make is whether you want a desktop system or a laptop. If you want portability, a laptop is your only choice. If you prefer or need to be tied to a desk, then either will do. Laptops can be just as powerful as desktops, but generally desktop computers are less expensive when similarly powered. You may want both, which is the Harlan route. Or you may want five (four desktops and a laptop), which is the Fisher way. (*Don't ask! —JPF*)

So which computer should you buy? Our advice for getting the computer you need to record, edit, mix, and deliver your voice is really quite simple. Buy the best model you can afford! Get the fastest processor, the biggest hard drive(s), and the most RAM you can for the money you have available.

Virtually any computer you purchase new off the shelf today will be more than adequate for voice-over recording. Even if you decide to expand into more complicated multi-track audio production—such as adding music and sound effects to voice tracks—today's desktop and laptop computers will serve you well.

Notice that we said "virtually"—that's our premeditated out for readers who e-mail us later whining that the computer they bought off some guy in an overcoat on a street corner didn't work for audio. Ditto for "business" computers. Those systems designed exclusively for business tasks typically are underpowered in the audio department. So shop for models that brag about their music, digital video/photo, and similar capabilities. These are the multimedia powerhouses that you should consider buying.

There is a caveat for those actors who may want to edit digital video. If that's your plan now or in the future, you'll need an even more robust system. It doesn't have to be super high-end, just more powerful than the typical audio-only choice.

After reading this chapter, toddle on down to your local brick-and-mortar computer superstore—Best Buy, Circuit City, Dell, Fry's, et al—or head online and see what you can afford. As of this writing (2008), desktops and laptops that hover in the $1,000 range are perfect for a budding voice-over career. Expect to spend a little bit more for video work.

Since everybody is on a budget of some kind, we suggest you watch for deals often offered by the major computer vendors. They regularly run specials and packages that include enticing payment options. Recently, Dell offered an 18-month, no-interest system with a great payment option. That enabled one of us to get a *very* powerful computer system for about $150 a month.

Software Drives the Hardware

Since software is such an important consideration, make it your first choice. Then you can buy the computer platform that it runs most efficiently and intuitively on. (Remember what we said about Macs and PC software a few paragraphs ago.)

Always choose software that makes sense for *your* brain; that's the intuitive part. Fisher loves Sony's *Sound Forge/Vegas*; Hogan loves Adobe's *Audition*. Both systems do the job, but we each intuitively prefer different audio software. Harlan tried and tried and tried to like *Mackie Tracktion*—lots of people love it—but for him, it just didn't click with the way his brain functions (*when it does—Prunella*).

Don't let anyone—including us—tell you the software to buy (though we'll give you some guidelines in the next chapter). You have to make a choice that *you* like. We don't care if it costs $50 or $5,000—if you can use it without fighting with it, you've made a good choice. If upon working with it for a little time, it still confounds you, it's not the best software *for you*. Try something else!

Ahhh, but how do you discover which audio software *you* like the most? The best way to find out is to download a demo version and start playing with it. Most audio software companies offer fully or nearly fully operational demos of their programs for free on the Internet. They may expire in a few days, and they constantly remind you to buy the software, but that's okay. The evaluation period is usually sufficient for you to see and hear if the audio software will meet your needs.

Often these same vendors sell "lite" or "dummed-down" versions of their flagship products for significantly lower prices. For example, you can buy *Sound Forge 9* (which is the Pro version) or get by with *Sound Forge Audio Studio*, which has fewer features but is about 20 percent of the price of its older, wiser sibling. Most VOs will find the less expensive version perfectly acceptable.

Note that most audio software is music-centric and aimed primarily at musicians and music-makers. This can often intimidate voice actors who don't need the myriad of music-related features built into their software. We've yet to see a voice actor using the metronome in Adobe's *Audition* or the Pan/Expand effect in *Sound Forge*. Relax. We'll help you wade through the muck of things you won't ever need or want and focus on the few things you do need to master later in the book.

And, let's face it, if even Harlan can learn to record and edit his voice on a computer, you can, too.

(Okay, so that was a cheap shot, but it makes a valid point and will hopefully reassure some readers. Besides, Harlan can and will take a cheap shot at me somewhere else, I'm sure. —JPF) (The gauntlet has been dropped. —H2)

In short, search for good, basic software that already seems logical to you, and stay away from a lot of the high-level pro software that you keep hearing about. Just because the big guys use this or that doesn't matter to you. Why? Because at the end of the day, you send them a digital file, one that is *totally compatible* with their system.

In reality, most audio engineers prefer to get just a simple well-recorded and well-acted voice track. They can then work their audio magic on the tracks. So resist the urge to play around with EQ and compression, for example, just because it was included with your recording software.

Here's the rub: how can you test software without first owning a computer? You thought you had us there, right? It's easy. Just borrow a computer from a friend or relative, or go to your local library, cybercafé, or even FedEx Office. There you can mess around with a Mac or a PC to see which programs and computer seems right for you and the way you think and work.

You could also ask audio engineers or other voice actors if you could watch them work and perhaps experiment a bit with their software of choice. Many community colleges and universities have classes and outreach programs where you can get inexpensive hands-on use of computers as well. Naturally, the library won't be too excited about your adding demo software temporarily to their machines, but a friend or relative probably won't mind.

So, the really key points to consider when buying a computer are the operating system (Mac OS or PC Windows), the hardware, and other software—including the audio recording/editing program, plus word processing, accounting, and so on. Currently, the Mac OS is Leopard, and Windows is running XP and Vista, but this will change—you can bet on it! But that really doesn't matter much, because most software packages follow the changes in operating systems, so compatibility usually isn't a problem.

Hardware Issues

The basic hardware in any computer system includes the computer's central processing unit (CPU for short), hard disc drive(s), USB/FireWire ports, a wired or wireless network connection, RAM, a CD/DVD writer, an audio interface/sound card, a monitor or two, speakers, a printer, the QWERTY keyboard, and a mouse. The information in this section applies whether you choose a laptop or desktop model, with a few distinctions.

CPU

In the past, your processor choices were different for Macs, but ever since Apple dumped Motorola and switched to the Intel chip, they have used the same processors as PCs. So, the same rules apply.

A dual-core processor makes for a powerful machine. This is what you should get. Dual-core means the computer actually has two—count 'em . . . two—processors in one. So, theoretically, it's like having two computers working for you at once for the same cost. Quad-cores are beginning to emerge, but that's overkill for the kind of audio work you'll do. Those dipping their toes into the video waters may like the speed and versatility of these powerful behemoths, though.

If you're laptop shopping, avoid the single Centrino processor, because it can't handle audio well, but today's dual-core Centrinos are plenty powerful for audio. AMD also makes some powerful dual-core processors, which are acceptable for audio work, too.

HDD

Get a large-capacity hard drive (HDD)—120GB or more—with a fast access time. "GB" equals gigabytes (that's *billions* of bytes), and that equals a ton of storage space for voice recordings, pictures of your pet poodle, the neighbor's Persian pussy cat, stupid e-mails from friends, and other whatever.

Even better is to opt for two hard drives, which make everything run smoother and faster. Your computer uses one drive just to store and run the operating system, your recording program, and other software you use. You use the second drive to record, edit, encode, and save the audio work you do. Like so many other electronic devices, the cost of hard drives has plummeted, so buy two—they're cheap! For a desktop system, dual drives are a no-brainer. On a laptop, you can't effectively do this internally. You can get an external drive, though (more later).

You might see the hard drive referred to as a 7200 RPM drive. That's a fast 7,200 revolutions per minute. Oh, a great many laptop HDDs spin at only 5,400 RPM. Relax. That's still fine for audio work. And you'll want a big drive, because audio files are rather large—10 megabytes (MB) for every minute of stereo audio and 5 megabytes per minute for mono audio, which is CD-quality. Record a 15-minute stereo piece, and you've used 150MB of space.

Delve into digital video, and the hard drive space necessary increases exponentially (at least 13GB per hour). Hopefully, you noticed how I—okay, we—managed to use "delve" and "exponentially" in a single sentence. I'll have to admit—albeit (*ALBEIT!*

My, my! —Prunella)—that Word-a-Day calendar Harlan bought me for Christmas has paid off.

External HDDs, such as the one pictured in Figure 3.2, come in two flavors: USB and FireWire. In either case, get one with a 7200 RPM drive and 8MB of memory cache (a sort of data buffer). These hard drives plug into an available USB/FireWire port on your computer and give you additional drive space. Unfortunately, it is increasingly harder to find the FireWire drives. That's acceptable, as USB-based HDDs will work fine both as a working drive and for storage—with an important distinction.

Figure 3.2 External HDD.

We *do not* recommend the pocket-sized drives that are flooding the market today. They are fine for storage, but they should *not* be used to record audio in real time. The same goes for thumb drives. While it's a real treat to have a gigabyte on a keychain in your pocket or on a lanyard (see Figure 3.3), you should *never* use a thumb drive to record your performances.

Always record your audio to traditional high-speed HDDs, and leave the pocket and thumb dives for storage and transportation of data only—not as active drives!

Figure 3.3 Pocket HDD and thumb (or flash) drive.

USB/FireWire Ports

Make sure any computer you buy has USB 2.0 ports—and the more, the better (see Figure 3.4). USB is the primary way to connect peripherals (other doodads such as printers, audio interfaces, and more) to your computer. While you can expand the USB capabilities via a hub, we do not recommend it when connecting other critical audio gear. For example, you want to directly plug an external USB-based audio interface into its

Figure 3.4 USB and FireWire ports.

own dedicated USB port. The same holds true for external drives; reserve a port just for them. USB-based keyboard, mice, coffee mug warmers, and lights often work just fine in hubs, though.

Here's an important and frequently overlooked detail. If you use a laptop, you might also have a base station that you plug your laptop into when you're home. Be forewarned that the USB ports on base stations are—in effect—hubs and consequently *should not* be used for an audio interface for exactly the same reasons we mentioned earlier.

FireWire ports (also called IEEE 1394) are important if you plan to do video work or use a FireWire audio interface (discussed in the next chapter). These ports are showing up less and less on modern computers due to USB's dominance.

Wired or Wireless Network Connection

Whether you use a DSL or cable modem to connect to the Web, your computer needs a wired network connection (called 10/100BASE-T or Ethernet by people who wish to confuse you). We prefer a wired connection at home. Wireless is nice and convenient—and usually the only route on the road—but wired is always more reliable if it's available.

RAM

The computer uses RAM memory to run the operating system, software programs, printer drivers, and other such tasks that are vital to keeping that hamster inside happy. Again, more is better—1GB is today's bare minimum, but 2–4GB is better (especially if you use Windows Vista). Your audio programs—indeed, virtually every program—will run substantially faster and with fewer problems if you install more RAM.

CD/DVD Writer

Although you'll most often be sending auditions as MP3s via the Internet, we still consider a CD or CD/DVD writer as another mandatory piece of equipment. Some clients want a "hard copy" of your work in addition to or in place of MP3s. A CD/DVD writer lets you create audio or data discs, load in software programs, make backups, and watch the occasional movie when times are slow.

Today, most computers have a CD writer and DVD player. Video users will want to create their own DVDs, so make sure you get a DVD writer.

One distinction that is very important to remember is that there is a big difference between making an audio CD and a data CD. Audio CDs can play in *any* CD player (car, portable, and so on), but a data CD can only be heard on a computer.

Software to operate the CD/DVD writer is usually included with your computer. Today, blank CDs cost just pennies, so a spindle of blank CDs will keep you well stocked for some time. Label making and printing software (see Figure 3.5) can make your home-grown CDs look professional—far better than scribbling on them with a Sharpie!

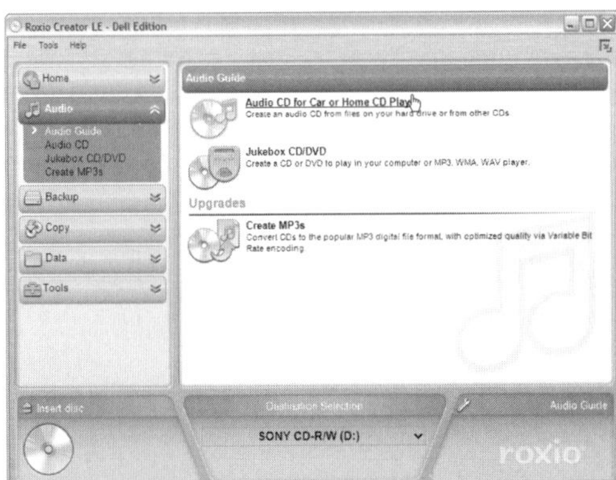

Figure 3.5 CD Writer software.

Blank DVDs costs a little more and vary in quality tremendously. Stick to well-known brands, or you will burn "coasters" (CD/DVD discs that don't work but can function under a sweaty glass of beer to protect your coffee table). Avoid sticky labels on DVDs you make yourself; the labels often prevent the DVDs from working well in certain players.

HP's LightScribe technology lets you make duo-tone labels using the same laser device that creates the audio/DVD/data disc. It's cool stuff, but slow; it sometimes takes longer to "print" the disc than to burn it.

Audio Interface/Sound Card

Every computer sold today comes equipped with a sound card—often called an audio interface—of some kind. As we mentioned before (unless you skipped the last chapter and now feel as shamed and embarrassed as we both often were when called on in class throughout our pitiful school careers), the problem is that most stock audio interfaces are completely unsuitable for serious sound recording. Laptop sound cards are particularly yucky. That said, with the right external gear (namely, a better-quality mic and preamp, the subject of Chapter 4, "Assembling Your Home Studio—Hardware"), a basic sound card *may* suffice, but only in a pinch.

Study the italicized *may* in the previous sentence. Some audio features built in to certain computers will *never* yield acceptable results. Never. Even plugging the best pro gear in the universe into these losers yields a muffled, tinny, garbled mess. The solution is to shop for a computer that brags about its multimedia features and specifications. Avoid any that hide or fail to mention their audio capabilities.

Even with a better-than-average internal sound card, we both recommend that you invest in an audio interface specifically designed to handle quality audio recording (see Figure 3.6).

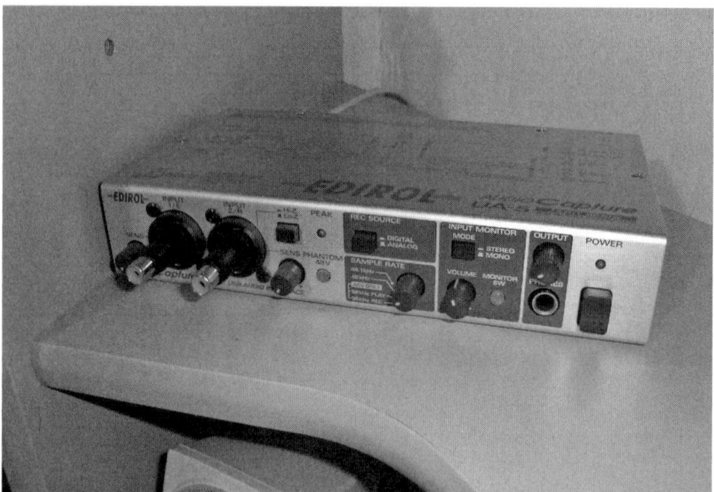

Figure 3.6 USB-based audio interface.

Some of these pro-level audio interfaces use a card that needs to be installed in the computer. If you are at all squeamish about the prospect of opening up the computer and putting something in it, hire a computer pro to do it for you.

Thankfully, many audio interfaces simply plug into your computer's USB or FireWire port, making it a snap to get up and running quickly. These connections are really, really simple—virtually plug and play—so don't worry about it. Chapter 4 includes a complete discussion about these devices.

Monitor(s)

Computer monitors are now all flat-panel LCDs in a variety of sizes. The thin, energy-conscious screens are not only beautiful, they take up a small amount of space compared to the old CRTs. Fisher found that it's much easier to work on 17-inch and 19-inch monitors, while Harlan prefers something in the 56-inch size due to his failing eyesight. If you have a small laptop screen, you may want to get a bigger desktop LCD to plug into when you are at your home studio.

Desktop users also have the luxury of using multiple monitors—if their graphics cards support this feature (see Figure 3.7). We both use multiple monitors to extend the desktop and keep our screens less crowded. Like power seats in a car, once you go multi-monitor, you never go back.

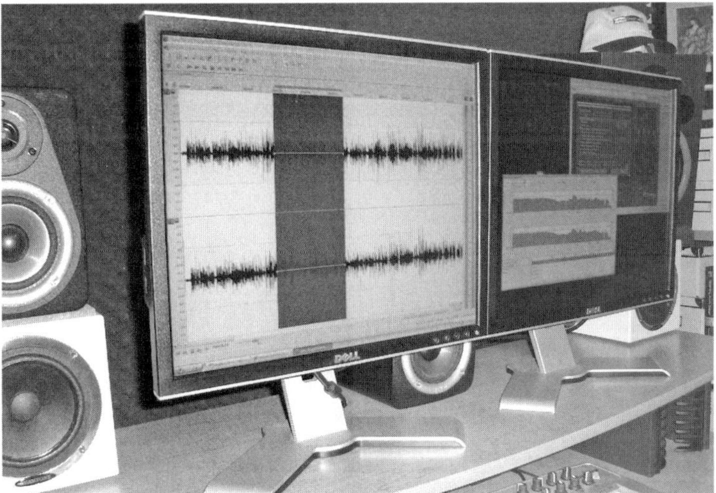

Figure 3.7 Multi-monitors.

We mentioned the computer's graphics card in passing, but suffice to say, computers need an extra bit of technology to clearly display what you see on the screen. Audio software does not really take advantage of this technology, but other software may (especially games). Choose the right graphics interface based on your lifestyle. If you will just record audio, any stock card will suffice. If having dual monitors sounds attractive to you, choose a card that supports this feature. Or if listening to and seeing Harlan as Thrall in the *Warcraft* series of games seems somehow important to your very existence, then you will need a more advanced graphics card.

Speakers

You'll need decent headphones while recording to hear yourself. However, when you are editing, you'll want to listen through speakers connected to your computer and trust them to give you an accurate representation of your voice.

Avoid junk like what's shown in Figure 3.8.

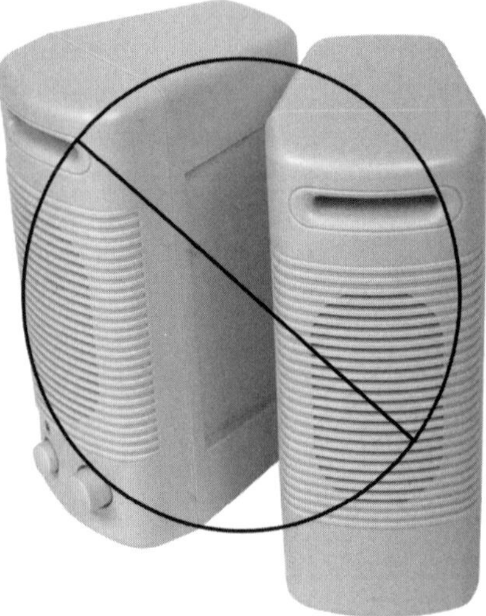

Figure 3.8 Cheapie speakers.

Laptops have built-in speakers that are equally no good. Instead, invest in better-quality speakers like the ones we'll talk about in the next chapter. Speakers are very important to professional audio engineers, which explains why you'll often see several kinds and sizes in a recording studio (see Figure 3.9). (*By the way: Speakers used in recording studios are referred to as monitors just to add to the overall confusion! —H2*)

Printer

A color printer is another great idea. You can make fancy labels for your CDs, mailing labels, print scripts, and more. There are lots of choices for less than $100. Get one. But be forewarned: the toner or ink cartridges can get expensive.

Other Fun Stuff

The mouse and keyboard are included with every computer. However, there are a couple of extra devices that can make recording and editing a little easier.

Figure 3.9 Lotsa speakers.

- The Keyspan Remote (http://www.keyspan.com) is a wireless infrared handheld TV/ VCR-type remote control for your computer. Since you'll often have to record and perform at the same time, this handy little device lets you control your recording software remotely.
- The Frontier Design TranzPort (http://www.frontierdesign.com) is another wireless remote that can make your life easier (see Figure 3.10).

Figure 3.10 TranzPort.

- The Contour Design ShuttlePRO V.2 (http://www.contourdesign.com) also gives you extra control over your digital recording software. The jog knob (see Figure 3.11) lets you move through your audio files with ease. Its 15 programmable buttons automate your most-used tasks. It's preprogrammed for most software titles and is easily customized to your workflow. And you can use it along with a mouse to really speed up your work.

Figure 3.11 ShuttlePRO V.2.

- An official Harlan Hogan mouse pad can make mousing so much easier. Optical mice just seem to float majestically over its smooth surface. Plus, it has Harlan's phone number in case you need to call him in a pinch about how to pad a chapter like this with superfluous content.

Software

Obviously, you'll need recording software, and since it's been a central discussion in our book, we'll cover recording programs in excruciating detail in the next chapter. But what other software might be useful for a professional voice acting career?

Well, essential to just about any business is a reliable word processor. You'll use it for everything—scripts, letters, promotions, résumés, and all the important information about every aspect of your career.

We also suggest that you consider a contact management system, called a PIM or personal information manager. You can use the information stored in its "database" to keep track of appointments, clients, and prospects and to generate mailing lists easily for your ongoing promotions. Harlan uses ACT!, and Jeffrey prefers a custom database he created himself. Harlan is clearly content to do without the whitewall tires, shiny red paint, and thundering exhaust pipes that feature prominently in Jeffrey's design. On the other hand, Harlan manages to get a ton of promotional stuff out whilst Jeffrey is busy fine-tuning shift ratios on his homemade miracle. (*Whilst! My, you boys are becoming such Anglophiles! —Prunella*)

There are even actor-specific career management scheduling programs, like *Actor Track* (http://www.holdonlog.com). For around a hundred dollars, this software keeps track of auditions, sessions, callbacks, and more, and it can interface with your PDA. What's a PDA? We thought you'd never ask. Read on, McDuff!

A personal digital assistant (PDA), like a PalmPilot, BlackBerry, iPhone, or equivalent, can really make your life easier. With its included address book, to-do lists, memos, and calendar, a PDA coupled with your computer is a one-two punch to keep you organized, letting you painlessly keep track of people, appointments, deadlines, and more. Plus, synchronizing data between the computer and a handheld PDA is a snap. Once you use one, you'll wonder how you managed to stay organized the old-fashioned way, when you wrote stuff in a notebook, on a wall calendar, or on bar napkins. We guarantee it.

Another software purchase might include accounting/bookkeeping software targeted for your small business. You can use it to keep track of personal and business income and expenses and manage all your financial affairs, including income tax preparation. Quicken and Microsoft Money are the leaders in this area.

Because you'll probably be burning CDs, and perhaps DVDs, you might want a program that helps you design, lay out, and print labels, booklets, and tray cards. You can put together a top-notch "physical" demo package with this software and a color printer, even one at a time. If you're graphically challenged, skip this program and hire a real designer to put together your package.

And Two Cautions ...

We live in a world where some people have little else to do with their lives than to make ours difficult. We're talking about those desperate souls who write viruses, spyware, and other malevolent software that wreak havoc with our computers. To combat this evil, invest in software (see Figure 3.12) to protect your computer and keep it up to date. Similarly, pay attention to other updates offered by your software vendors, including your operating system, to protect your computer and its contents from these potential risks.

Figure 3.12 Antivirus screen shot.

Oh, My Aching Backup

As great as computers can be, they can malfunction (remember our buddy HAL in *2001*?), and you can lose all your critical files. But if you regularly back up your data, there's no reason to worry, since you can quickly recover anything missing. Don't risk losing the best performance of your life or all your accounting records because of a power failure, a virus, or a computer hacker. We speak from experience; you'll never regret backing up your data and audio files—both raw files (unedited performances) and finished masters (what you send out for auditions and clients).

Blank CDs are cheap, and the few minutes it takes to make a backup on one is far less than the time it'll take to re-create all your work and records.

Another, even more convenient option is to create copies of your original files on a different hard drive. This drive could be inside your computer or an external drive connected via USB or FireWire. Hard drive prices have plummeted, and many come with automatic backup software you can "set and forget." Store your backup CDs/drives somewhere safe, away from your computer—offsite is the best, perhaps at a neighbor's or relative's house, or even in a safe deposit box.

You can also upload files to an online data backup and storage solution for just a few bucks a month. Some Web-based e-mail packages offer limited file storage, too.

Jeffrey also recommends using the small flash thumb drives for quick backups and for the ultimate in portability. Harlan cautions you to never be seen in public with one hanging from a lanyard around your neck—that's "geek bling"—akin to eating Thanksgiving dinner with a Bluetooth headset dangling from your ear.

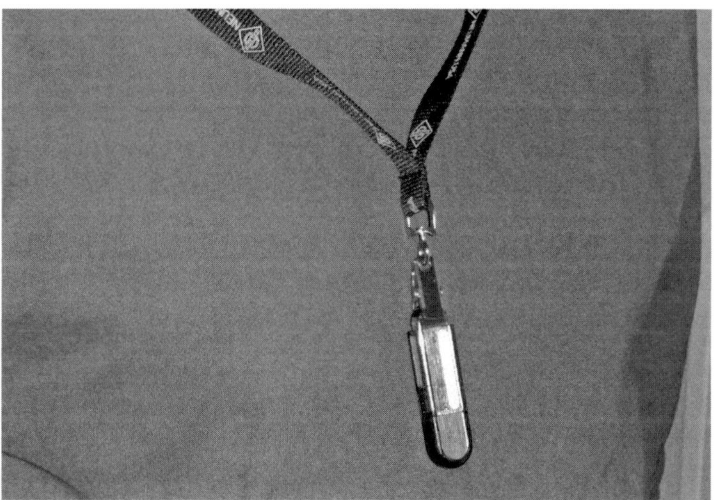

Internet Connection

This is another requirement. Having a computer without an Internet connection is like having a toaster and no bread. Essentially, you need four key items: a way to access the Internet, an e-mail address, a Web domain, and "cyberspace" to hold your Web site. The last two items are the subject of a later chapter; the first two are briefly addressed here.

We won't even mention dial-up access. (Oops, we just did.) Watching paint dry is far more rewarding than that antiquated technology. The files you'll be sending make high-speed access a must-have. Most likely, you'll sign up for high-speed Internet access with a phone company or cable provider. Regardless, you'll use a special modem (*mo*dulator/*dem*odulator) that attaches to your computer through its Ethernet port (the one that looks like a telephone jack on steroids) and then on to the phone line/cable connection. The phone connection is known as DSL, while the cable connection is just, well, a cable TV connection. There is the remote possibility that one or the other (or both) might not be available in your area. If that's true, we have a simple suggestion—move! Seriously, there are also satellite Internet services available. These aren't as reliable or as fast as the wired connections, but they're superior to painfully slow dial-up Internet! (*Mention number two. —Prunella*)

Neither solution (cable nor DSL; see Figure 3.13) ties up a phone line like traditional dial-up once did. (*Okay, three mentions, and you guys are out of here. —Prunella*)

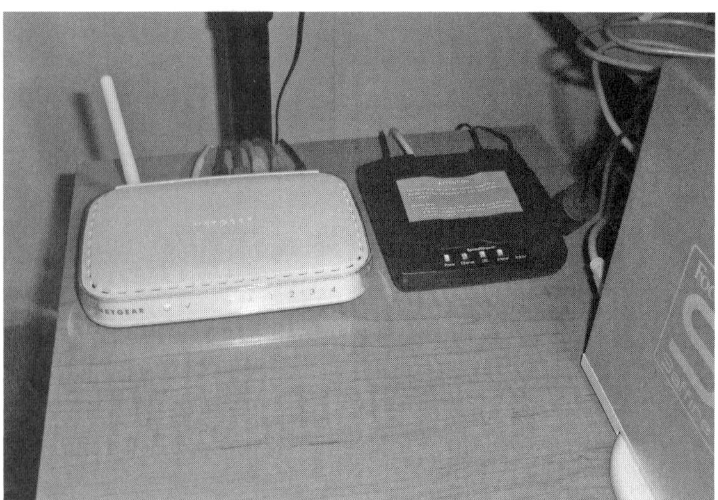

Figure 3.13 DSL modem and router.

When you sign up with an Internet service, you'll get an e-mail address. There are also free e-mail services that you can use, like Gmail and Hotmail. You may want to use one e-mail address for personal matters and another for your acting career.

Choose a username that's easy to remember, and avoid goofy, strange, incomprehensible, and otherwise bad choices. Studmuffin@suchnsuch.com is probably a wise choice if you're an idiot. 1$pxwWyzzzQf@suchnsuch.com is another great idea—if you never want anybody to remember your address or be able to type it correctly.

For good examples, see how our e-mail addresses are logical and easy to remember: harlan@harlanhogan.com and jpf@jeffreypfisher.com. Now, to get those specialized names, called domain names in Web parlance, you need to purchase them. We'll provide more detail on this subject in Chapter 11, "Working the World Wide Web."

The Internet is one of the main ingredients in your recipe for success. Learn to use it for research, to find sessions, to contact key people, to take care of personal and career matters, to establish a Web site of your own, and so much more. If you only use the Web on a cursory level (and by that, we mean you only go to Amazon, YouTube, and eBay), it's time to expand what the Internet brings to you. Go to the library or bookstore and get a few books on the subject, and spend several afternoons with geeky friends paying rapt attention as they surf the net. Or swallow your pride and sign up for a course at the local community college.

What you *can't* do is cop a plea: "Oh, I'm an actor and can't be troubled with trivial, revolutionary changes that affect the very foundations of society and communication." No go, kiddo, not—that is—if you want to make a buck or two in today's world of voice-over.

Still Worried?

Buying a computer can be a daunting task for the uninitiated. Thankfully, today you don't have to worry much about buying the wrong system. We can't emphasize enough that any computer you buy today that meets or exceeds the specifications outlined in this chapter will work for you. Lesser models might also work, but why risk it?

Take this book with you to the store and talk to a knowledgeable seller. Explain what you will be doing with your computer, and show the salesperson this chapter. Better still, take along a professional or a reasonably computer-literate person (geek) whom you trust and who understands *your* specific goals. It can be very reassuring to have a hand to hold as you shop, particularly if that hand is attractive to you. If not, well, then it's time to act! Stay in the moment, paying no attention to the seller's horn-rimmed glasses and the safety pin holding them together. And remember this:

> "He's a computer genius; he's supposed to be a little weird."
>
> —Jeffrey DeMunn, as Paul Wick, *RocketMan*, 1997, Caravan Pictures, 1997

4 Assembling Your Home Studio—Hardware

"Wait a minute, wait a minute, you ain't heard nothin' yet!"

—George Jessel as Jack Robin, *The Jazz Singer,* 1927, Warner Brothers

All right, you have your computer in place. So it's time to explore and choose the other pieces of the audio recording pie that connect to your computer. We'll slice and dice that pastry into individual servings, showing you all the hardware components you'll need to make top-quality sound recordings...and those you don't.

Thankfully, your audio equipment needs are minimal—just a few key pieces of gear. The basics include a microphone, microphone preamplifier, audio interface, and computer software so your computer becomes a digital recorder. Naturally, you'll also need an acoustically sound place to perform, too. That's pretty much it, although we'll turn you on to some nice-to-have not need-to-have items, too.

Because your "recording chain" is so simple, it's critical to understand that the quality of each link in that chain greatly affects the sound you record. A crummy microphone hooked to the best computer audio interface will still sound like a crummy microphone. Likewise, if you take a top-dollar vintage mic and plug it into a cheapie laptop mic input, your recordings will sound wimpy, thin, dull, and muffled. (That may be acceptable, even desirable, if the client has asked for tracks that sound wimpy, thin, dull, and muffled, but we don't advise counting on that happening. Not too often, anyway.)

Don't Skimp on a Solid Front End

It would have been easy for us to make some kind of lewd anatomy joke here, but we know Prunella would have nixed it. (*My red pen was ready, dearies. —Prunella*) The "front end" is audio geek talk for the elements that come *before* the computer—namely, the mic, preamp, and interface. While you don't have to spend vast sums of money to get a good front end, you can't get by with bargain-basement junk either. Investing wisely in the right components at this stage will pay off for you down the road.

Recording Overview

Caution: The following section contains material that might be considered "nice to know," not "need to know." We do know—from personal experience—that a thorough knowledge of the arcane intricacies of how recording actually works will *not* make you more charming at parties much less get you invited to them.

Recording, whether at home or on the road, has a single goal: capture the sound of your voice clearly, cleanly, and accurately while presenting and preserving your best performance.

To create sound, something must vibrate, like your vocal cords wiggling around in your throat. That vibration transfers its energy to the air that moves from your lungs out through your mouth and nose, making your own, unique sound.

You may have heard sound described as waves, moving out in all directions (see Figure 4.1). Drop a stone in a pond, and watch the tiny waves of water spread out. Sound waves, like water waves, have crests and troughs. At the sound wave's top, the air is compressed together tightly. At its trough, the air is loose. This is how sound energy travels through air, even though the air does not move. It's called acoustic energy.

Figure 4.1 Wave pattern.

To record the sound of your voice, you need to convert that acoustic energy into a form that can be recorded. Here's how it works. Your microphone captures acoustic energy and converts it to electrical energy. Inside the microphone is a tiny metal diaphragm that vibrates as it is struck by acoustic energy and converts that mechanical energy to electrical. You can chat up other voice actors at auditions by saying, "Ya know, a microphone is actually a transducer that converts one form of energy (acoustic) into another (mechanical)." It's sure to clear the room, leaving you with no competition!

Another analogy (*As if that weren't enough! —Prunella*) is to imagine a record spinning on a turntable. As the needle rides up and down in the grooves, it vibrates—just like the microphone's diaphragm. Once again, mechanical energy is converted to electrical energy and then amplified—made loud enough for us to hear. Likewise, electrical energy from your microphone is amplified and played back through headphones or speakers. Interestingly (at least to us), a speaker is really a microphone in reverse, converting electrical energy back into mechanical energy and then to acoustic energy that can be heard by our ears. Harlan says that makes speakers actually a Triducer. Prunella sent him to his room.

Electrical energy can also be converted to magnetic energy when we record on audiotape. Electricity applied to a magnet in the recorder arranges tiny grains of oxidized metal in a pattern that is analogous to—the same as—the electrical energy pattern from the microphone. That's why you'll often hear tape recording called analog recording. By the way, do you know why recording tape looks a lot like clear plastic tape with rust stuck on it? Because that's pretty much what it is.

Digital recording on a computer, on the other hand, converts the electrical energy from the microphone into information that your computer can understand. Amazingly, computers only recognize two numbers: 0 and 1. By manipulating these 1s and 0s, computers manage to perform all the tasks we ask of them.

Digital sound recording requires an analog-to-digital converter (ADC) to convert electrical energy into those 1s and 0s through a process called sampling. The ADC is part of the computer's soundcard/audio interface and the recording chain's front end. Essentially, the computer takes an electronic "snapshot" of the electrical waveform moment by moment and assigns this picture number values that represent the sound "frozen in time."

For CD-quality sound, the computer's ADC takes 44,100 snapshots per second! That number, abbreviated as 44.1kHz (kilohertz), is called the sampling rate. The higher the sampling rate, the better the quality of the digitized sound.

Once a computer takes its digital snapshot or sample, it needs to assign a value to the sound that represents its volume or amplitude (the size of the wave crest/trough). The number of bits used determines the possible values available. CD quality uses 16 bits—essentially a string of sixteen 0s and 1s. Since a computer only knows two numbers, the bit depth (as it is called) gets expressed mathematically as 2^{16}, and computers round or quantize all samples to one of those 65,536 possible values. As with the sampling rate, the higher the bit depth, the better the resulting sound. In your recording software, you'll see sample rates of 44.1, 48, 96, and higher, with bit depths of 8, 16, 24, and so on. For voice work, you'll probably stick to 44.1kHz/16-bit (see Figure 4.2).

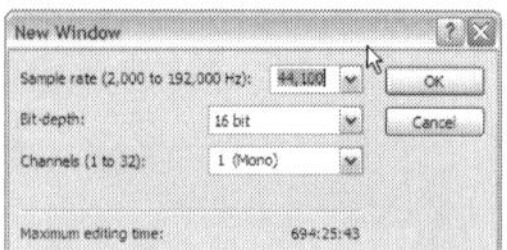

Figure 4.2 Sample rate and bit depth.

The process that the computer uses to sample your voice and represent it as numerals is known as Pulse Code Modulation or PCM, for short. This is uncompressed audio, uncannily faithful to the original sound. It is the format you should always record into and save for your masters. The PC stores audio in the WAV format, while Macs use the AIFF format; both are PCM, though. And both Macs and PCs can read either format.

MP3 is an inferior quality, highly compressed, and lossy way to store audio. Yes, you're right—lossy means loss, and a sizeable portion of the audio quality is sacrificed to make the size of the audio file smaller, or compressed. This smaller file size has made MP3 players popular and enabled actors to send auditions as simple e-mail attachments. Although MP3s are the standard for auditions, many clients expect an uncompressed, PCM file for tracks meant for broadcast.

It is best to always record at the highest PCM WAV/AIFF level and save that. Then save another file as an MP3. You can't do that the other way around because saving as an MP3 recording throws out (loses) much of the detail.

Whew! Don't say we didn't warn you! Now that we've rattled your brain with way too much information on how recording actually works, it's time to get practical. Here are the components you'll need to record yourself at home or on the road even if you really don't care how they work.

Microphones

As the first link in the recording chain, microphones are a critical component. Although it's possible to spend an arm, leg, and thigh on a good one, you'll be relieved to know that decent-quality mics can be bought for less than $100, with a myriad of even better choices between $200 and $500. Naturally, there are boutique mics available that sound extra rich and full and require you to be extra rich and have a very full wallet. We're not knocking expensive mics—on the contrary, some are well worth the investment—we're just saying that you can probably do well with a more modest investment, especially if auditions are all you plan to record.

By the way, that cute little microphone that looks for all the world like a tube of lipstick that came with your computer is—garbage. Yep, it's junk, trash, detritus.

Don't record your dulcet tones with garbage.

Throw it away.

Now.

We'll wait . . .

Thank you. That's a donation to the circular file you will never regret. Now we can get on to the main event: *real* microphones. There are essentially three types: dynamic, condenser, and ribbon (which is really a special type of dynamic mic).

Dynamic microphones create their own electricity. How, you say? (Now, don't deny it—Harlan and I distinctly heard you mutter, "Whaaaaaa?") Fair enough, remember Mr. Wizard on black-and-white TV doing this neat-o keen-o experiment where he made a tiny light bulb glow, just by spinning a magnet inside a coil of wire? No?

Okay fine. You're younger than we are, and we both resent that.

Anyway, a magnet moving in a coil of wire is a generator of electricity. From the turbines at the Hoover Dam to the most sophisticated nuclear power plant, we generate electricity by moving magnets in coils of wire, and that's precisely how a dynamic microphone makes its own electricity.

Inside that dynamic microphone is that thin metal diaphragm we talked about. It moves back and forth when struck by acoustic energy (your voice). But this diaphragm is attached to a coil of wire that moves over a strong magnet. Get the picture? The electrical energy that flows through matches the sound wave. That's why dynamic microphones are often called moving coil microphones. Not by anyone we actually know, mind you. When Will Shakespeare wrote his immortal lines about shuffling and mortal coils, we figure he was talking about dynamic mics—right?

No?

Maybe that explains why neither of us gets invited to dinner soirées ...

Moving on: A condenser microphone needs electricity to work. Once again, a thin diaphragm—often made of gold foil—moves when sound strikes it. But this diaphragm has a solid, fixed plate behind it and an electrical charge applied to it. The action of the diaphragm moving toward and away from the plate creates a varying electrical current that is analogous to the sound waveform. This tiny amount of electricity is then amplified and sent out from the microphone.

Condenser mics get their power from batteries, from separate power supplies, or from the next stage in the front end: preamps, mixers, and audio interfaces. Professional condenser microphones typically need 48 volts to work properly, and that power is known as phantom power. We know that's goofy-sounding, and even we can't bring ourselves not to make fun of it. This phantom power gets into the mic through your everyday mic cable, and for now that's all the information anyone really needs to know.

The inherent advantage of a condenser microphone is that it can capture the subtleties of sound. A dynamic microphone is akin to a piston—mechanical—and therefore is less able to "hear" the subtle differences, because dynamic mics need more energy to get things moving and overcome inertia. The gentlest of vibrations gets a condenser working, which is a primary reason they are chosen over dynamics for many uses. Large-diaphragm condenser models are particularly well suited to voice.

Generally, small-diaphragm condensers are better suited to musical instrument tasks, but there are notable exceptions, which we'll mention.

One other design element to consider with condenser mics is that they do not generate much electricity. So we need to boost the volume (level) inside the mic itself. Simple enough, but amplifying the volume of the mic at this stage greatly affects its sound, sometimes for the good, but sometimes not.

Some condenser mics are based on vacuum tubes; others are solid-state, transistor designs. Today, most condensers are solid state, but tube mics are still around, both vintage and new. The primary difference is this: tube microphones tend to sound fuller and warmer in a way that our ears appreciate. Plenty of solid-state mics sound just as good, though, making choosing just the right mic all the more difficult.

Ribbon microphones have a tiny corrugated-metal diaphragm (a ribbon with a bow, of course) that's suspended between two poles of a magnet. These dynamic mics generate their own electricity, too. Ribbons fell out of favor for many years but have recently started to make a comeback. They have a vintage sound that you may find flattering, but they are quite fragile and susceptible to wind—including normal breaths issuing from a voice actor speaking. One other warning: if you inadvertently send phantom power to a ribbon mic ... zzzttt! You have a lovely paperweight for your desk.

Since dynamic mics are rugged and often less expensive than condensers and ribbons, why not just use them? Seems like a no-brainer when you consider that when Electro-Voice introduced the EV 666 dynamic mic back in the late 1950s, mic salesmen would brag that it was so sturdy it could do double duty as a hammer just in case the station announcer needed to pound in some ten-penny nails to hold up the station's call letter banner on a remote broadcast!

Of course, a huge chunk of sound quality and nuance was "traded" for that kind of ruggedness.

Condenser and ribbon mics are fragile by comparison, but like a fine violin versus a fiddle, they bring forth rich tones and subtlety of sound. It's a trade-off.

Pickup Lines

How a microphone responds or "hears" where sound comes from is called its pickup pattern. There are four main pickup patterns: omnidirectional, Figure 8, unidirectional or cardioid, and hyper-cardioid (i.e., super-directional), more commonly called a shotgun microphone. They are illustrated in Figure 4.3.

Be forewarned. Chatting up (*Oh! Finally, a proper English phrase! —Prunella)* attractive strangers about the fascinating pattern available on microphone will not help your personal pickup pattern.

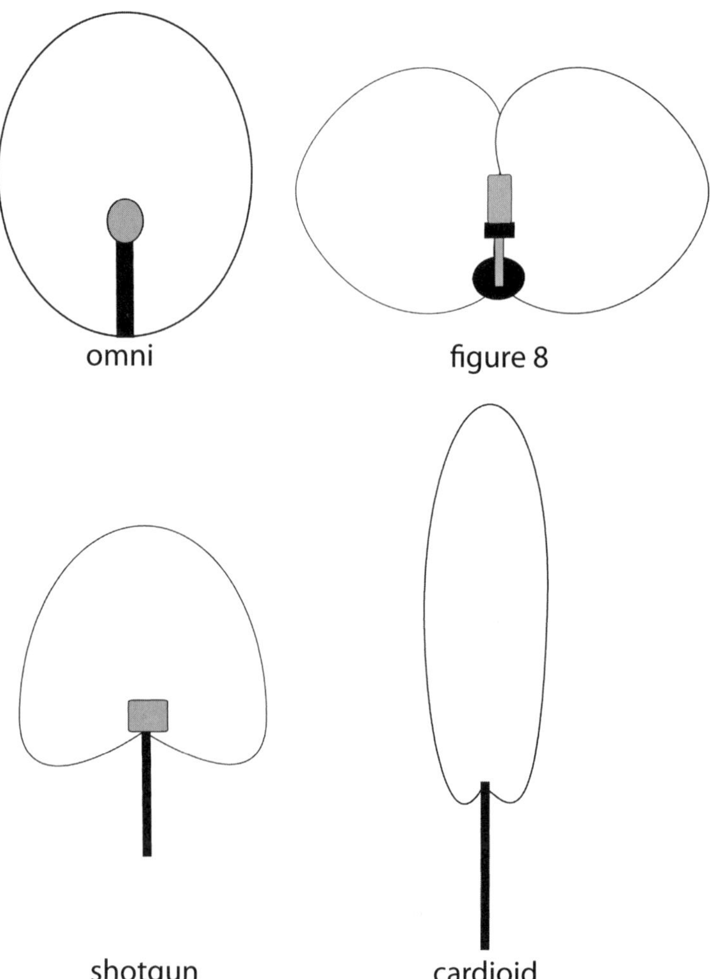

Figure 4.3 Microphone pickup patterns.

Omnidirectional microphones pick up sound in all directions. Picture the mic in the middle of a transparent globe, and you'll see how it responds to sound equally from all directions, including from behind what you might call the business end. Omni means "all," so the name omnidirectional is apt. The problem with omnis is that they "hear" all the background noise equally with your voice. They are useful for projects like in-the-street interviews and some music setups, but voice recording—especially in noisy environments—omnidirectional mics are usually a poor choice. It's not that omni mics are noisy; they just hear all the ambient sound around them and can *sound* noisier.

The Figure 8 microphone picks up sound in just two directions and rejects sounds coming from the sides, called—if you really need to know—nodes. We only mention this pattern because all ribbon mics are Figure 8. This means that this microphone will pick up sound behind it, so you may be recording unwanted noise from that direction. (*Is there such a thing as* wanted *noise? —Prunella*)

Unidirectional, or cardioid, microphones are more sensitive in just one direction and reject sounds coming from other directions. Picture a heart-shaped pattern, and you'll see how these mics pick up sound. This heart-shaped pattern is why these mics are called cardioids—cardio means heart. Cardioids are ideally suited to voice work because they focus on your voice and significantly reduce other background noises.

Caution: Giving a cardioid to a significant other on Valentine's Day will rarely have the same impact as a couple of dozen roses or a heart-shaped box of Godiva chocolates.

The shotgun microphone has an even tighter pickup pattern than a regular cardioid, letting you really zero in on the sound you want and reject the noise you don't want. Think of it as that cold-clammy-knurled-German-made-flashlight the doctor uses when looking down your throat and asking you to say, "Ahhhhhhh" as he laughs at the size of your tonsils and says, "Wow! The Hindenburg was a blip on the radar compared to these!"

A perennial favorite in the film industry for recording on-camera dialogue, the shotgun is a somewhat closely guarded secret in the voice recording world. A short-shotgun—such as the Sennheiser 416—gives that tight, omniscient announcer-quality tone so sought after for many radio and TV spots. The shotgun is not an inexpensive microphone, but its sound can really cut through. Guess which one of us has two shotgun mics—one for the road and one for home? (If you picked Harlan, give yourself 1,000 points.)

Now, some microphones have switchable pickup patterns that let you adjust the pickup pattern from omni, to cardioid, to Figure 8. How cool is that? Some sophisticated mics even allow various steps in between. This selection switch may be on the mic body itself or on a separate power supply (see Figure 4.4). The Lawson L47 that Harlan sometimes uses has this kind of variable pickup pattern, as does the Avantone CV-12 that Jeffrey likes.

Both cardioids and shotguns have a phenomenon called the proximity effect. Despite its name, we're not talking about that gnawing feeling you get in the pit of your stomach when stuffed into a crowded elevator. Instead, as you get closer to cardioid and shotgun microphones, the low frequencies or bass becomes more pronounced. This can work to your advantage, making a thin voice sound deeper and fuller. Or it might work against you, depending on your vocal quality. If you need the bass boost, get closer to the mic. If not, back away a little until it sounds right.

Figure 4.4 Variable pattern mic.

It's important that you understand how your particular microphone picks up sound, or you just might make the classic error of talking into the wrong place, resulting in an inferior sound called off-axis, or more commonly off mic. Some microphones are top address, while others are side address. A few microphones supposedly have unlisted addresses, but we're still researching that urban legend. If you glance at Figure 4.5, the left microphone, the Audio-Technica AT2020, is a side address condenser mic; in other words, you speak into the side with the manufacturer's name.

Figure 4.5 Side versus top address.

Many mics have an icon that looks like an upside-down heart indicating the correct address side. The mic to the right is a top address dynamic mic, the Heil PR40, so you speak into the top.

If you're unsure where to speak, consult the little owner's manual that came with your mic. (Yes, gentlemen actually *do* read instruction manuals.) It may be full of gobbledygook, but it'll also show you proper placement related to the mic's pickup pattern as in Figure 4.6.

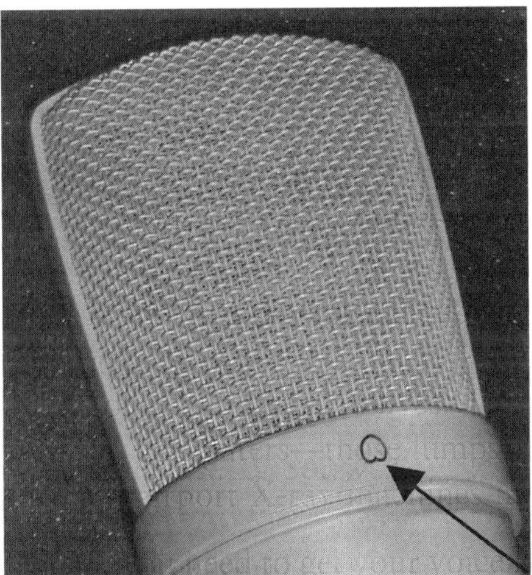

Figure 4.6 Cardioid icon.

We both find it funny—okay, mildly amusing—that the Heil PR 40 is perched on David Letterman's desk every night but is positioned as if it were a side-address mic. Since you now know it is actually a top-address mic, that means the microphone is—in reality—pointed *away* from the TV host! We know, we know, it's just a prop. We haven't bothered sending in any complaint letters—well, at least one of us hasn't.

Some other high-tech, high-trick features on some mics include a bass roll-off switch and a pad. Though these settings sound pretty esoteric, in fact, the bass roll-off switch simply turns down the volume on extreme low frequencies (rumble) that the mic might pick up as well as AC hum and infrasonic sounds (below the perception of humans). This can be a good thing.

The pad, aka an attenuator, simply lowers the sensitivity (volume) of the mic, usually by –10 to –20dB. When faced with recording really loud sounds, say a jet engine, this pad reduces the volume of sound going through the mic so it doesn't distort. Truth be told, you'd almost never need the pad for a voice-over session unless—perhaps—you were asked to scream Fay Wray–style for a couple of minutes straight.

Phantom Power

We mentioned that all condenser microphones need electricity to work and that power may come from a battery inserted in the mic body or more commonly from the same cable that connects the mic to the next part of the front end of the recording chain—a mic input on a dedicated preamp, mixer, or audio interface. It's called phantom power because it's transparent to the audio signal. This power to your microphone will not interfere in any way with your voice recording. The industry standard is 48 volts, and you may see references to that voltage on some of the gear you use.

The only thing you should remember is to make sure phantom power is off when connecting and disconnecting condenser mics (see Figure 4.7). Plug the mic in first, and then turn the power on. It's not a bad idea to also have your speakers turned down or your headphones off your ears, because turning on the phantom power oftentimes sends a loud "klunk" down the line. Ouch!

Figure 4.7 Phantom power switch.

Now this is a biggie, so pay attention. *Never* use phantom power with dynamic or ribbon mics. Dynamic mics don't need the power because they create their own electricity, remember? And ribbon mics will be destroyed by a jolt of 48 volts and be turned into doorstops.

Choosing the Perfect Microphone

Ever since we scribbled out the outline for the previous edition of this book on a few cocktail napkins, the one question we've been most asked is, "What mic should I buy?"

While it would be oh-so-easy for us to name a few models and call it a day, we both refuse to do that—for the following reasons.

1. There are so many microphones to choose from. There's a reason for this rich cornucopia of choices. Microphones have unique sounds—like musical instruments. You choose one model over another because of its sound and the way it flatters your voice.

2. Microphones are used to record a lot more than just spoken voice. So many mics are designed for specific applications, like recording singers and very specific musical instruments. There really are no general, all-purpose mics.
3. Never choose a mic recommended by anyone—including us!—*unless* you test it for yourself and decide it's the mic for you.
4. This is the biggie—you need to find the right microphone for *your voice*. We don't care, and neither should you, what the model is, what color it is, and whether it's a dynamic, condenser, or ribbon. It all comes down to you and the mic. Are you a good fit?
5. Like most of us, you probably have a budget, so you may need to keep your choices inside a certain price range. If all you have is $100, don't go testing Neumanns, okay?
6. Okay fine, we will fess up as to what we believe is the best voice-over mic. It's the venerable Neumann U47, which is a tube-based condenser that predates the Beatles era and is still sought after today (along with a few of its other Neumann siblings). see Figure 4.8. Unfortunately, at about $10,000+, this vintage mic is out of reach for most people. Of course, it will be difficult to even convince someone to sell you one and equally tricky to find a technician to keep it in pristine condition. It's not the *only* VO mic, but it serves as a standard to which other mics can aspire.

Figure 4.8 Holy Grail mic.

Tip: By the way, the newbie pronounces Neumann like *New-min*. The correct way to say it is *Noy-mahn*. There. Now you're already sounding like an old pro, and if you really want to sound like a hip professional (or a professional hippie), use the slang term *cans* when referring to your headphones, as in, "Dude, I can't hear myself in the cans." This is not the same thing as "going to the can," which is the subject of our next book. (*I refuse to even consider that cornball comment. —Prunella*)

Okay, with our six rules in mind, let's get picky.

The best approach to today's avalanche of microphone choices is to develop and implement a strategy when evaluating mics. Here are a few suggestions:

- You can listen to mic shootouts on CD, where various mics are auditioned. Beware of shootouts that feature musical instruments or just singers; these are not as valuable to us as ones comparing the spoken word. So-called blind listening tests are the best because there's no chance you'll be influenced by brand names and such. We have a blind voice-over microphone shootout on our *VO Success* DVD, and another we did (although not a blind test) called "New Microphones (and More) for Voice-Overs: What Is the Best Microphone for Voice-Over Recording?" at http://digitalprosound.digitalmedianet.com/articles/viewarticle.jsp?id=247299.

- You can test mics at large music stores. Guitar Center and Sam Ash Music let you step up to the plate—so to speak—and whack a few around. If you are near New York City, pay a visit to the audio department at B&H Photo/Video, and get ready to test a myriad of mics and preamps. We recommend taking your test recordings home for evaluation.
- Consider testing mics at a recording studio, preferably one that does a lot of voice recording (as opposed to a music-centric studio) and under the tutelage of a pro engineer. You can also judge preamps there. Ask the engineer to play back your takes blind, so you don't know which mic is which. There's nothing better than a pair of neutral professional ears, so ask what your engineer hears and recommends for you.
- You can also test mics by buying a few and bringing them home to give them a workout. Purchase from reputable merchants who will let you return the also-rans and keep the winner(s). Many online retailers offer such terms, but ask ahead to be sure. You don't want to get stuck with a restocking fee. Be upfront that you are auditioning a number of mics to see what fits you best.
- When testing mics, use the same script, and record a few short tests with each model you are contemplating. Play these recordings back and evaluate the best choice for your voice. You may want to enlist the support of another, such as an agent, producer, or audio engineer. Mothers and significant others should probably not be asked for their opinions, as their judgment will always be biased and skewed. What should you listen for? You want your voice to sound natural with no strange artifacts such as boominess, shrillness, Elliot Ness, or any other nesses. Seriously, listen for sibilance (excessive *S* sounds), poppiness (though that may be your technique or lack thereof), and other anomalies that don't flatter your voice.
- Now, some of you may say that your ears are not trained enough to notice subtle differences in microphones. We disagree. Sometimes the difference between mics is quite distinct; you'll notice it right away. Jeffrey does blind mic shootouts in his college audio classes, and students consistently notice the differences immediately. Of course, these differences are often subtle, so you need to really listen closely to arrive at the best solution. (And there can be more than one solution. See below.)
- Some voice actors seem to sound good on a lot of different mics. Harlan's voice gets captured quite nicely by many models, but he still sounds his best on a few

particular choices. Jeffrey has worked with VOs who only sound good on a single, specific mic (and some wannabe VOs who never sound good, ever, on any mic!).

- Some women, especially those with bright, sometimes sibilant voices, may have a difficult time finding a model that doesn't sound brittle and harsh. Many mics can bring out sibilance in a female voice and really mar a good recording. A few males will suffer this fate, too; there's no gender bias in the world of mics. If you qualify for this, search for tube-based or other warmer-sounding models (we'll mention a few shortly), and consider a tube-based preamp to help take the edge off that brightness.
- Also, realize that your choice of microphone preamp (coming up soon) will affect the microphone's sound.

With these criteria in mind, here are a few recommendations in each of the three categories and at different budget levels. We've used and tested the mics listed here and give them our stamp of approval for VO work.

Dynamic Choices

Because it is rugged and does not require power, a dynamic mic may be the right choice for you at home and on the road. If the preamp or audio interface you choose doesn't supply phantom power, using a dynamic mic is your only solution. If so, make the following models part of your evaluation. All of these have cardioid pickup patterns.

The Shure SM57 or SM58 dynamic mic is a solid choice for recording your voice (http://www.shure.com/index.htm). At less than $100, this mic sounds remarkably good on a variety of voices, but not all (see Figure 4.9). Generally, the SM57 is better suited to male voices, while the SM58 sings for females. However, your voice might be the exception to this rule so, if you can, record some tests and evaluate further before making a final buying decision.

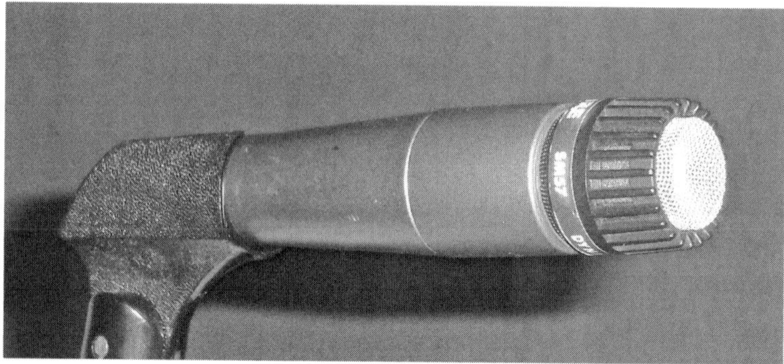

Figure 4.9 Shure SM57.

In the $200–$500 range, check out the Sennheiser MD 421 as a good dynamic choice (http://www.sennheiser.com/sennheiser/icm.nsf). Another would be the Electro-Voice RE20, a mainstay in the radio world (http://www.electrovoice.com/index.php). This dynamic mic is known for its warm, fat FM-DJ sound. Many broadcasters also swear by the similar-sounding and popular Shure SM7B.

Newcomers to the dynamic playing field are the Heil PR-30 and PR-40 (www.heilsound.com); they are growing in popularity as other go-to dynamic mics. Their cardioid patterns offer amazing off-axis rejection, which means they don't pick up much sound unless you talk *directly* into them. This attribute makes the Heil mics ideal for recording in noisier spaces. These two mics have very different audio qualities, though, so you must test them on your voice!

Condensers—Condensed

Assuming you are willing and able to invest in the components that supply the necessary phantom power, consider purchasing a large-diaphragm condenser microphone. We're confident that this is the route the vast majority of you will take. These mics are the VO recording standard, and you'll be quite pleased with how wonderful you can sound on a top-quality large-diaphragm condenser.

In recent years, there has been a flood of inexpensive large-diaphragm condenser mics. Many come from China and sometimes suffer from inconsistency in manufacturing, but as quality control continues to improve, we can recommend many of these microphones, particularly for those with a limited budget.

On the low end of the price scale, the Marshall Electronics (http://www.mxlmics.com) MXL 909, MXL 2001, and MXL 2003 all work quite well. The 909, in Figure 4.10, is particularly strong. (You'll learn why shortly.) The Audio-Technica (http://www.audio-technica.com/world_map/) AT-2020 is another economical alternative worth testing on your voice, as is the slightly higher-priced AT-3035. In that same price range, check out Australia's RØDE NT1-A (http://www.rodemic.com). It is an award-winning mic that sounds terrific on a variety of voices.

Moving into the middle price range, there are many more mic choices. This is really where the competition is fierce, but there are still a few standouts. RØDE's NT2-A is a step up from its less expensive little brother, the NT1-A. The Shure KSM line, particularly its KSM27 (good) and KSM32 (better), is ideally suited for voice work. We also like the Marshall MXL M3B "Silicon Valve" because of its balanced and smooth sound, but it may be a bit bright and accentuate sibilance too much for some (see Figure 4.11).

Figure 4.10 MXL 909.

Figure 4.11 MXL M3B.

The V88, again from MXL, was especially designed for voice-overs, and it gives you a tight in-your-face sound that some people crave.

The tube-based Audio-Technica AT-3060 (which adorned the cover of this book's previous edition) is worth testing, especially if you need to warm up a thin or overly bright voice. We'd also suggest the Avant Electronics CV-12 (http://www.avantelectronics.com/CV-12.htm), pictured in Figure 4.12, because it is warm and full with a pleasant quality that you can listen to for extended periods. If you do long-form narration, definitely consider this model on your short list of candidates.

Figure 4.12 Avant Electronics CV-12.

Another interesting mic from Marshall is the MXL 9090, which has two different mic elements: one brighter and the other warmer. This may be a good choice when you expect to record other people and need the versatility; it's like two mics in one.

For the just-under-a-grand prize, step up into the Neumann TLM 103 (http://www.neumann.com), and you will discover the rich sound of this legendary mic-maker and why this model is a popular mic for voice work. Another "sure" choice in this tier would be another Shure (ahem)—the KSM44.

The high end brings the AKG C414 (http://www.akg.com) and Neumann U87 http://www.neumann.com). Many engineers agree that the modern "descendant" of the U47, the Neumann U87, is a fantastic choice for voice recording—but at a high price. A less expensive alternative is the Lawson L47MP MKII (http://www.lawsonmicrophones.com), which comes close to the legacy Neumann U47 sound of yesteryear (see Figure 4.13).

Figure 4.13 Lawson L47MP.

Also in this range are the awesomely smooth and pleasant Blue Mouse and Blue Dragonfly (http://www.bluemic.com). Both of these really excel for long narrations and audio books, with the Mouse, pictured in Figure 4.14, better suited for males and the Dragonfly for females, generally. And both mics are beautiful just to look at.

Figure 4.14 Blue Microphones' Blue Mouse.

The only small-diaphragm condenser mic that we would recommend would be the Sennheiser 416 short shotgun (see Figure 4.15). For spot work, it's invaluable, but over time it can be ear fatiguing. It seems to work better on male voices, giving that kind of in-your-face omniscient announcer quality. Harlan uses this mic for the majority of his work. Some females can benefit from this mic, too. (Test it, ladies!) Also, since the 416 has a small and tight pickup pattern, it sounds really weak if you are off-axis. So if you're a talent who needs to move around a lot, the 416 isn't a good choice.

Figure 4.15 Sennheiser 416.

Remember that MXL 909 mentioned earlier? In blind mic tests, we found it sounded nearly as strong as the 416 (especially when coupled with a superb mic preamp). It's uncanny that the 909 ($60 from http://www.musiciansfriend.com) can compete head-to-head with a $1,500 mic, but it is nevertheless true! Everybody should test this mic; it's hard to beat the price.

It's important to note that many expensive mics (and cheaper ones, too) can be found at a discount online on sites such as eBay. Just remember: *caveat emptor.*

It's also fun to collect vintage and other unusual mics as Harlan does. Many of these don't actually work anymore, but they sure look good.

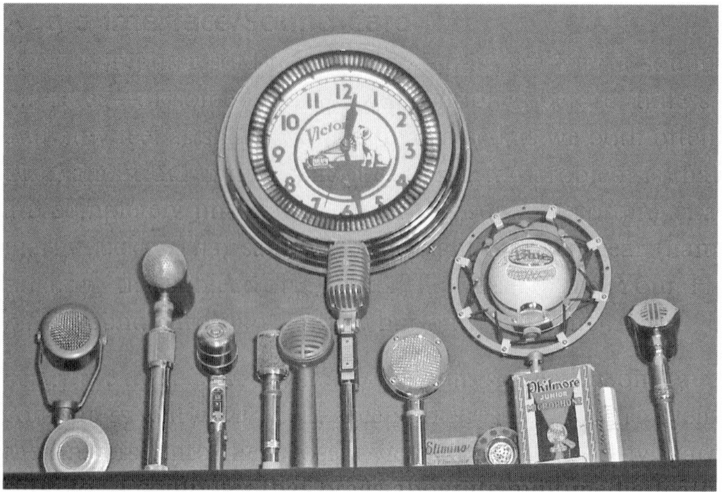

Ribbon Cutting

We both have to admit that we're latecomers to the recent ribbon resurgence (*Lovely alliteration, fellows. Lovely. —Prunella*) and at this time can recommend a fine emulation of the vintage RCA 77DX—the Edward R. Murrow microphone. Cascade makes the Victor (http://www.cascademicrophones.com), which is an inexpensive ribbon mic that is well worth considering, especially if you want a warm, full tone. It also looks really great; you can see it perched on Jeffrey's desk in Figure 4.16. Actually, it looks retro, so make that the recent retro ribbon resurgence. Really ...

Figure 4.16 Cascade Victor.

Mic Accessories

After investing in the best mic for your voice, you'll need a few more things to get everything working together.

Cables and Connectors

Don't underestimate the value of a good-quality cable. Professional mics use cables with XLR connectors. These three-pin "balanced" connectors are less susceptible to radio frequency interferences (RFI) and electrical noise (hum to you and me and even Harlan, who is, admittedly, tone deaf). Know how most modern electrical appliance wires have a third—ground—plug? Well, an XLR connector works pretty much the same way. These cables can also supply the phantom power that condenser mics need.

Spend the few extra dollars to get a quality cable from a top manufacturer like Mogami (http://www.mogamicable.com). Choose a cable just long enough to reach from your recording area to your gear, but no longer. Excess cable can degrade sound quality. Also, be sure to keep your microphone and other cables away from household electrical wires. They are a classic source of hum. Never run an audio cable parallel to a power wire, and if you must cross an electrical cord, do it at a right angle (90 degrees).

These cables will *not* eliminate the noise from cell phones. You will hear—and record—the unmistakable *dit-dit-dit* sound when your network tries to find your phone (usually just before it rings or you get a text message). Turn off your phone when you're recording at home or you're at a recording studio.

Mic Support

You'll need a microphone stand to hold your mic. Almost all voice performers prefer to stand rather than sit when performing, so you'll probably want to purchase a boom arm as well. Boom arms make positioning the mic easier and more precise. Some stands have big, heavy, solid bases, while others use a tripod configuration. Check out On Stage's (http://www.onstagestands.com) line of freestanding mic supports. Some mics are quite heavy and can overpower an inexpensive stand, especially when the boom arm is extended. This is another area where investing a few extra dollars really does make a difference. Use a counterweight on the opposite end of the boom to balance an especially heavy microphone.

Broadcasters and voice actors who want to have several microphone choices ready at a moment's notice often use spring-loaded mic booms like the Heil PL-2 (http://www.heilsound.com). Harlan uses three inside his booth, making it quick and easy to swing one mic out of the way and bring in a different model as needed. In Figure 4.17, you can see the Heil boom arm supporting the Sennheiser 416. (Another unseen boom arm is supporting the aging, decrepit Harlan.)

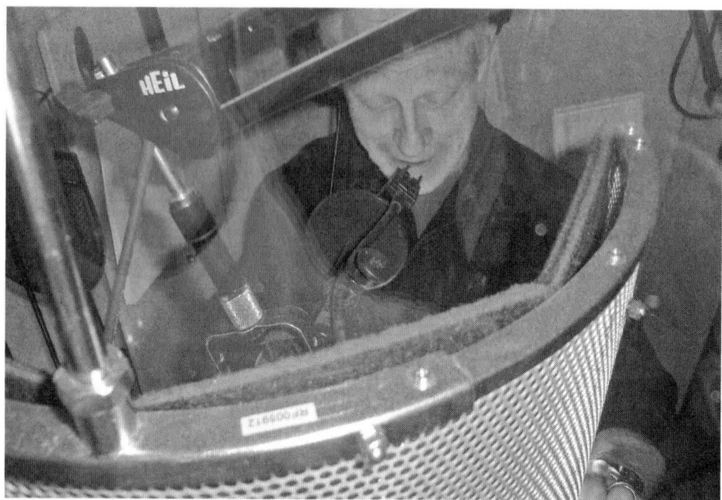

Figure 4.17 Heil boom.

If you will use a portable sound booth, like the Harlan Hogan Porta-Booth, to record at home or on the road, you need a small footprint desk mic stand that fits inside. There are lightweight versions, like the K&M/AKG (http://www.akg.com) low-profile desk stand or the Blue Snowball Mic Stand (http://www.bluemic.com/). These collapsible devices fold up for travel. For more permanent applications and heavier microphones, desktop devices like the Atlas Sound DS5 (http://www.atlassound.com) work great. We'll explain how to build your own Porta-Booth in Chapter 7, "Home Recording—Away from Home."

Shock Mounts

No, a shock mount is not—contrary to what one of us thinks—a stampeding stallion. Shock mounts, which are a good idea, simply attach your microphone to the stand but keep it acoustically uncoupled. In other words, these Web-like contraptions, sometimes referred to as spider mounts, effectively isolate the mic from picking up minor bumps and thumps. Some microphones come with a shock mount, but often it's an additional purchase. Mounts are typically custom-designed for the mic; they are not universal. Also, you'll be amazed and probably shocked to see just how much a shock mount costs for a Neumann microphone!

In Figure 4.4, the shock mount is next to the power supply, and in Figure 4.15, it is wrapped around the shotgun mic.

Pop Filter

Here's one more important accessory. Invest in a good pop screen to keep moisture (that's right, spit) out of your expensive microphone. Moisture that gets onto that vibrating diaphragm in a condenser microphone can damage it permanently.

These devices also do a good job of reducing plosives, such as popped Ps, Bs, and Ts, and can often save an otherwise great recording. Get the kind that attaches to the mic stand and can be positioned easily between your mouth and the mic. Don't use those foam "clown noses" (they actually muffle the sound); if one came with your mic, go toss it in the wastebasket or give it to the kids to play with. The nylon screen models are fine, but we both prefer pop filters that use a metal mesh design.

Check out the Avantone Pro-Shield (http://www.avantelectronics.com), with its oversized, arch-shaped face that mirrors the curvature of most large-diaphragm studio condenser mics. It's all metal, and positioning it is a snap. There's a mic stand or mic boom C-clamp attached to a sturdy, flexible gooseneck that keeps the filter exactly where you want it. More importantly, the Pro-Shield, in Figure 4.18, does its job extremely well, with no perceived loss in high-frequency sounds. The metal mesh attacks only those pesky low-frequency plosives and keeps moisture off the mic element.

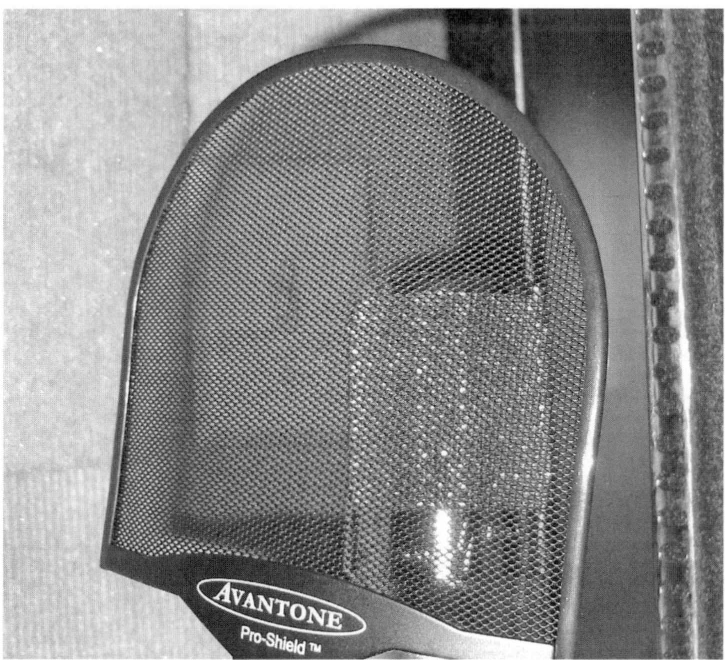

Figure 4.18 Pop filter.

An added perk to the all-metal designs is that you can easily clean the filter with soap and water or an antibacterial cloth between sessions and talents.

In a pinch, you can make a pop/spit filter from a coat hanger and some pantyhose, but professionally made ones are quite inexpensive and look a lot better!

Other Gear

Stedman (http://www.stedmancorp.com) supplies some neat-to-have accessories that attach to your mic stand and make your life easier. Its ProClip script holder and studio headphone hanger are invaluable. On Stage (http://www.onstagestands.com) also offers many handy-dandy doodads.

Microphone Care Handle your precious mic carefully. Don't blow into it, drop it, immerse it in water, play ring toss with it, or generally abuse it. Harlan feels strongly that you should never taunt your microphone or blame it for a lousy interpretation but ... well, that's just his opinion. When it's not on its stand working for you, put the mic away in its case. If it didn't come with a case, use a cloth-lined pouch or wrap it in some lint-free cloth or plastic and store it in another container.

Moisture and dust are your enemies; keep the mic away from both of those evils. Jeffrey packs his mics away with those "Do Not Eat" silica packs. They absorb excess moisture easily, with no fuss and no muss (and no snacking).

Ribbon mics are quite fragile, susceptible to wind damage and, as we warned you before, will be destroyed if phantom powered is accidentally applied to them. Also, always store a ribbon mic *vertically*, not on its side.

Plugging/unplugging any mic with phantom power already on is a bad idea. Turn off the power, plug in the mic, and then power it up. When unplugging, power down first (wait 15 seconds for the power to fully dissipate), and then disconnect the mic.

Microphone Preamps

Remember when we said that microphones deliver electricity that can then be processed by the computer? That's true, except the amount of electricity is too small. You'll need to boost or amplify a microphone's output before you can do anything else with it. For this, you need a microphone preamplifier whose purpose is to amplify the low-level microphone signal up to a useable volume called line-level. This higher level can then feed other components, such as your computer. Preamps come in three basic flavors:

mixers, standalones, and as part of many all-in-one computer audio interfaces—devices that combine the analog to digital converter, phantom power, and mic preamp.

Do we hear you saying, "What about the tiny little microphone input jack right on my computer?" Guess what? That little hole is designed to use the toy microphone we made you throw in the garbage. You did do that, right? We'll be checking the recycling bin. As you can guess, the preamplifier attached to that jack inside your computer is *not* a high-quality, low-noise microphone preamp suitable for serious voice recording.

Mixer

As its name implies, a mixer lets you hook up many different sound sources and combine or mix them in new ways. Mixers, like the one in Figure 4.19, come in all shapes and sizes (and dollar amounts!), and many include the proper input and preamp you need to work with your microphone. Quality microphones use those round tube-shaped three-prong XLR connectors we discussed, so make sure the mixer you're considering has XLR jacks. If it doesn't, move on (see Figure 4.24). Because you will probably use only one microphone at a time, most mixers will have more inputs than you'll ever need. That's okay; the extra knobs and switches can really impress people who need impressing, and that alone can be worth the price of admission.

One very important point: if you selected a condenser microphone, you must make sure the mixer you buy supplies phantom power. If the mixer you buy lacks this feature, your cool mic won't work. Dynamic and ribbon microphones don't need phantom power, so

Figure 4.19 Mixer in use.

any mixer that accepts a microphone input will suffice in that case. Some condenser mics work on batteries, but they are more the exception than the rule.

Many people erroneously believe they must have a mixer. It's not true. There are other choices today that work as well as or better than having a dedicated mixer. For most of you, choosing a mixer really depends on its sound, specifically its mic preamps. If you like the way mic preamps sound with your mic and voice, go with a mixer. If not, read on for other ideas.

Also, note that you may see references to powered mixers. These are for live sound reinforcement and are unsuitable for voice work. Skip 'em.

However, if you will be doing phone patch and ISDN sessions, having a mixer is a key component for making that work. In Chapter 8, "Basic Production Techniques," we'll give you all the details for long-distance work. Also, if you will juggle a lot of different microphones as Harlan does, a mixer is handy for keeping everything plugged into one central location and then letting you choose which mic you use to record without a lot of plugging and unplugging (see Figure 4.20).

Figure 4.20 Mixer inputs.

Many manufacturers make mixers with mic inputs, phantom power, and low-noise microphone preamps. You can't go wrong with models by Mackie (http://www.mackie.com). Mackie is well known and respected for the quality of its microphone preamps. Both its Onyx line and VLZ models are very good. Mixers with too many inputs are usually overkill, so the Mackie 402-VLZ3 with four inputs is a good choice.

Behringer (http://www.behringer.com) is another company that makes dedicated audio mixers. Check out its XENYX line, specifically its model 802. And the Alesis MultiMix (http://www.alesis.com) models are equally strong for VO work.

The output of a mixer can go directly into a computer, but as we've mentioned, most computer audio interfaces are not top quality. You may need to invest in a better audio interface. However, some mixers include a USB hookup and serve as an audio interface, too. This can make for an all-in-one solution and be the cornerstone of your recording chain.

Standalone Microphone Preamp

Instead of a mixer, you can use a dedicated microphone preamp, which is built for one purpose: to provide a clean, low-noise preamp for high-quality microphones. Some of these models, called boutique preamps in the audio trade, are much sought-after for the particular "sound" they have. Most preamps also supply phantom power.

Entry-level dedicated microphone preamps include the ART Tube MP Studio V3 Mic Preamp (http://www.artproaudio.com), in Figure 4.21, the PreSonus TubePRE (http://www.presonus.com), and Studio Projects VTB1 (http://www.studioprojectsusa.com). You'll notice all three of these devices reference "tube" technology. That means they use a vacuum tube in the amplification stage instead of a solid state (transistor) amplifier. So what? Many pros agree that tubes add pleasing warmth to the microphone's sound. Anything that helps present your voice in the best light can't be bad, right?

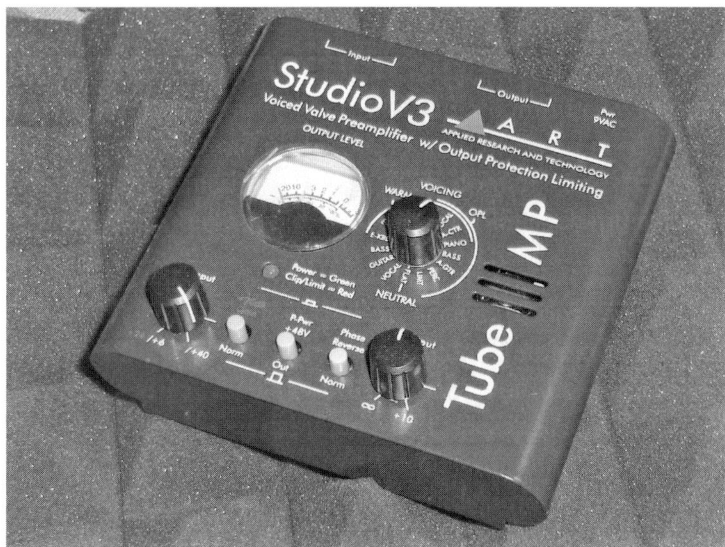

Figure 4.21 ART dedicated tube preamp.

As mentioned before, if you suffer from a bright tone that creates excessive sibilance, a tube preamp (along with the right mic choice) can make you sound great. Female voices in particular often benefit from the fullness that a little tube preamp can add. But—test, test, test.

Moving up in price brings some terrific choices, such as the Focusrite TrakMaster PRO (http://www.focusrite.com) and two of Jeffrey's favorites, Universal Audio's (http://www.uaudio.com) SOLO/610 (Tube) and SOLO/110 (solid-state).

In the upper tier, you'll find the Focusrite VoiceMaster Pro, Grace Design model 101 (http://www.gracedesign.com), the John Hardy M1 (http://www.johnhardyco.com), and the Avalon M5 (http://www.avalondesign.com). The John Hardy M1 is shown in Figure 4.22, and the Avalon is pictured in Figure 4.23.

Figure 4.22 John Hardy M1.

Figure 4.23 Avalon M5.

The M1 and Avalon preamps, when paired with a solid microphone, provide a wonderful tone. Mr. Fisher feels that just about anything plugged into the John Hardy sounds fantastic and, in oh-so-rare accordance, Mr. Hogan agrees!

Choosing a dedicated preamp is an aesthetic decision—you love the way it sounds on your voice. Be sure you invest in a quality audio interface, though; you wouldn't plug your lovely "pre" into that ten-cent audio interface built into your computer!

Audio Interface

Speaking of audio interfaces, we *highly recommend* you use an external audio interface in your studio, and there are a number of external computer audio interfaces available today that include a mic preamp. These all-in-one solutions (see Figure 4.24) accept balanced microphone inputs, supply phantom power, include headphone outputs and speaker connections, and use a top-quality analog-to-digital converter (ADC) with higher sampling rates and greater bit depth. Once again, the sound you record will be far superior to what you'll get from the el-cheapo sound card already installed in your computer.

Note: Even if you opt for a standalone preamp or mixer, we still suggest that you invest in a quality audio interface. You may not use its preamps, but you will still plug the output from your preamp into its line-level input and use it for the conversion to digital, headphone/speaker monitoring, and so forth.

Figure 4.24 Audio interface.

Note: If you select ProTools as your software of choice, you *must* use its hardware audio interfaces. Digidesign does not support any of the interfaces mentioned here (with the exception of some M-Audio hardware). For example, you can get the USB-based MBox2 mini, which includes ProTools LE 7.4 software. The MBox2 mini has one mic input, with phantom power, and a preamp that will record into the ProTools software. You can plug in headphones and hook up speakers. If you prefer, you can still use a dedicated preamp with your mic and plug its output into the MBox2.

Although some audio interfaces require installing a card inside your computer, others simply plug into USB or FireWire (aka IEEE1394) ports on your computer. This gives you everything you need in one compact box. The only real difference between the USB- and FireWire-based models is that FireWire supports a greater number of inputs and outputs. You'll probably need only one input (your microphone); more inputs may be unnecessary.

Another big bonus of the plug-and-play devices is that these interfaces can be used on multiple computers. Harlan uses his on his home computer, on his wife's computer the day that a virus brought his fiefdom to a crashing halt, and on his laptop when he's on the road. Jeffrey has several interfaces that also move from computer to computer depending on what he's doing and where he's currently parking his derrière.

USB Based

The price range for decent models is about the same for all the devices mentioned here. Check out the M-Audio Fast Track Pro (http://www.m-audio.com), Edirol UA-25 (http://www.edirol.com), or the Lexicon Lambda or Omega (http://www.lexiconpro.com). You can also get the convenient ART Tube MP Project Series USB, which uses the same tube preamp we spoke of along with a USB audio interface. On the higher end of the price range is the equally high-quality Sound Devices USBPre (http://www.sounddevices.com).

For the ultimate in at-home and on-the-road functionality (and portability), the CEntrance MicPort Pro (http://www.centrance.com) is a mini audio interface that plugs directly into your mic and has a USB cable out the other side (see Figure 4.25). It delivers phantom power to mics that need it and—this is important—has a headphone jack for monitoring while you record. This clever device even offers 24-bit/96kHz recording and includes a volume knob for setting the microphone level and another for your headphone volume. The MXL USB Mic Mate is a similar-looking unit, but it lacks a headphone jack.

The MicPort Pro's ability to supply 48V phantom power through your computer's USB port greatly expands its usefulness. Now, any mic you own or purchase in the future can

Los Angeles

DPN

CESD

SBV

TGMD

WILLIAM MORRIS

New York

ATLAS

BUCHWALD

ACCESS

PARADIGM

CESD

Word of Mouth.
V.O. Tales of Techniques
VORG

ROUNDABOUT
ENTERTAINMENT, INC.
Video Mastering & Duplication

DUCK DUNN
WILLIE WEEKS
CHUCK RAINEY
JAMES JAMERSON
JERRY JEMMOTT

More legato, less staccato
less melody
End lines flat or down

From HOME

3915 W. Burbank Blvd, Burbank, CA 91505, Tel: (818) 842-9300 Fax: (818) 842-9301
E-Mail: roundabout@roundabout.com Web Site: www.roundabout.com

Figure 4.25 MicPort Pro.

be a USB mic. We've tested it with a dynamic, the Shure SM57; condensers, including MXL 909 and MXL M3B; and even a Sennheiser 416 short shotgun. The preamp is low noise and perfectly acceptable. It doesn't have a unique "sound" like some boutique mic pres, and it's not warm like a tube pre for those who need it. The preamp is clean, clear, and natural sounding, and the A/D audio interface is quiet so you record your voice, not the electronics. This is one amazingly handy device at an equally amazing low price.

FireWire Based

There are many possibilities here, but the ones we'd most recommend include the PreSonus FireBox (http://www.presonus.com); M-Audio FireWire 410 and M-Audio FireWire Solo; Focusrite Saffire and Saffire LE (http://www.focusrite.com), which Jeffrey uses and is shown in Figure 4.26; and the Mackie Onyx 400F. Both Focusrite and Mackie preamps are terrific, so these models are well worth investigating.

USB Microphones

If you don't already have a mic, audio interface, or mic preamp that you love, consider the simplicity of a USB microphone. These mics plug into and get power directly from a USB port, where it appears to your recording software as an audio interface. So, you get a mic, preamp, and A/D audio interface all rolled into one, spitting out 0s and 1s right into your computer—no extra gear required. This is a reasonable solution for the technically challenged.

Like most USB mics, you can't monitor the sound in your headphones as you record with the MXL .008 (see Figure 4.27). You can, of course, keep a watchful eye on the volume meters in your software or on your mixer, but you can't actually hear and evaluate what's happening as you record. You have to wait until you finish recording and listen to the playback. Most VOs prefer to hear themselves on headphones as they

Figure 4.26 Focusrite Saffire.

Figure 4.27 MXL .008.

record. Unfortunately, only a few USB mics allow you to do that. That's why we're so excited about the MicPort Pro approach mentioned earlier.

New mics that arrived as we were putting the final touches on this chapter include the MXL USB.009 24/96 (http://www.mxlmics.com) and the USB (http://www.seelectronics.com/USB2200a.html).

The USB.009 is a surprisingly heavy and robust mic that sounds fantastic on a variety of voices. It supports 24-bit/96kHz recording, has level knobs onboard, and has a separate, zero-latency headphone jack with volume control for monitoring.

Based on the studio standard sE2200a, the USB2200a records via USB directly to your software and includes zero-latency headphone monitoring, mix control playback/record path, and more. The neat thing is that it works with an XLR as a regular mic or as a USB. The folks at sE claim the electronic guts in this mic make it less noisy than other USB mics.

If you were only going to choose one mic, these two new entries are well worth testing. They're the best USB mics available right now.

USB mics without headphone monitoring:

- Audio-Technica AT2020USB (same mic as the 2020 mentioned earlier)
- Blue Mics Snowball (it not only looks cool, but it has a three-pattern switch (cardioid, cardioid with –10dB pad, and omni)
- MXL .008

USB mics with headphone monitoring:

- MXL USB.009 24/96, which couples a terrific mic with a great digital converter and includes the crucial headphone connection
- RØDE Podcaster
- Samson G Track
- USB

Final Necessities

Enough already, right? You've already drained your savings by buying a microphone, shockmount, stand or boom arm, preamp, computer, audio interface, cables, and (coming up in the next chapter) software. What else could you possibly need?

Well, you need ways to listen to what you record. That means a pair of quality headphones and good speakers. Accuracy is our goal. You need to be sure that what you record will sound the same when people play it back in their homes and offices. So you can't risk letting cheap speakers and headphone lie about how your home studio recording sounds.

Headphones are useful, but they're not for making critical audio judgments. In other words, don't rely on headphones for the final recording. Most people listen on speakers, and the difference between what sounds good on headphones and what sounds right on speakers can be completely different. Instead, just use your "cans" when you record—so you can hear what's being recorded. Headphones can also be useful when checking your finished recordings for background noises and other junk you might miss when listening on speakers. Don't let them have the final word, though. *Always* check your recordings on real speakers before you decide what sounds right.

Of course, if you do phone patch and ISDN sessions, you'll need headphones so you can hear direction from the remote producer.

Headphones

Avoid the cheap ear buds you use with your MP3 player, and also stay miles away from open-ear design headphones. Noise-cancelling headphones are fine for air travel, but keep them out of the voice-over booth. This is a case where you *want* and *need* to hear any noise so you can take steps to eliminate it!

Instead, use closed-ear models that sit closer to your ears, surrounding them. They shut out outside sounds so you can hear yourself better and hear what the microphone hears. Their design also keeps the sound in your headphones from feeding back through the microphone. Ouch! That can really hurt your ears, not to mention your equipment.

The recording studio standards are the Sony 7506 or the Sennheiser HD280 Pro. Both are under $100 and well worth the price.

You might think—as Harlan once did—that high-end wireless headphones would be a good choice because they make it easier to roam around your studio unencumbered. However, wireless devices often pick up extraneous noises, like cab dispatchers, nearby radio stations, and general hum and buzz. They simply don't sound nearly as good or as accurate as plug-in phones like the kinds we mentioned. After trashing his wireless headphones, Harlan simply bought a very l-o-n-g curly headphone extension cable so he is now "free to move about the building."

Another handy tool is a separate headphone amplifier/volume control such as the Rolls HA43 Headphone Amplifier Mixer (http://www.rolls.com), pictured in Figure 4.28. Since you will want to record at a distance from your noisy computer, it won't be convenient to turn up and down the headphone volume when needed. This is especially true on remote sessions, where you'll need to balance the producer's volume in your cans with your own. Similarly, if you need up to four performers on headphones at the same time, this little and inexpensive device is invaluable.

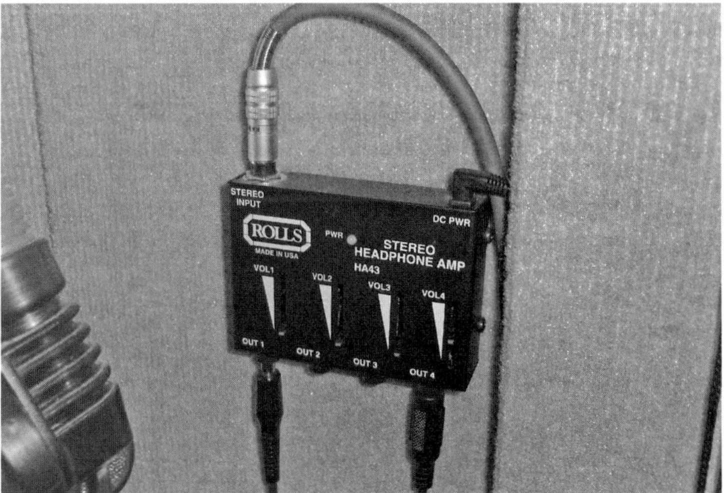

Figure 4.28 Rolls headphone amp.

Speakers (aka Monitors)

You also need a set of speakers to monitor your sound recordings and to make critical judgments about their quality. You know already, of course, that we're going to trash the little speakers that came with your computer. Ditto for laptop speakers. Frankly, they just won't cut it. You won't really be sure whether what you're hearing is an accurate reflection of what you've recorded. One thing computer speakers are useful for is to hear how your voice will sound on—computer speakers! Many times, auditions in particular will be played only on desktop or laptop speakers, so in that case checking your tracks on computer speakers makes sense.

That said, you still need a better set of quality speakers for your other voice work, especially if you are recording finished, air-quality tracks. Ready for more slang? Speakers are called studio monitors in the audio trade. And monitors don't come cheap.

You have two choices: passive and active monitors. Passive monitors require a separate amplifier to power them. Active monitors include an amplifier right in the speaker cabinet. Active monitors are often called powered monitors, and they are really the way to go. Powered monitors are so popular that it's actually hard to find studio-quality passive monitors. One of the reasons for that is that monitor manufacturers prefer designing the whole shebang for better quality control. Do remember that, though you can play your monitors in a hall, they are not hall monitors! (*I'm sorry? Was that a sophomoric American joke? I dozed off. —Prunella*)

Here are some powered, active studio monitors that are suitable for voice-over recording, editing, mixing, and quality control. The difference between a 4-6 model and an 8 is a larger bass driver on the 8, called a woofer, that makes the speaker/monitor fuller range. Choosing the larger model is more a matter of taste; the smaller versions are acceptable.

- Alesis Monitor One, Mk2 (http://www.alesis.com)
- Behringer Truth B2031A Active (http://www.behringer.com)
- Event TR8XL Tuned (http://www.event1.com)
- KRK VXT6 Active or KRK VXT8 (http://www.krksys.com/)
- Mackie HR624 or Mackie HR824 (http://www.mackie.com)
- M-Audio DX4, BX5A, or BX8A (http://www.m-audio.com)

Harlan is enamored with his Mackie HR624s (see Figure 4.29), while Jeffrey loves his passive, but discontinued, Event 20/20s, in Figure 4.30 (now replaced by the TR8XL active version). Jeffrey also uses the M-Audio LX4 system for surround sound work. Therefore, Harlan is active despite his age, while Jeffrey, though marginally younger, is—as long suspected—passive.

Also, be sure to invest in Auralex MoPads (http://www.auralex.com) to slide under your monitors. These rigid foam pieces isolate the speaker from the surface it sits on and greatly improves the sound. Trust us when we say that spending $40 for a set of these will make a huge positive impact on what you hear. You can see them under the Event's in Figure 4.30.

Figure 4.29 Mackie-powered monitors.

Figure 4.30 Event passive monitors.

Don't Be Shy: Ask for Help

Consider asking an experienced local recording engineer for help in selecting equipment and setting up your studio. You should offer to pay for this expertise, either with money or some like/kind trade. Perhaps the engineer needs a voice for a project, like the studio's answering machine.

Reputable audio dealers can also be a good source for assistance. Do keep in mind that most dealers are music centric and don't always understand the needs of a voice-actor. Their gear recommendations may have more to do with musical instruments and singers sounding good than working with the spoken word.

Finally, where do you get all this equipment? We recommend the following online sellers:

- American Musical Supply (http://www.americanmusical.com)
- B&H Photo Video (http://www.bhphotovideo.com)
- Full Compass Systems (http://www.fullcompass.com)
- Musician's Friend (http://www.musiciansfriend.com)
- Sweetwater (http://www.sweetwater.com)
- Voice-Over Essentials (http://www.voiceoveressentials.com)

Well, there you have it. You now know everything you need (and might want) to put together the front end of your own recording studio. Time to go shopping!

5 Assembling Your Home Studio—Software

"You guys created me, I didn't come from anywhere. Before you started messing around with your computer, I didn't even exist. By the way, you did an excellent job. Thank you."

—Kelly LeBrock as Lisa, *Weird Science*, 1985, Universal Pictures

Okay, fine, so maybe your computer software *can't* create knock-down-gorgeous creatures like Lisa. But, it *can* make knock-down-gorgeous-looking and *-sounding* audio right at home. Really.

So far, we've discussed the importance of a quality computer to serve as the center of your recording studio. And we've explored—perhaps a little too extensively—the need for a solid audio front end. The next critical component is your recording software—the computer program you'll use to record, edit, and deliver your performances.

You'll want something that's easy to use but still powerful enough to handle the job. Most voice actors will be perfectly content with a simple recorder/editor program, although you may discover that you want and need more bells and whistles (*Is that a sound audio double entendre? —Prunella*) as your studio skills improve and the scope of your audio projects get more complex.

Digital Recording Software

We said earlier that software itself has little effect on the quality of sound recordings, because quality sound needs to be captured *before* your software does anything. But audio software does let you manipulate and, to some degree, alter the audio you've recorded after the fact. Some software providers claim that their software sounds better, but that's usually in reference to the quality of the hardware connected to it. Granted, some software programs handle the processing of audio data differently, which *can* result in a better sound if extensive audio manipulation, like noise reduction, is necessary. But most voice recordings won't need that kind of firepower.

There are two primary types of audio recording software: sound recorder/editors and multitrack systems. Sound editors such as in Figure 5.1 essentially let you record and edit individual mono or stereo files. A multitrack environment can combine several recordings on separate, fully synchronized tracks. This gives you the greatest control over all of a project's different sound elements, such as music and sound effects. All multitrack software functions as a recorder/editor, too.

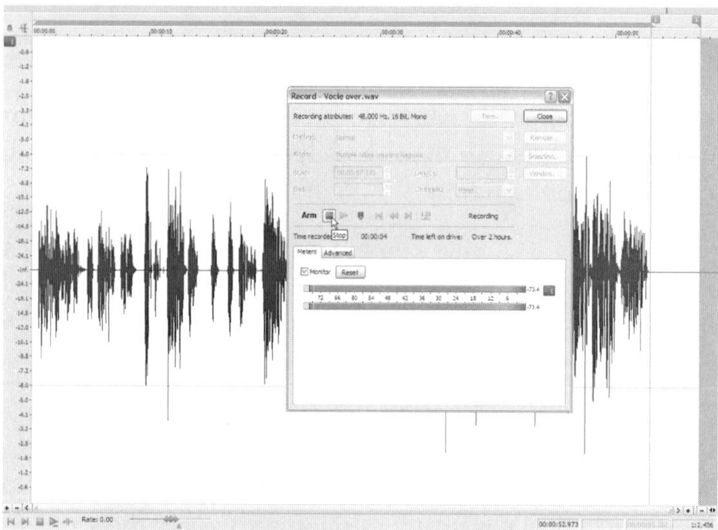

Figure 5.1 Audio recorder/editor.

If all you will record will be voice-only projects, such as auditions, radio/TV/Web spots, nonbroadcast work, and so forth, an audio recorder/editor is all you really need. However, should you plan to do more extensive sound recording, such as producing finished spots, sweetening video soundtracks, and more—then solid multitrack software is mandatory (see Figure 5.2). This kind of program is known as a *Digital Audio Workstation,* or DAW for short.

Be forewarned: some DAW software is complicated beyond belief. The owner's manual for one comes in at over 1,000 pages. (That one thousand is not a misprint!) And most of you would use less than 5 percent of its capabilities, if even that much. That doesn't mean you should avoid all DAW software. You just need to shop around.

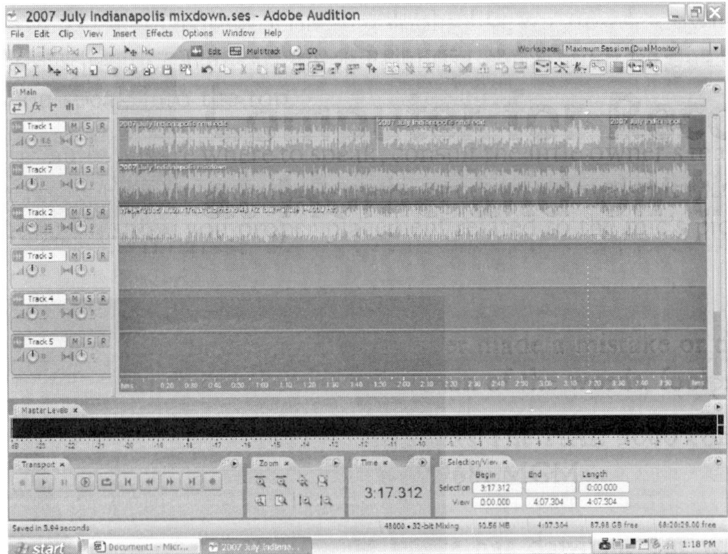

Figure 5.2 Multitrack software.

IMPORTANT! READ THIS! Now, you may ask other people what software they use, and they may tell you that everybody uses XYZ (not its real name) and that you have to use XYZ to compete in the voice-over world or to be compatible with other studios. This is complete balderdash. (*Okay if I use that word, boys? The one you chose with the initials B.S. did not fit my delicate sensibilities. —Prunella*)

Your finished recordings will be either WAV/AIFF or MP3, all of which are 100 percent, totally, absolutely, completely, and utterly compatible with *every* audio software program, including XYZ. Any studio on the planet can open and play these files no matter what audio recorder/editor or DAW it uses.

So save yourself the expense, and save yourself the headaches of having to learn programs that are way too complicated and way too sophisticated for the average voice-actor.

Fair warning. Don't make it hard on yourself. There are plenty of powerful *and* easy-to-use recording software programs to choose from.

Here's the real skinny: the only way to choose the right software for your needs is to try out various programs. Just like choosing a microphone, experimenting with various products will enable you to find the program or programs that suit your needs and "feel right" for you. Luckily, you can shop for software from the comfort of your computer, by visiting recording software Web sites like those listed next, and then downloading free trial versions. Play around with several programs before getting out your wallet. If the software feels natural and intuitive to your way of thinking and working, it is a good choice. If you are befuddled or find yourself fighting with the software, trying to get it to conform to your thought patterns, try another program. Remember: *all* the products out there will produce *all* the same audio formats: WAV (PC), AIFF (Mac), and MP3s suitable for e-mailing.

It should never be a struggle to learn the basics of the software. You should be able to pick it up quickly without a lot of paging through the manual or FAQs, especially for recording and basic editing. If, after an hour, you still feel lost, intimidated, and generally displeased, don't blame yourself; it's probably the software. Move on to the next demo, and see if that one clicks.

So what do you choose? Here's a list of popular programs to consider:

- *Audacity* (http://audacity.sourceforge.net; Mac/PC)
- *Adobe Audition* (http://www.adobe.com; PC)*
- *Bias Peak* (http://www.bias-inc.com; Mac)
- *Apple GarageBand* (http://www.apple.com; Mac)*
- *Goldwave* (http://www.goldwave.com; PC)
- *Apple Logic* Pro (http://www.apple.com; Mac)*
- *n-Track Studio* (http://www.ntrack.com; PC)
- *Steinberg Nuendo* (http://www.steinberg.net; Mac/PC)*
- *Digidesign ProTools* (http://www.digidesign.com; Mac/PC)* #
- *Magix Samplitude* (http://www.samplitude.com; PC)*
- *Cakewalk Sonar* (http://www.cakewalk.com; PC)*
- *Adobe Sound Booth* (http://www.adobe.com; PC)
- *Sony Sound Forge* (http://www.sonycreativesoftware.com; PC)
- *Apple Soundtrack Pro* (http://www.apple.com; Mac)*
- *Mackie Tracktion* (http://www.mackie.com; Mac/PC)*
- *Sony Vegas Pro* (http://www.sonycreativesoftware.com; PC)*

* = Indicates that software is a full-fledged, multitrack Digital Audio Workstation

= ProTools requires using their dedicated hardware audio interfaces as mentioned in the previous chapter. This limits your choices somewhat.

Many of these programs have two versions: the fully featured professional model and the stripped-down "light" consumer version. Though you should test the demos to be sure, most of the lighter (and therefore far cheaper and easier to use) versions are more than adequate for your needs. One choice—Audacity—works great on both Macs *and* PCs, and it's free (see Figure 5.3). That's right, *free*ware—hard to beat that price!

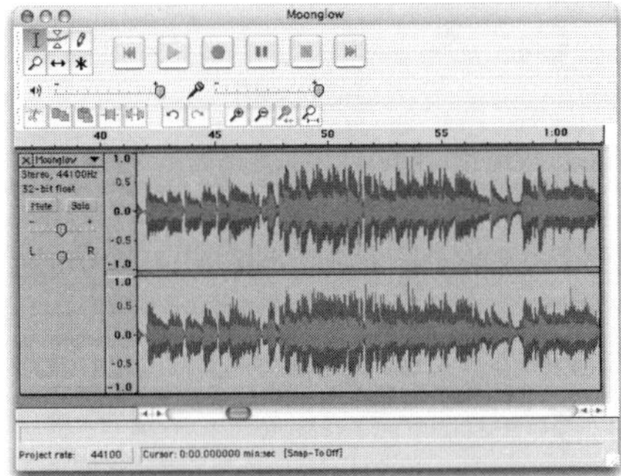

Figure 5.3 *Audacity.*

Recording software—like all computer programs—is constantly changing and improving, so there are bound to be new versions of the software mentioned here after this book is published. Typically, the latest version is the best choice. It's a good habit to regularly check your software's Web site for updates and fixes even after you've chosen it.

Note: You may see references to something called MIDI in some of the software available. Contrary to Harlan's belief, MIDI is not a conservative miniskirt *(! —Prunella)*. MIDI stands for **M**usical **I**nstrument **D**igital **I**nterface. Unless you are a music maker and a voice talent, you can just ignore this functionality with no hard feelings.

Here is what we use and recommend to you, with the caveat that you should still consider the many other choices available, because everybody works and learns differently. Since you'll spend *a lot* of time living with your software choice, don't just take our word for it.

PC

Sony's *Sound Forge Audio Studio* is a light version of its popular, full-featured, and professional *Sound Forge 9* (see Figure 5.4). This is a recorder/editor program only that is very capable and easily mastered. The software lets you record, edit, process, and deliver your finished voice tracks. We've recommended this software (and its Pro version, which Jeffrey uses) to hundreds of people and have been pleased with their reaction to its features, ease of use, and quickness to catch on. It doesn't get in the way of what's really important—performing, recording, basic editing, and creating finished files. You will be up and running quickly with either version and find it a willing partner in your success.

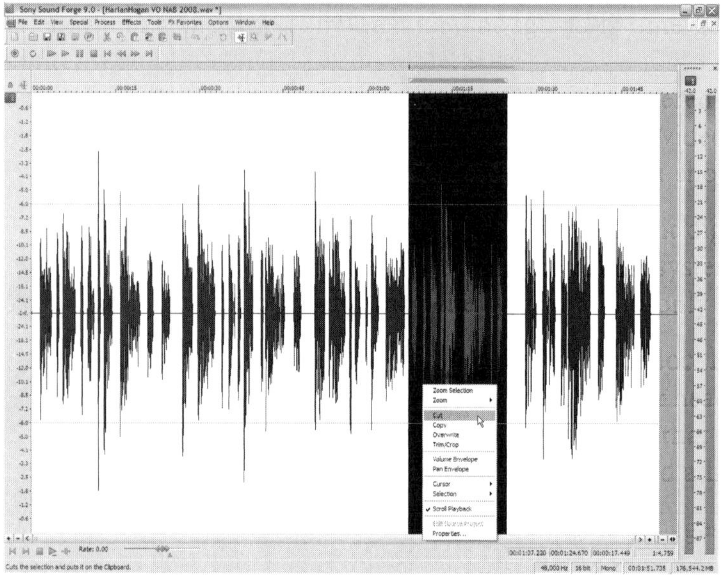

Figure 5.4 *Sound Forge* (Pro).

Adobe's *Audition,* in Figures 5.5 and 5.6, is Harlan's recording software choice, with its complete DAW features of recording, editing, multitracking, and mixing. *Audition* combines a powerful audio/editor with complete multitrack capabilities. Those audio recorder/editor functions may be all you ever need; you may never use its advanced multitrack functionality. (Harlan only occasionally does.) For a lighter version, check out Adobe's *Sound Booth,* which just has Audition's recorder/editor utilities.

Sony *Vegas 8 Pro* (see Figure 5.7) is Jeffrey's choice for a multitrack DAW. It's also a full-fledged nonlinear video editing system (NLE), which Jeffrey needs for the other work he does (video editing, audio post-production, music projects, and such). *Vegas Pro* has a powerful audio engine that can be used on its own; you can ignore the video features. Though Vegas Pro does have audio recorder/editor functions, Jeffrey prefers to work in *Sound Forge* for some tasks and *Vegas* for others. This means owning two different software programs, but they do complement each other and play together nicely.

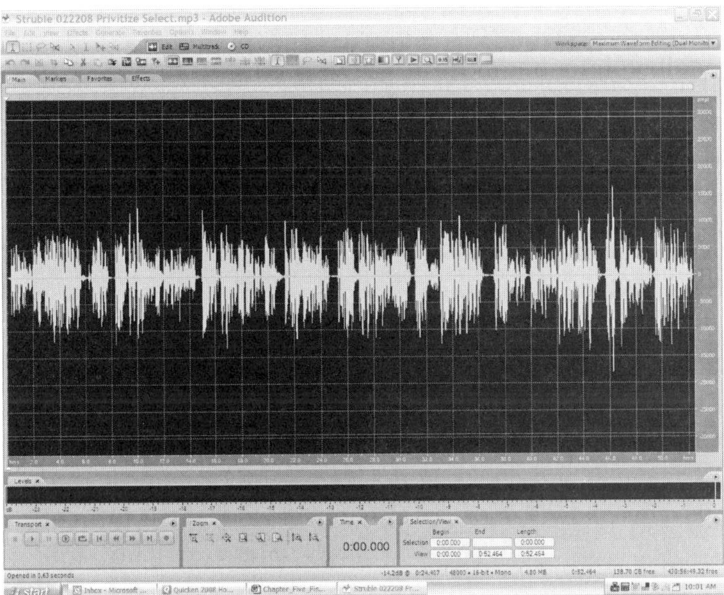

Figure 5.5 Adobe *Audition* mixer.

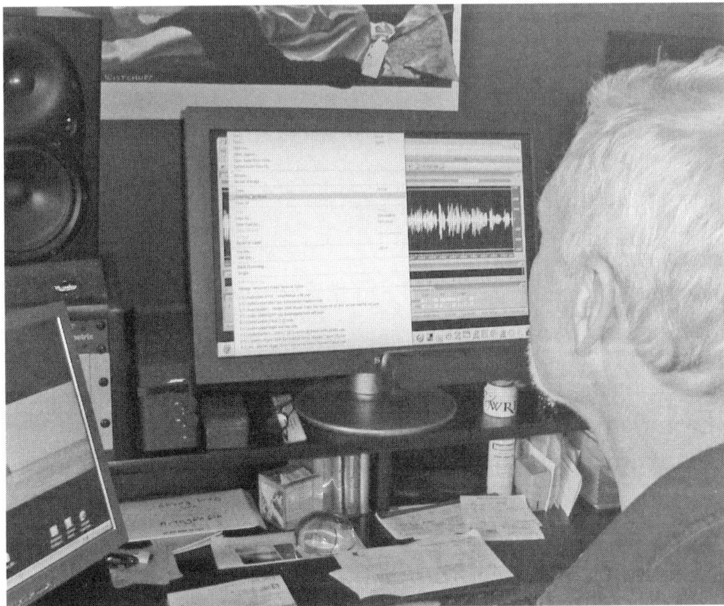

Figure 5.6 Harlan using *Audition*.

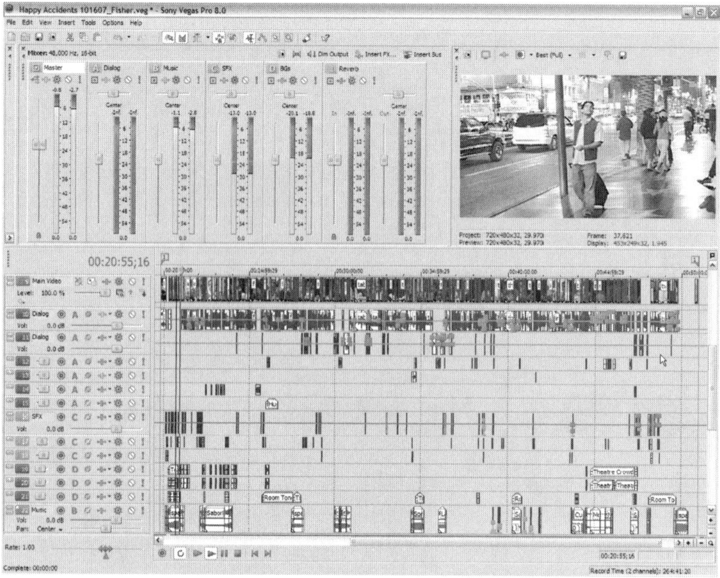

Figure 5.7 Sony *Vegas Pro*. (Screenshot from El Percance Perfecto courtesy of Xristos Productions.)

If you can conceive of yourself ever dipping your toes into the video waters, we highly recommend you take *Vegas Pro* for a test drive.

Mac

For those of you who use the other computer platform, you probably already have the best choice—*GarageBand*. The program, shown in Figure 5.8, is included with the iLife suite on every new Apple computer (and is separately available). Though the program was

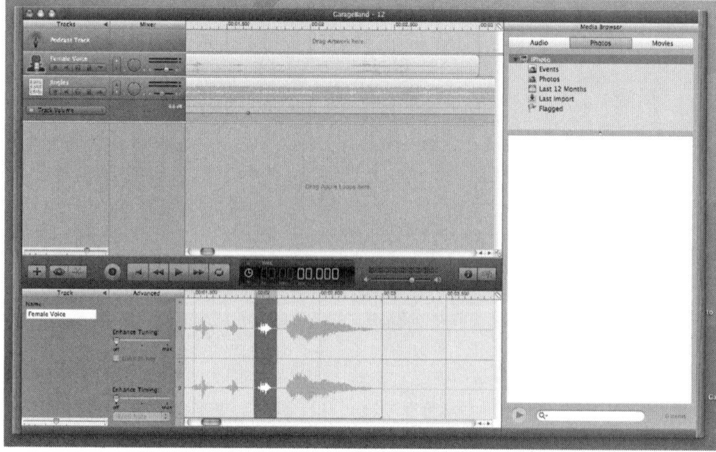

Figure 5.8 *GarageBand*.

primarily designed to be a music composition program, it includes all the tools you need to record, edit, and deliver your voice tracks, too. In fact, it even has some podcasting features that are suitable for voice work. It does have a lot of music references, but if you can look beyond that to its core audio toolset, you will be up and running fast.

GarageBand is also a multitrack DAW, so you can use it for more sophisticated audio work should you decide to take that direction.

For something more single purpose, like *Sound Forge* on the Mac, look at the LE (light edition) version of *Bias Peak*. And don't forget to eye and ear the freeware *Audacity* either.

A step up in functionality and sophistication is *Soundtrack Pro* (see Figure 5.9), which is part of the *Final Cut Studio* package, Apple's NLE.

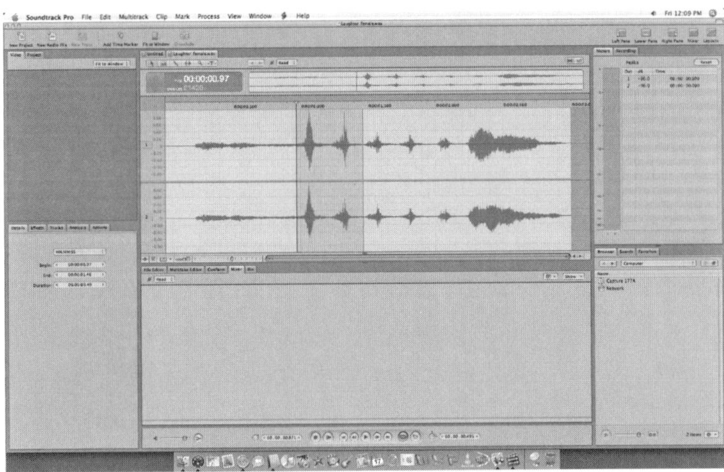

Figure 5.9 *Soundtrack Pro.*

Other Software

There are some other audio-related software programs that you should be aware of. Some are built in to your computer, while others come from outside venders.

Audio Interface/Soundcard Software

All the audio software recorder/editors and DAWs mentioned earlier need to "see" your audio interface/soundcard to work correctly. Most do this automatically, but you may need to adjust this manually (see Figure 5.10). Since this is controlled by the operating system (Windows or Mac), you access it through the Start, Control Panel (PC) or the Apple menu, System Preferences (Mac). Here, you can set up how your computer uses sound. If you use an external audio interface (as we recommend), connect it before checking or adjusting the settings here.

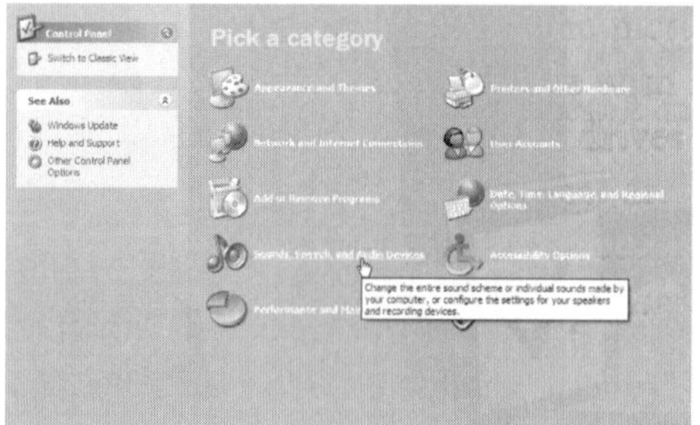

Figure 5.10 Windows Control Panel.

You may also need to adjust this setting directly in the audio software you use. This is typically in the program's Preferences. For example, in Figure 5.11, you would access these functions in *Sound Forge* using Options, Preferences, Audio tab and then select the proper input from the available options there.

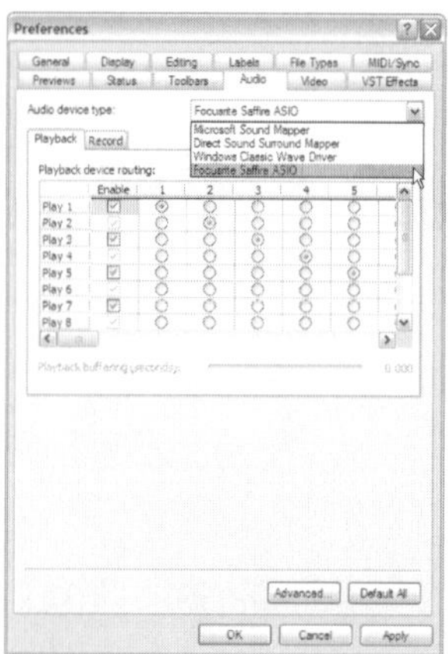

Figure 5.11 Set up an audio device.

A few audio interfaces also have their own software to control their functionality. The Focusrite *Saffire* that Jeffrey uses has a sophisticated software mixer shown in Figure 5.12 that provides access to various recording and playback scenarios.

Usually, the initial setup is all that needs to be done. After that, it is typically set and forget and get on with your work.

Effects and Plug-Ins

All the programs mentioned here come with the tools you need to record, edit, fix, sweeten, and deliver high-quality voice tracks. They include many processes and audio effects that are useful to fix mistakes, adjust volume, tweak tone, eliminate some noises, and create special effects. For example, you could apply a reverb effect to make your voice sound as if you were talking inside a large parking garage or use a filter effect to make it sound as if you were talking over the telephone. These various effects and tools will be discussed in greater detail in Chapter 12, "Advanced Production Techniques."

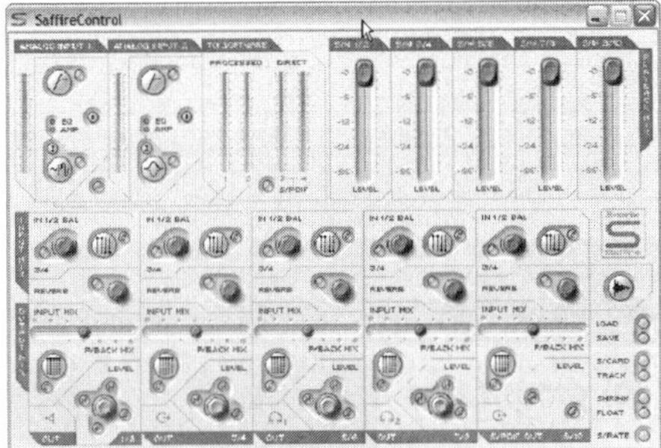

Figure 5.12 SaffireControl.

There are also third-party audio effects that "plug in" to your software and give you access to even more functionality and flexibility. For example, there are plug-ins that can duplicate the sound of expensive, vintage, and hard-to-find audio equipment and those that emulate the sound of hundreds of different microphones. For example, Jeffrey uses the audio effect plug-ins available from Universal Audio (http://www.uaudio.com), such as the LA2A in Figure 5.13.

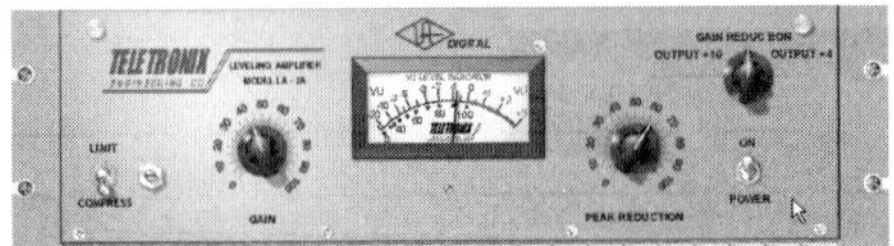

Figure 5.13 UAD LA2A.

Some audio effects are single purpose, designed to do one job. Others, such as iZotope Ozone 3 (http://www.izotope.com), combine several functions into one plug-in to handle a myriad of processing duties (see Figure 5.14).

Processing your voice is not for the beginner. While some special effects are easy to master, others, such as compression, take experience and knowledge. Most people reach for effects in an attempt to make their voice sound better. Frankly, if you have to resort to audio effects to make yourself sound right—whatever right may be—it might be smart to rethink your microphone and mic preamp choices. Get the sound down correctly in the first place, and leave the effects out of it!

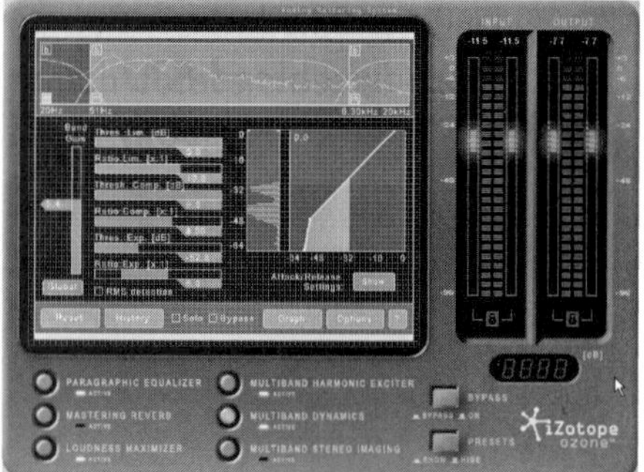

Figure 5.14 iZotope Ozone 3.

Most clients prefer plain, unprocessed voice tracks devoid of any special effects anyway. Remember that your voice is just one element in the overall soundtrack—a soundtrack with sound effects, music, and perhaps other voices. Audio engineers who mix these soundtracks often need to apply different effects to these diverse elements to fit them together into a cohesive whole. If you start adding effects, you make it harder for these professionals to do their jobs.

Computer Audio Tune-Ups

To get the most from your audio recording/editing software, follow these tips:

- When you record, disconnect from the Internet. E-mail, chat, and Web sites with constantly updating active content can interfere with recordings. You will hear glitches or little dropouts on the final tracks.
- Temporarily disable antivirus and other security programs while recording. Obviously, disconnect from the Web before turning off your protection.
- Shut down other programs you have running to free up the computer's resources.
- Keep your computer HDD running smoothly by defragmenting it regularly. Files get scattered all about the disc, making it inefficient to access the data. A defrag run puts stuff back together and frees up contiguous space for your recordings.
- Raise the priority of your recording software. For example, Windows enables giving your recording application the highest priority, which means lesser tasks won't interfere with it (like when you are recording).
- Keep software up to date, as manufacturers' bug fixes may solve your problems.

- Keep drivers updated. Drivers are little programs that control (uh, drive) your hardware. If you've invested in a quality audio interface, make sure it's working its best. Visit the manufacturer regularly, and look for driver updates for your particular model.

We've got our computer, hardware, and software decisions out of the way. Now you'll need a place to record—the subject of the next chapter.

6 Sound Space: Finding/Creating/Tweaking the Right Location

"It is my job to keep this very, very, very, very QUIET!"

—Fred Ward as Walter Stuckel, *The Player,* 1992, Avenue Pictures Productions

People need a place to create their art. For painters, that's a room with good light. For the culinary inclined, it's a dream kitchen. For writers, it's usually a quiet place free of distractions (or crowded coffee shops, though neither of us understands how anyone could write well [*or edit —Prunella*] in such an environment). Voice-actors are no different. You need a place to perform, too. And although almost any space will do, some choices are much better than others.

This chapter looks at designing a more permanent setup in your home or office. That doesn't mean you can't take it with you (should you relocate, for instance). But generally, the discussion here is about a fixed recording space. A truly portable solution is discussed in Chapter 7, "Home Recording—Away from Home."

You need enough room to record in and house your computer and other recording gear. This space can be one and the same or located in separate rooms. Spare bedrooms and basements work well, but even a corner of your living room can suffice. We recommend keeping the work away from where you sleep for psychological and sanity reasons; finding the odd sock dangling from your $1,000 TLM-103 is as disquieting as it is disgusting.

In any case, you need to put some distance between your microphone and the computer that records it. Computers are noisy beasts. The whirrs, hum, clicks, fan noise, and that pesky squeaky wheel that the little hamster runs on to power it all create a background noise that will ruin your voice tracks. Throwing a blanket over the computer will not effectively eliminate this din either and could actually allow the computer to overheat and, well, ... that's just not a good thing at all. There are soundproofed enclosures with silent cooling fans that you can place your computer into, like the Silent PC and XRack-Pro (http://www.xrackpro.com) lines; however, the cost of these devices is often as much or more than the computer itself!

So, whatever space you choose, it's most practical to consider dividing it into two distinct areas: one for the geek gear and another for your mic and related paraphernalia. The more distance you can put between these two, the better your recordings will be. From now on, we'll call the former your office and the latter your vocal booth (whether it's an actual booth or not).

Your Office

Invest in a decent desk that's designed to hold a computer and the right height for using your keyboard. There should be enough room for the CPU, monitor(s), keyboard, mouse, and printer. If you'll just use a laptop, your desk space needs are a bit smaller. Don't forget, you may need extra space for the audio interface you're using and for your monitor/speakers. Invest in a quality chair, too. You'll spend a lot of time working at the computer, so you deserve to be comfortable. The office superstores and places like Ikea have plenty of furniture to choose from.

Your desk needs space to hold your monitor/speakers and perhaps regular vanilla computer speakers as well. If there isn't enough real-estate available, you'll need to invest in stands to hold them.

Proper positioning of your monitors is critical. You want the speakers at ear level with *no obstructions* in their way. Position them so that the two speakers and your head form the three points of an equilateral triangle. (*Ah ... that explains why Jeffrey's head is so abnormally pointed. —Prunella*)

In Chapter 1, "The New Paradigm—A Home Studio Is a Required Tool of the Trade," you can see snapshots on pages 2 and 3 of Harlan's and Jeffrey's offices. H2 uses a desk made specifically for audio gear by Omnirax Studio Furniture. A single desk works for Jeffrey, too, with some other audio gear located nearby.

Your Vocal Booth

With the basic office space ready, find a nearby area to record your voice. An echo-y space, such as a large room or tiled bathroom, just won't work. Even most bedrooms are too bright and bouncy—what audio engineers call "live" sounding—for recording. You don't want the sound of the room to overwhelm your voice; you want to minimize the room's impact. And you already know that sound—the hollow, mushy, and noisy quality of everybody's home videos (and quite a few YouTube ones, too). Voice work is better served by a tight, intimate quality, so try to find a suitable recording space that already possesses those qualities.

However, keep these issues in mind:

- You need to keep unwanted sounds from being picked up by the microphone when you're recording. Noise may come from outside your recording area (street traffic) or originate inside it (your furnace and air conditioner). To keep the clatter of real life out of a room, you need to try to eliminate as much of those extraneous sounds as possible.
- You need a quiet, acoustically dead space that you'll add sound-shaping acoustic treatments to so that it sounds good.
- Soundproofing a room—which is quite a feat—will not make the room itself sound good, only quieter.
- Adding sound-shaping acoustic treatments will make a room sound good, but it will not keep noise out of your recordings.

It's neither easy nor cheap to keep noise entirely out of a space, so don't even bother trying to soundproof a room. That requires some special construction techniques that you can't take with you if you move. And renters will have a hard time convincing their landlords of their soundproofing needs.

The Web site http://www.minewurx.com/echos/the-monster-sound-isolation-booth/ will give you an idea of what's involved in building a soundproof vocal booth. Warning: this is a serious building project requiring money and skill that surpass even trying to type in that crazy Web address!

Soundproofing requires mass—big, thick walls—and room-within-a-room construction. Hanging a blanket across your window that looks out over the rail yard is ineffective (and looks plain tacky to the commuters on the trains passing by your house).

Instead, look for a space that's reasonably quiet already and set up your recording area in it. Then work to *reduce* noise. It's best to choose an interior space away from windows and outside walls/doors. A walk-in closet is a popular choice for many voice actors.

Preventing noise within the space itself may be as simple as telling other housemates to be quiet when the recording light is on. Sometimes recording at a different time of day can make the difference between quiet and noisy recordings. Turning off the heat or air conditioning temporarily can help, too. If you live near a train or highway and moving isn't an option, you may need to invest in a professional soundproof booth—it will be the *only* answer.

Remember that many microphones are directional, so be sure to point the "dead" side (its less sensitive side) toward the source of any noise. Point the business end at your mouth (duh!). Your voice will be louder by comparison and help minimize the sound of the unwanted noise onto your final recordings.

Closet Comments

Since many of you will use a spare bedroom as your office, consider a nearby closet for the booth itself. The fact is that a typical closet filled with clothing should sound just about fine for recording your voice. If it's fairly empty, though, the closet will sound boxy. Move some soft furnishings into it, such as pillows, sheets, blankets, towels, and more clothing. Consider this our permission for you to go shopping:

New clothes and stuff = acoustic treatment for home studio

Now, we aren't accountants or tax attorneys (*Really? Your pedantic prose sounds like you are. —Prunella*), so we are not advocating this formula as a viable business tax deduction.

"We only meant it as a clever comment, Your Honor..."

Of course, you can buy acoustic treatments for the closet, and that could quite likely be a legitimate tax deduction for you. (*See your tax advisor, always read and follow label directions, void where prohibited, members FSLIC, professional driver on closed course, always wear your safety belt, Rotary meets here Wednesday.*)

For those without a spare closet, or for the claustrophobic among us, we'll give you some specifics on constructing a booth a little later in this chapter.

Years ago, when the sound of a landscaping crew's leaf blowers made their way into one of Harlan's sessions, he knew he needed a better acoustic solution than just a spare bedroom. Though he lived in a quiet neighborhood, he couldn't take the chance of critical work being ruined. Rather than build a recording space, he opted for a ready-made moveable sound enclosure designed specifically for voice work, as shown in Figure 6.1. These little 3.5 × 5-feet booths can both keep noise out and provide a dead space for recording. And since they set up and break down easily, Harlan was able to take the booth with him when he moved. The modular design also allows these booths to be expanded later on if it becomes necessary. You can't do that with permanently installed, expensive soundproofing or acoustical treatments.

Figure 6.1 Harlan in Whisper Room.

Ready-made sound enclosures work well for serious voice recording. They provide both soundproofing *and* sound-shaping. Noise outside the booth is reduced (attenuated or turned down in volume) significantly by the booth, which helps to keep noise out of your recordings. And, perhaps more importantly, the recordings made inside the booth sound good. Noise outside the booth, created by heating and air conditioning, computer fans, traffic, and the everyday sounds of life, is reduced.

Unfortunately, your wallet must be prepared to pay for the luxury of a ready-made booth. A Whisper Room, depending on its size and features (http://www.whisperroom.com) can cost several thousands of dollars, as do similar products from VocalBooth (http://www.vocalbooth.com).

Whether you use a spare closet or a ready-made booth to record in, it can get warm inside, and the heat from incandescent lights doesn't help any. Enter the Mighty Bright

LED music stand light (http://www.mightybright.com), which is cool, portable, inexpensive, and battery operated. Another illuminating idea from your buddies Harlan and Jeffrey. (*Ouch! —Prunella*)

If a ready-made sound booth is beyond your budget or needs right now, here are several inexpensive but effective sound enclosures you can build yourself. These are mostly designed to shape the sound in the room (so you sound good in it) and are relatively ineffective as noise reducers. They will help *reduce* some unwanted sounds, but not nearly as well as a booth or extensive soundproofing.

Building a "Recording Booth"

Here are some additional and alternative ideas that you can try to make your recordings sound better.

The Tent

Set up a three-sided enclosure in a corner of the room by simply hanging three heavy, thick, quilted moving blankets from the ceiling. You can hang a fourth blanket in the corner itself or stack up some pillows there instead. Buy a few hooks and screw them in to the ceiling. Then, using heavy-duty picture-hanging wire, loop it over the hooks, punch the other end through the blankets, and tie it off. To keep the wire from ripping the blankets, install metal grommets. (Your local hardware store sells a kit with everything you need.) For best results, hang the curtains loosely. You can double the enclosure with another set of blankets about six to eight inches outside and away from the first set to make the space even quieter. This creates a tent (see Figure 6.2) within another tent. If you have young children around, they'll love this idea.

If your floor is a hard surface, be sure to put a heavy throw rug underfoot. Set up your mic inside this enclosure with your back to the corner, and then start recording. Experiment to see if facing the corner sounds better. (It may.) When you're finished, you can remove the blankets, fold them up, and put them away. Of course, the hooks in the ceiling will remain, but a little paint will help them blend in.

This approach creates a suitable recording space around your microphone for capturing the full tone of your voice, and although it can't stop loud noises from ruining a take, it will remove the sound of the room from your recordings.

The site http://www.palmcitystudios.com/timobrien/music/soundbooth/simplesoundbooth.html has a twist on this idea, using PVC pipes to build a frame on which to hang the moving blankets.

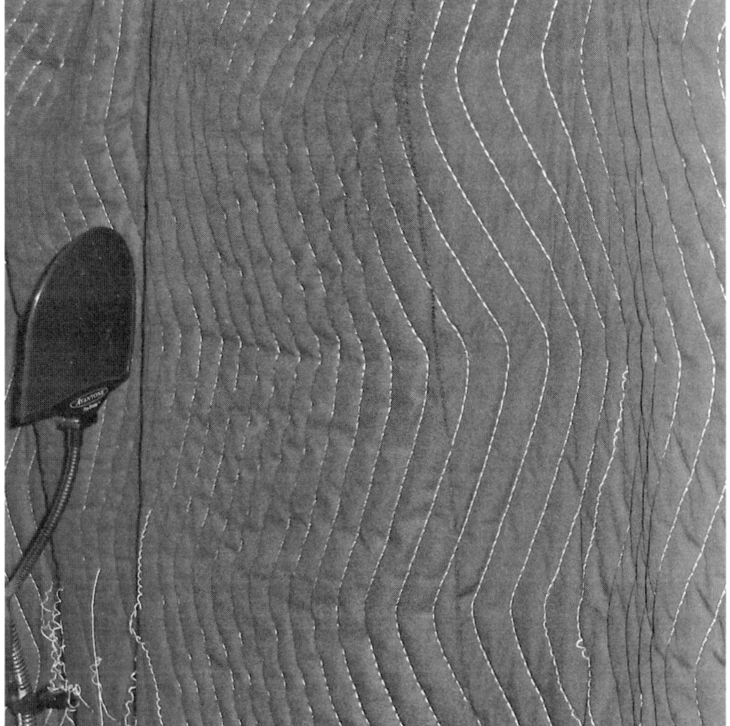

Figure 6.2 Moving blanket tent.

Corner Space

With the application of acoustic foam—specially made high-density foam that absorbs sound readily—you can turn just about any area into a great recording space. Cheap mattress foam won't work. Acoustic foam is relatively expensive and comes in sheet form (see Figure 6.3) and tile form (see Figure 6.4). There are often different colors, styles (pyramid, blades, and other shapes), and densities/thicknesses to choose from. Mixing foam thicknesses, such as placing 3-inch foam on one wall and 4-inch on an adjacent or opposite wall, can improve results and create a better sound.

In addition to the regular sheet/tile foam on walls, add in dedicated corner solutions, often called bass traps, such as the Auralex Lernd (http://www.auralex.com). These work differently and help eliminate pesky bass frequencies that can make a room sound bad. Together with standard sheet/tile foam, the corner pieces (see Figure 6.5) create a terrific overall solution.

Parallel walls are always a problem because sound bounces between the two surfaces. That's why a room corner is a good location to record in. Place the mic so you will face *into* this corner. Put the acoustic foam or bass traps directly on the walls in that corner. Start with the corner pieces and then the sheet/tiles. If you prefer not to mount the foam directly to the walls, attach it to wood panels or strips and hang it on the wall like a picture frame. Assuming you will stand when you record, start the foam at about knee level and go up to a few feet above your head. Extend into the room about 50 to 60 inches back. Essentially, you want to surround the mic with foam, not the whole room. Here, too, a heavy rug underfoot can help prevent sound bouncing off the floor.

Figure 6.3 Acoustic foam sheet.

Figure 6.4 Acoustic foam tile.

Figure 6.5 Corner bass trap.

Auralex foam is very good and highly recommended. Sonex (http://www.sonex.com) is another well-respected brand. Also, Marketek (http://www.markertek.com) makes large 54 × 54-inch sheets of 3-inch-thick acoustic foam. Two sheets would be enough for a typical corner setup. Add a couple of their Markertrap 23 × 11-inch corner units, and you'll be good to go. Marketek also sells 16-inch square blade tiles, which can be more easily placed than large sheets.

This same acoustic treatment recommended for a corner space works well in a closet. Again, place the soft acoustic foam around you and the mic. (It's acceptable to have an open space behind as you face the mic and foam.) Closets tend to be boxy—and sound boxy—so breaking up the parallel surfaces into fewer angles will improve the sound. You can use a well-stocked bookshelf covered in books, chatzkes, and such (messy is better)—even boxes of different shapes and sizes—to help "break up" the sound.

For problem areas, consider using a higher-density acoustic foam like Owens Corning 703 (http://www.readyacoustics.com). This stuff really traps sound well. It can help deaden a live room and make a boxy room sound less so. It's a decent soundproofer, too.

Three-Sided Booth

Alternatively, you can build this standing portable booth, using supplies you can buy at a local home center and from an acoustic foam supplier.

Purchase three 36-inch bifold doors (the kind you might use for closet doors). These come unfinished in kits, complete with hinges. Flat, *hollow-core* doors are best but increasingly difficult to find. If you can't find them, go ahead and buy the readily available half-louvered doors, with flat lower sections. You'll be covering up the louvers with acoustic foam anyway. Cheap ones are the best for our purposes, with 36-inch bifolds coming in around $50. Avoid solid wood doors. Not only do they weigh a ton, but hollow-core doors work better for our purposes.

Buy one sheet of 54 × 54 × 2-inch Markerfoam acoustic foam and one sheet of 54 × 54 × 3-inch Markerfoam acoustic foam. Cut the foam pieces into six 18-inch-wide sections. Also, buy one tube of Markerstik foam adhesive and use it to attach the foam to the inside of the closet door panels about 4 to 6 inches from the top. Put a 2-inch piece on one panel and a 3-inch piece on the other until you have foam on all six sections of the doors. Adjust where you place the foam depending on whether you'll stand or sit when recording. You want the foam to surround you and your mic, not the bare door panels.

Insert the hinge pins into the two-section doors and stand them up by bending the foam-covered doors in slightly. Set up a booth around your microphone using the three door sections. This booth reduces extraneous noise around the mic and creates a dry, quiet space. Remove the hinge pins to break down the booth, and store the sections when not in use. Better still, decorate the outside of the booth and use it as functional room divider. Chic!

Prebuilt Freestanding Walls

You might also consider the Auralex MAX-Wall solution. This is a manufactured acoustic wall or baffle that can be arranged into a simple booth around your mic. It costs more, but it does look more professional.

VO Box

Douglas Spotted Eagle, Grammy-winning artist, producer, sound designer, videomaker, writer, and respected authority on all things musical, sound, and video, designed and uses a simple, inexpensive VO box, as shown in Figure 6.6. It's perfect for reducing room noises around the mic while producing a fuller, more natural-sounding voice. You can make a 24-inch (or bigger) three-sided box out of 1/4-inch plywood or even sturdy foam core. Line it with 2–3-inch pyramid-style acoustic foam, and set it on a desk. It's a good idea to put a folded towel or moving blanket on the table under the box. Place the mic mounted on a desk stand inside the box about 10 inches from the front. Deliver your performance into the mic while it's inside the box. This device will keep many unwanted sounds from ruining your recordings, and it will make your voice sound great.

Figure 6.6 VO box.

For an equally great-sounding, collapsible, and easily *portable* version of this idea, see Chapter 7. A number of actors use the portable version in their office *and* on the road.

Other Standalone "Vocal Booths"

There are three competing products available today that help to isolate your mic and give you a tighter, fuller sound. These items work best *in addition to* other options mentioned here and not in lieu of. For example, you can see the Reflexion Filter in Figure 6.7 through the window of Harlan's Whisper Room. This device makes the booth sound even better than it already does, but it is not a replacement for the booth as a whole. (By the way, it's hanging upside down from the ceiling in Harlan's booth for space reasons, not acoustics.) There's another view in Figure 6.8.

The choices for standalone vocal booths include the RealTraps Portable Vocal Booth (http://www.realtraps.com), SM Pro Audio "Mic Thing" Microphone Isolator (http://www.smproaudio.com), and the SE Electronics Reflexion Filter (http://www.seelectronics.com/rf.html).

We've covered the basics of finding a space to record in at home. Next, we'll take our show on the road and look at the why's and how's of home recording even when you are far from home.

Figure 6.7 Reflexion from outside booth.

Figure 6.8 Reflexion inside the booth.

7 Home Recording—Away from Home

"Hey, hey, easy kids. Everybody in the car. Boat leaves in two minutes ... or perhaps you don't want to see the second largest ball of twine on the face of the earth, which is only four short hours away?"

—Chevy Chase as Clark Griswold, *Vacation*, 1983, Warner Brothers Pictures

In this brief chapter, we'll talk about some specialized travel recording accoutrements and a little philosophy, too. Luckily, most of the gear you use in your home studio can and will be used on the road, but before we discuss that, let's talk about the *why* ...

Why would you even want to record on vacation, on location, or between acts at the theatre?

Two big reasons: customer service and opportunity.

Okay, opportunity sounds nicer than the unvarnished truth—money.

Countless times, Harlan has saved a job (and gotten the money) by having the ability to record from his hotel room and, occasionally, more exotic locales like a ship's cabin on the Atlantic, while shooting a movie in Vail, and at The Parador de Ronda in Spain perched on the edge of a 300-foot gorge. Tight schedules often don't allow the luxury of finding a nearby recording studio, if such an animal even exists.

Of course, much of the time we voice actors are simply recording auditions when away from home, and these are *potential* money opportunities should you eventually book the job. But just as important as money (and potential money) is the first reason we mentioned: customer service. The customer in this case is your agent or agents, direct clients you have, or Internet casting services you subscribe to.

Let's start by examining our actor/agent relationships. Most of us don't view this partnership as a supplier-customer one, but we should.

For a booking, you are the supplier of talent for the session; your agent is your direct customer and the end client the second. A good analogy is a manufacturer's representative who sells several different products and services—supplied by others—to the final client.

For auditions, agents serve the same function, but instead of booking you, they select you to participate from their list of "products"—all the other actors in their roster that fit the talent description. Most agents handle many people who might fit the bill and whom they may or may not choose to include in the audition. So when they choose to include you, you have a responsibility to (within reason) promptly record and send your audition back to them ASAP, regardless of where you happen to be physically.

This is important with all agents and is especially critical with those who represent you outside your immediate geographic area. Building a long-distance actor/agent relationship is hard enough since there is rarely—if ever—a face-to-face connection. If you are lucky enough to have "out of town" representation, prepare to invest even more effort in building trust and fostering a win/win business partnership. Auditioning in a timely manner is one way to show your dedication to your relationship.

The simple fact is this: if you consistently can't or don't respond with your MP3 auditions to your "hometown" or "out-of-town" agents, before long they'll stop sending you the scripts. Wouldn't you?

All of this applies to your direct clients and subscription casting sites, too. Fast turnaround translates into good customer service.

Of course, there are times when all of us "book out" for various reasons, from health issues, unreachable locations, and insurmountable time zone differences to "I really need to just sit on the sand and suck my thumb for a week."

But skipping auditions frequently just because you're visiting friends for the weekend, shooting on location, taking a road trip, rehearsing a play, or because it sounds like too much trouble isn't reason enough. Besides, you already have most of the recording gear you need.

Remember this: ten or fifteen minutes out of your day will make your agents/customer(s) happy and just might land you that gig that otherwise would have passed you by. Plus, the successful voice actors we know love this work, and when they devote an hour or so a day working during a vacation, they enjoy the remaining 23 hours all that much more.

Assembling Your Portable Studio

Gone are the days of lugging around tons of equipment like some pack mule. You'll be pleasantly surprised how a simple portable recording rig can help you turn out quality work.

As you've seen, the cost and complexity of equipment for your home studio largely depends on whether you are simply auditioning or recording studio-quality audio for finished productions. The same premise is true for your road warrior recording kit.

For simple auditions, your rig may consist of just a USB microphone or any microphone you like, teamed with a relatively lightweight audio interface. Harlan has a Samson C01U USB mic (http://www.samsontech.com) permanently packed in his motorcycle side case. It's rugged and has a decent enough sound to have gotten him several jobs he might have missed otherwise, including a long-running stint as the voice of BioGuard.

The MicPort Pro audio interface we described in Chapter 4, "Assembling Your Home Studio—Hardware," converts *any* microphone you like into a USB mic. It's hard to beat when you consider its minuscule size and weight, reasonable price, phantom power, high-quality preamp, and all-important headphone jack. Remember that most USB mics do not let you monitor your performance as you're recording, but the MicPort Pro does. Although the MicPort can plug directly into the end of the microphone, we find it easier to adjust the volume controls by plugging it into a short microphone cable and the cable into the microphone itself. Of course, you'll need your laptop computer and audio software, small headphones/earbuds, and a relatively quiet space.

Ahhhhh ... the recording space and its acoustics will be your major challenge.

It's important to keep in mind that most auditions are listened to on computer speakers and sometimes even the teeny-tiny laptop computer speakers. So yes, you want decent acoustics and sound quality even on the road, but for auditions, the acoustics don't have to be perfect studio quality. A decent directional mic, close-up, and awareness of some obvious sound issues—like getting the microphone as far away from your noisy laptop as you can—will probably be enough.

For studio-quality sessions just about anywhere, we'll show you a simple do-it-yourself solution to making a cavernous motel room sound like a tight sound booth in just a minute. (This idea will also make an already good room sound great!)

Although as Figure 7.1 shows, you can handhold your microphone—*carefully*—so you don't make noise, a small microphone stand is a good investment. Your local Radio Shack and Atlas Sound have simple, inexpensive, classic desktop microphone stands that will work just fine, although they are a tad heavy for travel. We like the AKG/K&M tabletop mic stand (see Figure 7.2), because it folds up, weighs only a few ounces, and costs about $10. B&H Photo/Video in NYC (and online) has them, as do many other audio equipment suppliers.

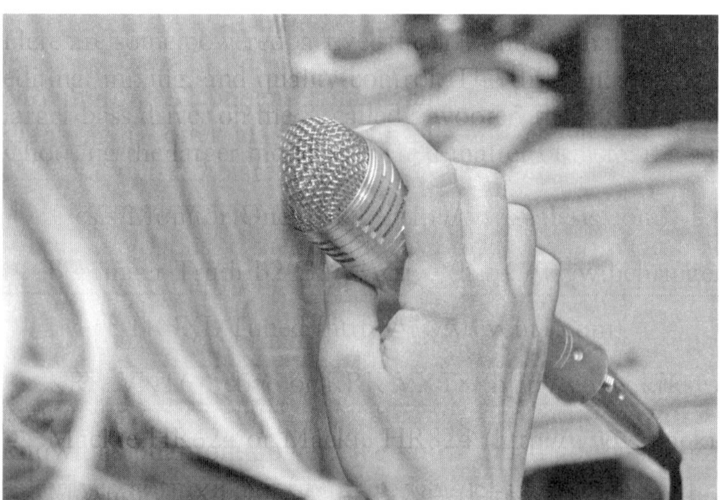

Figure 7.1 Handheld mic.

A pop filter is another item in your road-worthy arsenal. You can bring along the one from your home studio, but it's simpler to pack a travel screen in your kit. (We know from experience how, in the heat of a deadline-induced packing frenzy, it's way too easy to forget to take one along.)

The rugged and lightweight Popless Voice Screens (http://www.popfilter.com) are a good choice on the road. They are a little more expensive than some brands, but they include a flexible suspension mount clamp and come in several sizes to match your particular microphone. Harlan uses the smallest version with his Sennheiser MKH 416, as you can see in Figure 7.3.

Figure 7.2 Folding desktop stand.

Figure 7.3 Sennheiser 416 with screen.

This brings up the question of why you would haul along a $1,000+ microphone like the 416 on the road.

It's simple, really. If you may be doing finished, final, air-quality sessions from your hotel room, cabana, or second cousin-twice-removed's guest house, you'll need a higher level of road gear like the 416, and you'll have to devote more serious attention to the acoustics of the room you are in.

There are two major sound issues you need to deal with once you've left the comfort of your home studio: general noise that can get into your recordings, and the spatial sound of the recording space you find yourself in and how it can adversely affect the quality of the recording.

Recently, while speaking at Dan O'Day's International Radio Creative & Production Summit, Harlan had to record a political spot for an important client *now*! The event was being held at the LAX Hilton, conveniently located next to the Los Angeles International Airport.

Convenient? Very. But a plane zooms in to land about every 90 seconds right overhead and, though the jet noise isn't all that noticeable for the hotel's guests, a microphone hears every decibel. There's no way to mask that sound in a recording so—as the comics say—timing is everything. Despite beads of sweat on his brow, Harlan managed to record usable tracks between landings, with nary a trace of jet noise or even jet fuel.

Extreme examples like that aside, you will often have to deal with common sound makers like elevators, so insist on a room away from the elevator shaft. Then there are those huge, lovely-to-look-at-but-horrible-to-hear glass windows in your room and the proverbial ice maker or vending machine lurking just outside your door. We've found that these noise makers often become mysteriously unplugged moments before a recording is about to start.

Harlan says it's leprechauns; Jeffrey says it's targeted rolling blackouts (*I say one of you ne'er-do-wells unplugged the bloody things! —Prunella*), but who will ever really know?

Now, depending on your client, if you're doing an actual session on the road, you may be required to use a phone patch for direction, an Internet solution, such as Source Connect, or even ISDN. All these options—pro and con—we will discuss in excruciating detail in Chapter 8, "Basic Production Techniques," so we'll spare you the details for a few more minutes. But be assured, there's more!

So how do we make the No-Tell Motel's drywall-encased, cheap-wood-grain-paneled cavern—practical and inexpensive though it is—sound like our nice, tight recording booth back at the manse?

Creativity.

> "Hi! My name is Brad Majors, and this is my fiancée, Janet Weiss. I wonder if you'd mind helping us. You see, our car broke down a few miles up the road. Do you have a phone we might use?"

We agree that Dr. Frank N. Furters's dungeon in the *Rocky Horror Picture Show* would be next to impossible to record in. It's fairly unlikely that Barry Bostwick or Susan Sarandon would find even POTS telephone lines down there, much less high-speed

Internet or ISDN. Then there's the problem of chains rattling, moaning, and whips cracking, to say nothing of the breathtaking but noisy production numbers like "Time Warp."

But scary spaces that tough are the exception, not the rule, and most of the time we can make even a mediocre room sound decent with—as we said it before—creativity.

The big tip-off that you aren't in a sound booth is the roomy/boomy sound of an open, acoustically untreated room.

Start by walking around the space clapping your hands systematically. This not only compliments the room (couldn't hurt . . .), it lets you hear what areas sound "deader," with fewer noises and echoes. Often a corner is the best place to set up shop. Sometimes using the back of an overstuffed couch or armchair works as a sound baffle. Almost certainly, you'll stay away from glass windows. And closing the drapes should keep some of the street sounds out. Also find the air conditioning/heating thermostat and shut it off while you are recording.

Just remember to turn it back on.

Really.

One of us (unnamed) has forgotten several times over the years, narrowly escaping a divorce decree from a chilled/sweating significant other.

Pull the pillows off the bed and check the closet for more. You can call housekeeping and ask for more pillows and blankets as well. Now your kindergarten skills will pay off as you build a pillow fort to surround your microphone so that it doesn't hear the room.

Don't want to spend this much time "taming the rogue room?"

We have just the answer—the Harlan Hogan Porta-Booth.

The Porta-Booth

We've described Douglas Spotted Eagle's brilliant idea of putting a microphone inside an open, acoustic foam–lined box in Chapter 6, "Sound Space: Finding/Creating/Tweaking the Right Location." He discovered that *we* didn't need to be inside the box; the mic does. The mic "hears" the sound of a tight sound booth as you speak (and sing into the box). A few years ago, Harlan was describing a particularly noisy hotel room he'd tried to record in to his friend and Los Angeles voice talent, Steve Schatzberg. Harlan had built himself a quiet igloo from sofa cushions and pillows and had gone so far as to throw a down comforter over the whole shebang, including himself.

> Harlan: "It sounded good, Steve, but I had to read by flashlight and couldn't breathe after a couple of minutes."
>
> Steve: "Maybe you ought to carry one of those VO boxes along."
>
> Harlan: "Too big to pack, so it'd have to break down."
>
> Steve: "Maybe one of those fold-flat storage cubes or the mesh kind that twists flat and pops up."
>
> Harlan: "Bingo!"

You see, creativity comes from many places, even Los Angeles.

So the journey of experimentation began to make a practical, lightweight portable booth that would sound great and pack small.

After a few false starts trying wood, plastic, and a "pop-up" mesh cube that sounded like, uh, a flimsy mesh cube, Harlan finally settled on "The Folding Home Box" manufactured by Reisenthel. It twisted flat and sounded quite good, but soon after Harlan discovered it and made several for friends to try, the manufacturer stopped making that model. Luckily, he discovered an even better box—"The Whitmor Collapsible Cube."

In several blind A/B comparisons, this new Porta-Booth constructed using the Whitmor cube sounds even better but is lighter, 1 inch larger, folds flatter and, amazingly, costs half the price of the original Reisenthel box. The improvement in sound is primarily because the Whitmor cube has solid sides instead of fabric like the home box.

Figure 7.4 shows the complete Porta-Booth with an MXL 909 mic with shock mount and the K&M/AKG low-profile desk stand.

Building Your Booth

The Whitmor collapsible cube is readily available at around $10 from many sources, including Target and Amazon. It's shown folded and unfolded in Figures 7.5 and 7.6, respectively.

The box alone is just part of the story, though. You'll need professional-quality acoustic foam to line it. You'll get the best sound by using 2-inch-thick, Pyramid-style foam, not the less expensive wedge style. Cut the foam so there are three pieces: one for the back wall and top and two for the sides. Cutting soft foam is harder than it might seem. If you use scissors or a mat knife, the foam compresses as you cut, and you'll get ragged edges. That won't affect the sound or practicality of the Porta-Booth, but it sure looks ugly.

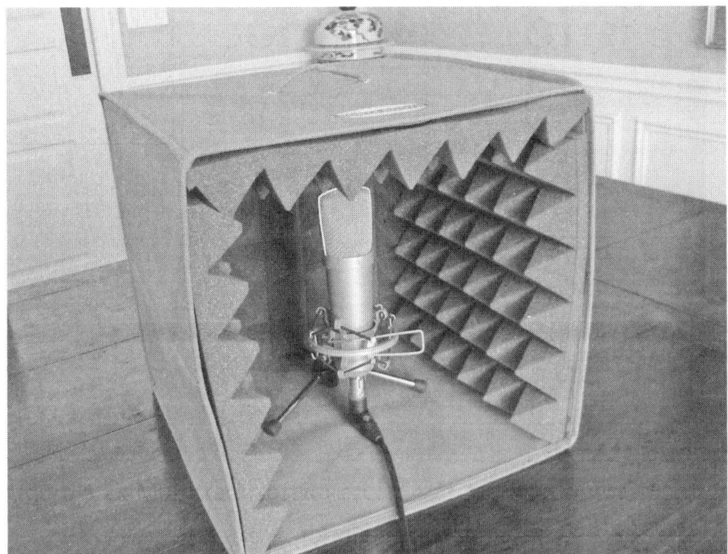

Figure 7.4 MXL and Porta-Booth.

Figure 7.5 Whitmor booth folded.

Instead, cut the foam with a serrated knife. Take your time, and be patient as you saw—not slice—through the foam. Of course, a professional foam cutter—a hybrid jigsaw—is best for this task, but it's financial overkill unless you already own one.

Figure 7.6 Booth unfolded.

You may also consider scrounging around garage sales and flea markets until you find an electric knife (see Figure 7.7). Harlan's is a lovely shade of Harvest Gold and dates back to the 1950s. Best of all, it cuts through foam like butter, all for a $2 investment.

Figure 7.7 Cutting foam.

Some popular brands of foam from Sonex and Auralex can be purchased from suppliers such as Markertek, B&H Photo, American Musical Supply, and Musician's Friend. Ask your favorite friendly recording studio if it happens to have some scrap pieces lying around, because the foam will be your biggest expense (see Figure 7.8).

Figure 7.8 Foam pieces.

For example, Auralex Studiofoam 2-inch Pyramids are sold in 2-foot by 4-foot panels, which is perfect to make one box. It yields two 12 × 12-inch panels for the sides and one 26 × 14-inch piece for the top and back. The only problem is that most sources sell that particular foam in boxes of 12 for around $400! Similar-sized Sonex foam is sold in 8-packs for roughly $300. You can make a lot of Porta-Booths with that much foam, and it's one of the reasons Harlan started assembling ready-made booths for friends and clients.

If you use a shotgun microphone, like the Sennheiser 416, you'll want to cut a slit or a small hole in the back of the box and the foam. This way the mic can be placed back far enough. Fortunately, the fabric on the Whitmor cube can be easily cut with a mat knife, and it doesn't fray. No sewing necessary! Figures 7.9 and 7.10 show the modifications in detail.

Using and Traveling with the Booth

The foam pieces nest together for travel. To save even more space in your suitcase, you can shrink the foam in thickness with an Eagle Creek Large Compression Sac, available at camping and luggage stores or online. See the amazing before and after results in Figure 7.11. You roll the bag (or sit on it!) to remove the air, but the foam regains its size and shape in about 5 minutes when you open the sac. Don't store the foam compressed for long periods of time, however, because it will eventually warp. Many talents put all or some of the foam to good use instead by wrapping their microphone and audio interface in it, providing perfect protection for delicate equipment.

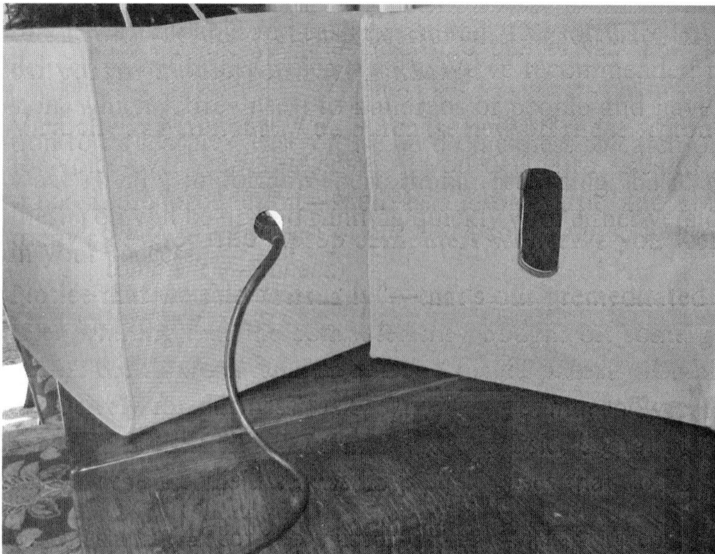

Figure 7.9 Shotgun modification back.

Figure 7.10 416 in Porta-Booth (after modification).

The box will accommodate most microphones. Place the mic 30 to 50 percent of the way back from the outer edge for the best sound. Talk into the box; you don't need to stick your head in there. Hold your copy just slightly to one side of the Porta-Booth or inside it. If you need better visibility, use a battery-powered LED light inside. If the

Figure 7.11 Foam compressed (and not).

room is particularly noisy, Harlan leans in (see Figure 7.12) so that his forehead just touches the top of the booth, and then he moves back a few inches. Putting a quilt or a few pillows behind you can also help in a "difficult" environment.

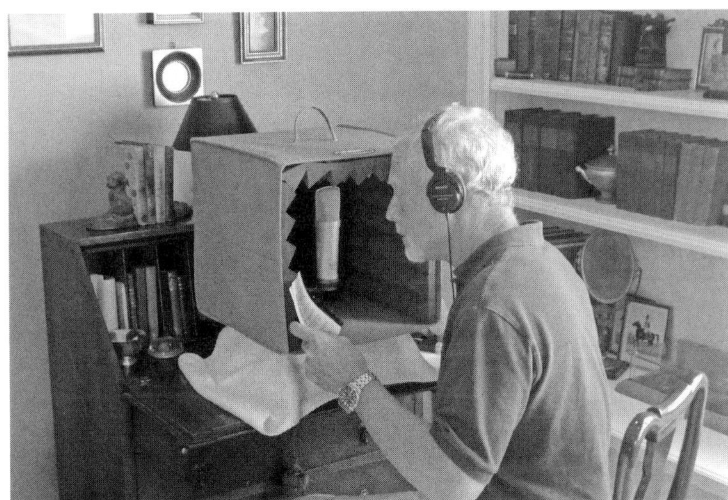

Figure 7.12 Harlan using the Porta-Booth.

Harlan often reads scripts directly off his iPhone. Unlike a laptop, an iPhone is both silent and small enough to hold right up to the microphone inside the box. It also saves him the chore of having to find a printer at the hotel.

One tip: turn your iPhone to Airplane Mode; otherwise, you'll hear the whining and buzzing of the GSM cell phone system sending and receiving data. This applies to other smartphones, too. Actually, it's a good idea in all sessions to turn off your cell phone, rather than risk ruining a take with GSM buzzing or, worse yet, that embarrassing ringing while you're performing.

Another road warrior technique that really helps with long scripts is Amazon's electronic book, the Kindle. You can scroll through the longest script with nary a noisy page turn. (*Nary a noisy! Dear God! —Prunella*)

That's it! The Porta-Booth is a simple, practical, and inexpensive way to sound good anywhere, at home or on the road.

Keep in mind, though, that all the Porta-Booths, pillows, and blankets in the world won't eliminate noise. What the Porta-Booth does is to eliminate/reduce that telltale boxy sound when you are—in fact—recording in a big untreated box rather than a proper studio.

If you still find that the room you're stuck in sounds bad, ask your host or call the front desk to see if you could move or at least use another room for a few minutes. Many hotels have small conference rooms that sound better than guest rooms, and most will let you use the room for free as long as you don't overstay your welcome. If you are getting desperate and the room you are stuck with still sounds awful, read on for a tip we learned from a movie soundman.

When All Else Fails

One of the best-designed acoustic spaces on earth is the modern automobile.

So, get in that rental car and find a nice scenic rural roadside. Pull over, shush the cows, plug in your mic, and press Record.

8 Basic Production Techniques

" ... and if you use voice-over in your work, my friends, God help you. That's flaccid, sloppy writing. Any idiot can write a voice-over narration to explain the thoughts of a character."

—Brian Cox as Robert McKee, *Adaptation,* 2002, Sony Pictures

That said, let's hope that writers never stop writing voice-overs! We know there's little chance of that happening, so let's get all our gear connected and record our first home-studio voice-over—one that's not flaccid or sloppy!

We've already talked about the basic recording chain, or signal path, a fancy way of saying that the sound goes from your mouth to the microphone, then on to your microphone preamp next into the audio interface, and then to your computer software. Figure 8.1 illustrates the idea nicely. The reverse of this signal path is when the output of your recording software goes back through the audio interface arriving at your speakers/monitors or headphones.

Figure 8.1 Signal flow. (Illustration by Tony Santona)

Now, we won't spend time going through the machinations of setting up your particular computer—the manufacturer of that device has no doubt felled countless trees showing you—with all the requisite legal warnings—how to hook up your mouse, keyboard, printer, and so on. But we will show you how to connect your audio equipment and the other things you need to do to get your voice into and ultimately back out of your computer.

First, follow the manufacturers' instructions *exactly* when you connect your new audio interface to your computer. Yes, that means actually reading the instructions! These devices often have to be installed in a particular sequence to work correctly, especially USB and FireWire connections.

Audio interfaces also require special software, called drivers, to work with your computer. Windows users should use ASIO drivers if available, and Mac users should match the right drivers to their particular operating system (OS). It's a good idea to hop on the Internet and go to the manufacturer's Web site to download the latest driver version. The CD that came with your interface may be out of date and not as good as the newest version, which will be available for free. In addition, check to see if general operating system updates are available for your computer from Microsoft or Apple. These updates and other fixes often solve both minor and major issues you may experience with your computer.

Now it's time to install the audio recording software you chose. After installation, open the program. Try not to be intimidated by the seeming endless rows of little buttons and icons. One of the first things you'll probably have to do is to tell the software what audio driver you have installed. This instruction to your program is typically "buried" in the software so, once again, you really need to read the instructions. For example, Figure 8.2 shows that in Adobe's *Audition*, you click on Edit, Audio Hardware Setup and choose the *Audition* ASIO audio driver from the list.

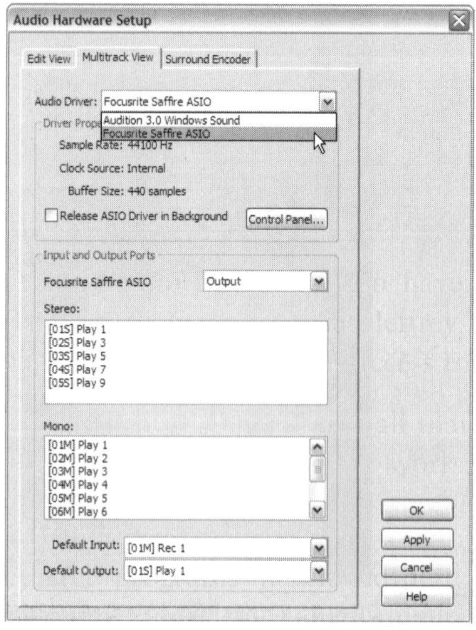

Figure 8.2 *Audition* Audio Hardware Setup.

Generally, you won't want to use one of the generic device drivers on your computer. In this same setup area, you'll click on the audio interface hardware you want the computer to use.

In *Sound Forge,* choose Options, Preferences, Audio tab, as shown in Figure 8.3, and again choose the driver from the list that matches your particular audio interface.

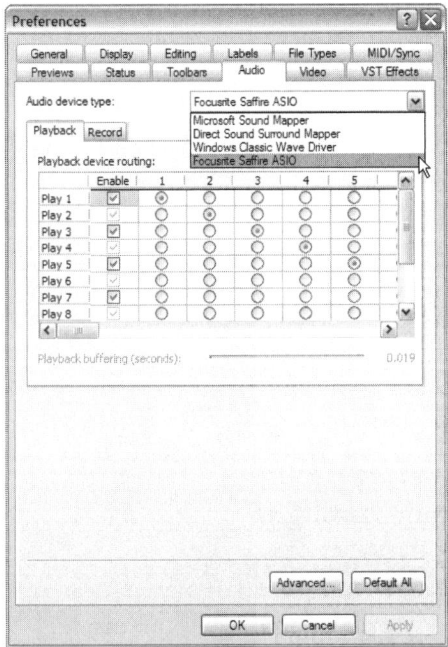

Figure 8.3 *Sound Forge* Audio Device Type.

Now it's time to assemble your sound booth, if you have one, and get all your gear—microphone and its shock mount, mic stand, music stand, headphones, and a chair or stool if you prefer to sit while recording, although most VOs prefer to stand while performing.

Note: It's a good idea to get in the habit of closing other computer applications—especially Web and e-mail—when you record. You may also want to *temporarily* turn off antivirus protection. Do this after you disconnect from the Internet, of course.

If you do need a chair, for example when recording "long-form" narrations or audio books, make sure it's quiet and free of squeaks. Noisy fabrics, such as leather, and antique wooden chairs will mar your recordings as they compete with your voice for attention. Imagine JFK's speech if it had been, "Ich bin ein—SQUEAK!—Berliner." Doesn't have the same impact, does it? (*Of all the presidential quotes you boys could've chosen, you went with one in German! Ach du lieber! —Prunella*)

Buffering for Headaches When you're using some audio interfaces and their drivers, there is an additional setting you may need to adjust. If, when playing back your recordings, you hear gapping (a miniscule dropout or loss of audio) or loud clicks or crackles, you may need to adjust your recording buffering. Figure 8.4 shows an example of buffer settings from within the *Sound Forge* software. Essentially, a buffer holds some data back briefly before presenting it to the software. If the size of the buffer is set too low, your software may not be able to keep up, and the result is an audible gap. It's not uncommon, but it's easy to fix, and you'll only have to go through this drill once. Simply increase the size of the recording buffer. This may be in milliseconds (ms), so the best way to do that is to increase the buffering number in .25 ms increments. If your buffers are in samples, try doubling them. Each time you increase the number, stop and make a sample recording. Once the gapping/clicking goes away, stop. You've found the right buffer size for your computer, software, and audio interface.

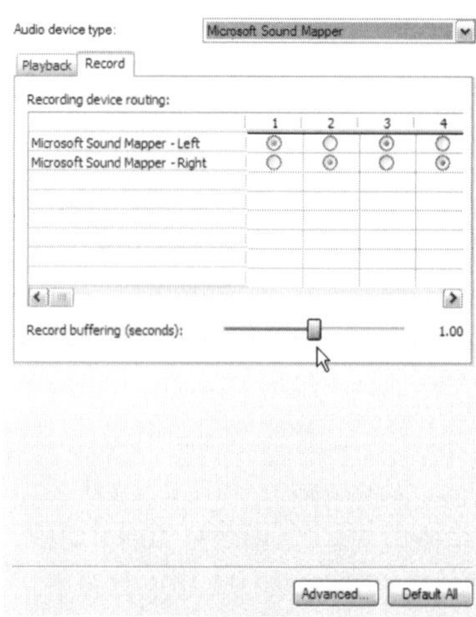

Figure 8.4 Buffer setting.

A common problem with music stands (most voice artists call them *copy stands*) is that your voice often "bounces" off them. That sound ricochets back into the microphone and can adversely affect the quality of your recording. The easy fix is to drape a heavy cloth, a fluffy bath towel, or a carpet remnant on the stand to reduce or eliminate this bounceback.

Also be careful of nearby hard surfaces, such as walls and windows, because they, too, can reflect sound back to the microphone. Move away from walls and windows if you can, or minimize audio reflections by using fabrics and acoustic treatments. Refer to Chapter 6, "Sound Space—Finding/Creating/Tweaking the Right Location," for tips on making your room sound great.

First, attach the microphone mount or (preferably) its shock mount to the mic stand. Now carefully put the microphone in the mount, making sure it's secure. Next, attach one end of your microphone (XLR or USB) cable to it. Wrap the cable loosely around the boom and stand all the way to the floor. This prevents accidentally catching the cable with your arm, clothing, or foot. You don't want to trip and pull the microphone down with a crash. Condenser and ribbon microphones are fragile, so treat them carefully. Also, make sure the cable isn't bent or crimped and that there isn't too much pressure on the connector where it attaches to the mic.

Run the cable to your external microphone preamp or directly in your audio interface. If it's a USB mic, plug that into an available USB port. Direct is better; avoid using a USB hub. It's always a good idea to make sure any phantom power is switched *off* before plugging or unplugging XLR microphone cables. The sudden jolt of electricity *can* ruin a condenser mic and definitely *will* destroy a ribbon mic!

Caution: It's also imperative at this point to keep all volume controls on your mixer, preamp, or interface off. If you don't, you risk sending a loud pop through your gear that can destroy components and your expensive monitors, to say nothing of the potential damage to your ears. Get in the habit of turning your speakers or headphones down or off when unplugging cables and when turning on/off phantom power.

If you are using a standalone microphone preamp or mixer, connect your microphone using the other end of the XLR cable to it. Use tape or a throw rug to hold down the wire, and keep yourself and others from tripping over it. Take the line out of either device, and plug that into the corresponding line input on your computer audio interface.

Using an external audio interface? Then connect your mic to its microphone input. You already connected it to the computer in the earlier steps. Don't forget to connect the audio interface's line output to your powered monitors or to a speaker amplifier if you're using passive (nonamplified) speakers. You should connect headphones to the headphone jack.

If your microphone is positioned too close to your speakers, you risk creating the high-pitched whine, called feedback, that preceded every announcement over the loudspeakers in your high school and ruined those perfectly good naps you were enjoying during homeroom. Feedback occurs when the microphone sends sound to speakers and then picks up the same sound coming from them and sends it back around again and again. Feedback is an oscillating sound loop that is hell on the ears and your recording gear.

So just turn the speakers off, and use your headphones in your recording area when recording. When you play back recordings, turn down or mute the mic, and bring up the speaker volume to listen.

With the volume down on both the mic preamp and the speakers, make sure all the connections are secure, and then turn on phantom power if you're using a condenser microphone. (Leave it off if you're using a dynamic or ribbon mic.) Although the microphone should begin working immediately, most people agree that letting it warm up a bit results in a better sound. One minute is usually sufficient, but wait longer if you're using a tube microphone, tube preamp, or both. And it couldn't hurt to turn off the phantom power when you are finished recording. Leave a few seconds for the power to dissipate before unplugging any mics or other gear, too.

If you're truly stumped, refer to the instructions that came with your gear or ask a knowledgeable friend or relative (or hire a pro) to get everything up and running correctly.

Setting Levels *Outside* the Box

Proper gain staging is important. Gain staging, of course, refers to those highly choreographed pseudodance numbers featured in every weight-loss workout video ever created. (*Not! —Prunella*)

Gain is just a fancy name for volume; we need to make sure the volume level going into and then out of our mic/preamp/interface is correct. Too loud, and there will be distortion; too quiet, and there won't be anything to record. Here's how to make sure that the volume of all your equipment is properly set. First, we'll set up the external volume controls, and then we'll turn our attention to the internal ones. Note that these two activities are directly related to each other, so read through *both* the outside and inside sections to fully understand the procedures.

Start with the source—your voice. Position your mouth relatively close to the microphone. A good starting point is to leave about the width of your hand—with the thumb extended—between the mic and your lips. Touch the edge of your pinky finger to your mic and your thumb to your lips. This is about six inches or so, as you can see in Figure 8.5. This may seem close at first (you'll get used to it), but the sound will be so much clearer and cleaner and will reduce much of the ambient room sound you don't want on your recording.

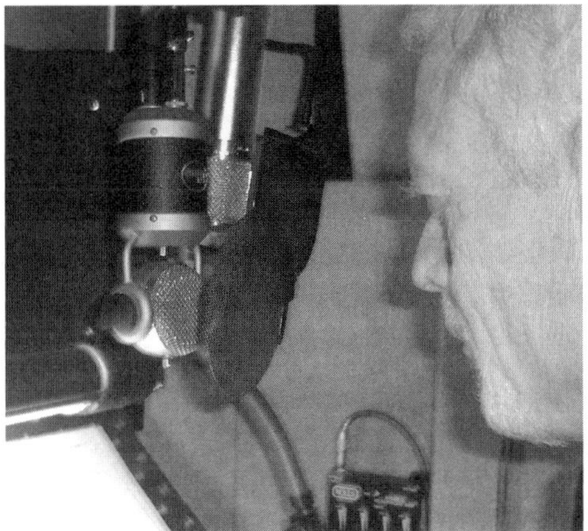

Figure 8.5 Mouth to mic.

When using your microphone and setting your unique gain levels, you'll want to maximize what audio geeks call the signal-to-noise ratio. That just means you want a loud, clean signal (your voice) and little or no noise (hum, hiss, background sounds, paper rustles, and so on). Getting close to the mic and using a directional mic helps, as does correctly setting your recording levels (discussed in a minute) to be as loud as possible without distortion or clipping. You want your performance to be louder in relation to everything else going on around you, which also reduces the effect your recording space has on the final product. You don't want to sound like you recorded in a bathtub, a tunnel, or a parking garage.

Now comes the tricky part. How do you set a level for the microphone going *into* the computer and the volume in your headphones coming *from* the computer when you have to be in two places at once—at the mic *and* at the computer? Harlan's solution was to have his arms surgically lengthened. (*Ah, so that explains why his hands drag on the ground when he walks! —Prunella*) A cheaper, less drastic, and more aesthetic solution is to simply record some tests adjusting things step by step until you get it right. Like our previous discussion about setting up and adjusting the recording buffer, this takes some time. Thankfully, once you've got it, you've got it! You can, of course, move the microphone temporarily out of your sound booth/recording area and test some basic levels while nearer to the computer. But eventually, you'll need to return it to the booth and refine the levels to get it just right.

It'll save lots of time if you can press a relative or friend for help in setting levels. Better still, hire a professional sound engineer to hook up your gear correctly and help you set basic levels. A few dollars spent here can make your life so much easier later.

Thankfully, once you determine the optimum recording level for your voice, it's pretty much set and forget. Once you do have your optimal levels picked, use a china marker, pieces of tape, or sticky notes to mark the settings directly on your gear and write down your settings, just in case you forget or some innocent person diddles with your knobs unexpectedly. Store this piece of paper where you can find it in a pinch. Both Jeffrey and Harlan have seen how tempting it is for a child to turn all those shiny knobs and slide those faders up and down while your back is turned. Cleaning ladies? It's one of the required skills of the trade to spray Pledge on the mixing board and wipe it down while simultaneously turning off all those little switches. So take it from us—write those settings down!

How to "Work" a Mic

Stop.

Before you even begin speaking, turn slightly away from the mic, take a breath, exhale, and then take another breath. *Now* open your mouth, turn toward the mic, and start talking. This simple procedure reduces the risk of recording sharp intakes of breath and lip smacks as you start to talk. Of course, those sounds can be edited out, but why not do it right in the first place?

A great technique is to pull your head back or even rock back slightly on your heels, so you move about 8 to 10 inches away from the mic during loud passages. If you double the distance between your mouth and the mic, you'll cut the volume down accordingly. Be aware that you'll pick up more room sound and less voice the farther you speak from the mic.

A wonderful tip is to bring your index finger up to your lips if you are having problems with "popped" sounds called plosives on letters like P and B. Better still, learn not to pop your Ps or Bs through practice. Put your palm in front of your mouth and say, "Peter Piper picked a" over and over, and you'll feel the air from the Ps strike your hand. Now practice until you can recite it with no air hitting your hand. Voilà!

Be kind to yourself by turning off your cell phone or putting it into "airplane" mode to stop those *dit-dit-dit* sounds from being recorded. Also, remove that jangling jewelry! Avoid polyester, leather, or overstarched clothes that rustle, too. And please, don't turn away from the mic or put your hands (or other objects) in front of your mouth while you speak (other than the popped P trick we just taught you). These bad habits interfere with getting a quality recording.

Many performers suffer from the dreaded dry mouth and the clicking and popping sounds it creates. The best solution is prevention. One thing you can do is apply some lip balm to your lips. And never drink milk or eat salty foods before recording. Harlan has found through embarrassing experience to eschew Chinese food before a session due to its high salt content and the resulting mouth noise. Another good idea is to have some tepid room-temperature water handy. (Cold water can freeze your vocal cords, which is a bad thing.) You can take a plastic bag with a few apple slices into the booth, too. That really helps get the juices flowing and the clicks removed before they even start. What could be better? A healthier diet and better VOs!

And here's a secret that really helps with dry mouth, hoarseness, and raspy throats. It's called Entertainer's Secret Throat Relief. (*Well, I guess it's not a secret now, is it? —Prunella*) Anyway, this handy little spray bottle shown in Figure 8.6 contains some magical ingredients like Aloe Vera that really help, particularly if you are doing long sessions. It's available online at http://www.entertainers-secret.com and from Voice Over Essentials (http://www.voiceoveressentials.com). There you'll find other throat sprays many singers and voice actors swear by, like Pro's Choice and Vocal eZe.

Figure 8.6 Entertainer's Secret.

If you use a standalone preamp, there is most likely a single knob for setting the volume level. This knob may be labeled Gain, Input, Mic Level, or something similar (see Figure 8.7). Always start with that knob completely down and off, and then slowly turn it up as you speak.

Figure 8.7 External level knobs.

Some audio devices include a meter that helps you set the optimum level. It may be a peak meter with a row of little lights, called LEDs, with number markings: –20, –10, –5, –3, 0. It's important to realize that 0 is the important marking. As you speak, you should stay *well below* the 0 and *never* light it up. In digital recording, unlike analog recording like on a tape recorder, once you go over 0, you pretty much record a distorted mess.

If the meters are analog VU (such as on the far left in Figure 8.7), you want the level of your voice to peak at or just below this 0. That means the majority of your speaking should stay below the 0 and only occasionally, such as on a particularly loud word or phrase, go past it. If you're seeing the needle hover between –5 and –3 continuously, you're doing fine. Setting levels with a VU meter is more difficult than a peak meter. Be patient.

Once again, it is worthwhile to actually read your owner's manual to see what your meters are trying to tell you.

If you use the preamplifier built in to your mixer, there are even more controls. First, there is probably a switch labeled Mic—Line. Switch this to mic to tell the mixer you've plugged in a microphone. Along the lower edge of the mixer, there will be a channel volume knob or sliding fader (as in Figure 8.8) with adjacent negative number markings leading up to 0. Set this at 0 to start.

Now look for another knob, usually along the upper part of the mixer near the Mic—Line switch. It might be called Input Trim, Gain, Mic Level, or something similar. This controls the mixer's preamp volume. Start with this knob fully counterclockwise, and slowly increase the preamp volume while speaking. Use the mixer's meters to set the optimum level, as described earlier.

Figure 8.8 Mixer optimum.

The process for setting a level going from the preamp or mixer to the computer can vary greatly. A mixer might have an output or master level adjustment. If so, set it to 0 (like the fader in Figure 8.8) and make level adjustments with the mic preamp volume or input trim. A standalone mic preamp or external audio interface may also have an output knob. Set it to its optimum (middle) position. Use the input volume control to set a good recording level.

Let's go over that one more time because it is so important. You want to control your levels at *one* place—the mic preamp—and leave other controls at their middle or optimum position (0 on a mixer, for instance). This gives you the best sound. Note that some output knobs only control the volume going to the speakers or the headphones and may have *no effect* on what you record.

Congratulations! You've hooked up the mic, powered it up, and set the correct recording level at the input stage of your recording. If the output of your preamp or mixer is connected properly, you can now check the level going into the computer.

Setting Levels *Inside* the Box

Make sure you hook up the output of your mixer or separate preamp into your audio interface (sound card). This is your analog-to-digital converter. Typically, that's going to be the Line In connection. If you use a USB- or FireWire-based recording interface, the corresponding cable carries your signal down that line to the computer. These devices do their analog-to-digital conversion *outside* the computer and only send the little digital 0s and 1s to the computer. A USB-based mic works similarly, sending binary data down the cable.

Be sure you understand this *really* important point. There may be two or more places to set the level of what you record going into the computer: your audio interface's external controls or perhaps some software program that controls your interface/sound card directly. *But* you won't find level adjustments in the audio recording software you use. Let's repeat that for simplicity: there are no level adjustments in the audio recording software. You won't find an input level knob in *Sound Forge, Audition, GarageBand, Audacity,* or *XYZ*. You may find an output level control, but that is for the volume of what you hear on headphones or speakers. The actual adjustments of what you record—louder or softer—are made by your audio interface controls or the separate software that controls it.

Most audio interfaces have hardware level controls (knobs) and no additional settings in software. So you simply set your recording levels there, outside the computer.

On the other hand, depending on the hardware you use, some internal sound cards make you set levels with special software installed on your computer. This software typically "talks" to the sound card and sits between the hardware outside or inside the computer and the recording software you use. This includes the standard software controls for audio shown in Figure 8.9 included with Windows XP, Vista, and Mac OS. It can be confusing, baby!

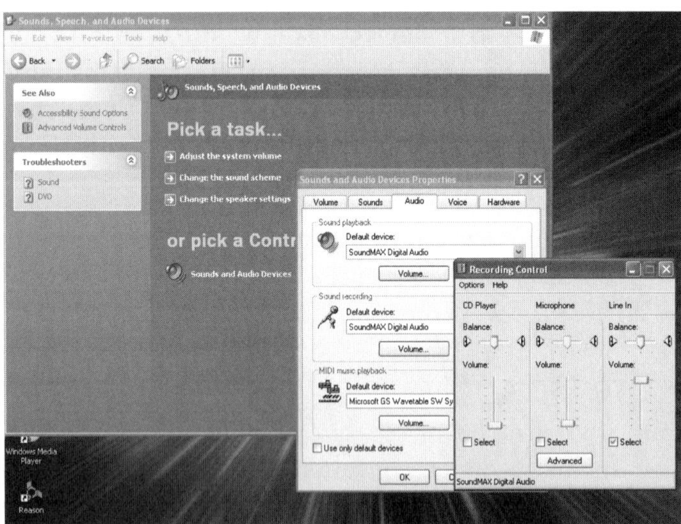

Figure 8.9 Software level setting.

If this applies to your situation, set the input source—what the sound card records—to Line In. Then set the volume control between 75 and 100 percent. Adjust the volume going to the audio interface input using the mixer or preamp stage instead. If you know you've set the level there correctly, fiddle with this software control knob until the levels work. Usually all the way up is best; set it and forget it, and then control levels outside with your hardware.

Here's another example. While the Focusrite *Saffire* software appears to give a lot of control over setting levels (Figure 8.10), these settings are actually used only for monitoring (to headphones and speakers). In the foreground is what appears to be a setting for the device volume, but you'll notice it is grayed out and unavailable. This differs from the generic sound card software pictured in Figure 8.9. That's because you set the volume of your microphone physically on the front of the Focusrite hardware unit with a Gain knob and not in software, like our previous example.

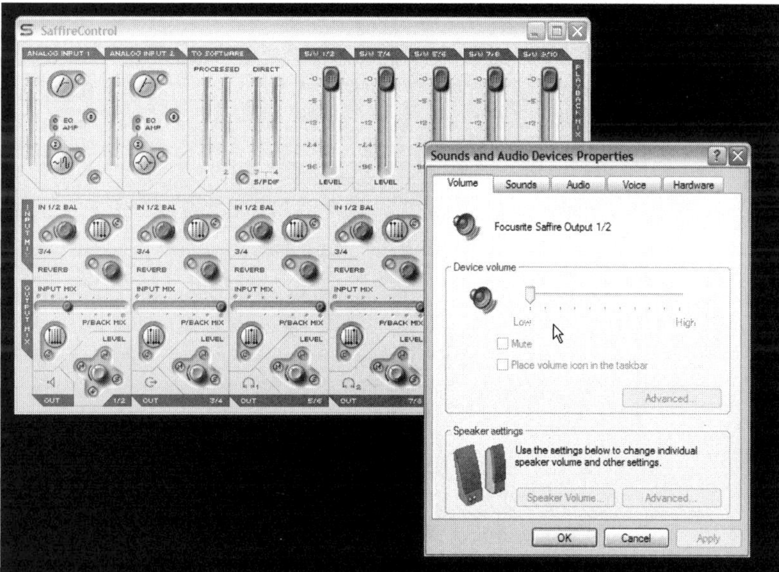

Figure 8.10 *Saffire* levels.

The best way to set levels is with a test tone to match levels between these external and internal devices. See the later sidebar titled "VU for Vous?" Also, refer to the manuals that came with your computer or audio gear for suggestions.

With your levels matched, it's time to start recording. Your software might differ somewhat from the examples used here, but the differences are usually subtle and often cosmetic in nature. Understanding basic recording concepts is far more important than learning a specific application. Once you set levels and get a decent sound down, it really doesn't matter which software you use, and you'll quickly begin to feel comfortable with the software you chose.

In the next examples, we're using the Sony *Sound Forge 9* package. We're also assuming that you have a basic understanding of working with software on a computer, including how to navigate, open, and save a file. If you don't, take some classes at a local community college, online, or ask your nine-year-old nephew to show you. He'll know more about this stuff than anyone. (*Certainly more than you two! —Prunella)*

Most recording software requires you to set some kind of project or file attributes. Figure 8.11 is one such example. In other words, you need to tell the program what level of quality you want to use in recording. We always recommend that you record and edit your voice at the highest sampling rate and bit depth your computer hardware can handle. Be aware that the limitations of your audio interface (and even your recording software) will dictate the sampling rate and bit depth you can actually use. Because CD quality has a sampling rate of 44,100Hz and a bit depth of 16 bits, this should be the *minimum* setting you record at. By the way, the last time we checked, most humans had only one mouth—so that makes us a *mono*phonic instrument. There's no need to record your voice in stereo—ever. If you do, you're using *twice* your computer's resources for absolutely no reason. Choose mono!

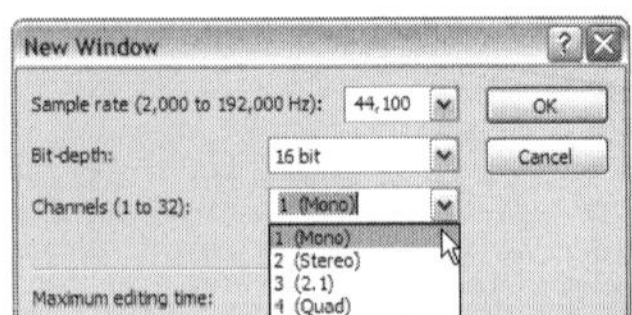

Figure 8.11 New file attributes.

If 44,100/16/mono is the *minimum* setting, what is the *optimum* sampling rate and bit depth? We both feel moving up to 48,000Hz and 24 bits is ideal for serious recording, editing, and processing. The sound is more natural and open. You can always save the final version to another format, such as a CD-compatible file (44,100Hz and 16 bits). And, although you will probably "dumb down" your recorded files to the popular MP3 format (for e-mailing), it is still better to start with the highest quality first. MP3s are a lossy format, and that means exactly what it sounds like—audio information and detail are *lost* so that the file can be small enough to simply send along. That's fine, but we want to start with the best quality and then "dumb it down." Have you ever heard your computer-savvy friends talk of GIGO? No, it's not a movie starring Leslie Caron. (That's *Gigi.*) GIGO is geek-speak for garbage in, garbage out. We don't want to start with garbage!

Once you've created a file or project, you need to get into record mode. *Sound Forge* and all other software audio recording applications have a set of transport controls that should look familiar. If you've ever used any kind of recorder, you've seen similar buttons—play, stop, pause, and the big, red Record button—so go ahead and click it.

Adobe's *Audition* has you click Record and then choose file attributes you want, like 48,000Hz and 24 bits, and then you can start recording. In contrast, clicking Record in *Sound Forge* opens a dialog box that provides a plethora of options in addition to file attributes; that's pretty much the same thing as a cornucopia of choices. In *Sound Forge,* you have to click the Record button in the dialog box a *second* time to actually start recording. Also, notice how the dialog box also shows a pair of recording level meters. If they aren't actively moving and your mic is active, just click to select the Monitor check box. When you start talking into your microphone, you'll see these meters jump around in response to your voice.

There are no level adjustments within the *Sound Forge* or *Audition* applications. You need to set levels at your outboard equipment or within the software that controls your audio interface. Hopefully, you followed our advice from earlier and have reduced or increased the level of your preamp/mixer/audio interface as needed. The most efficient workflow is adjusting and tweaking levels in just one location while keeping an eye on the recording program's meters like those shown in Figure 8.12.

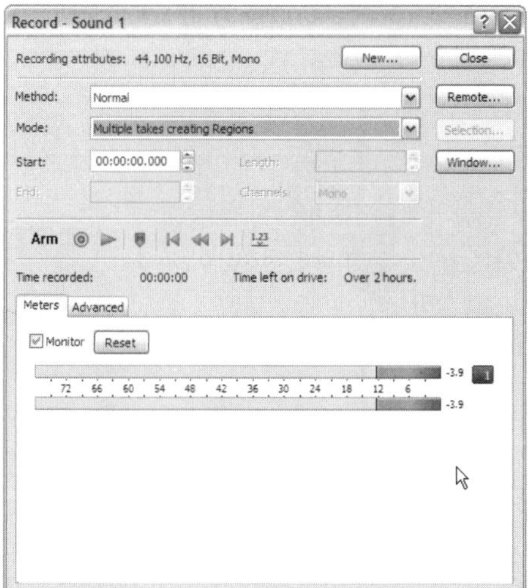

Figure 8.12 Record meters.

We know that all this may have been a bit confusing, but once you get everything set—well, you're pretty much set. Just remember that any adjustments you make to your microphone, its preamp (input and output, which may be part of your audio interface), and the software that controls the audio interface affect the level of the sound you record.

Caution: Don't be fooled by the volume of sound you hear in your headphones and speakers. Since they are controlled separately, you may be hearing something really loud (or soft) but actually recording just the opposite, so monitor your gain levels with your meters!

Let's go ahead and do a test recording. With all the levels set, click the red Record button in the dialog box and begin to speak. Try to avoid for the sake of tradition saying, "Mary had a little lamb." Try something like, "Wow, I'm actually recording my own voice—professionally—right here at home thanks to Jeffrey Fisher and Harlan Hogan. Maybe I should send them each a couple hundred bucks in gratitude." Record for about 15 seconds, and then click the Stop button. Close the dialog box, and you'll see a file on your screen that looks something like Figure 8.13.

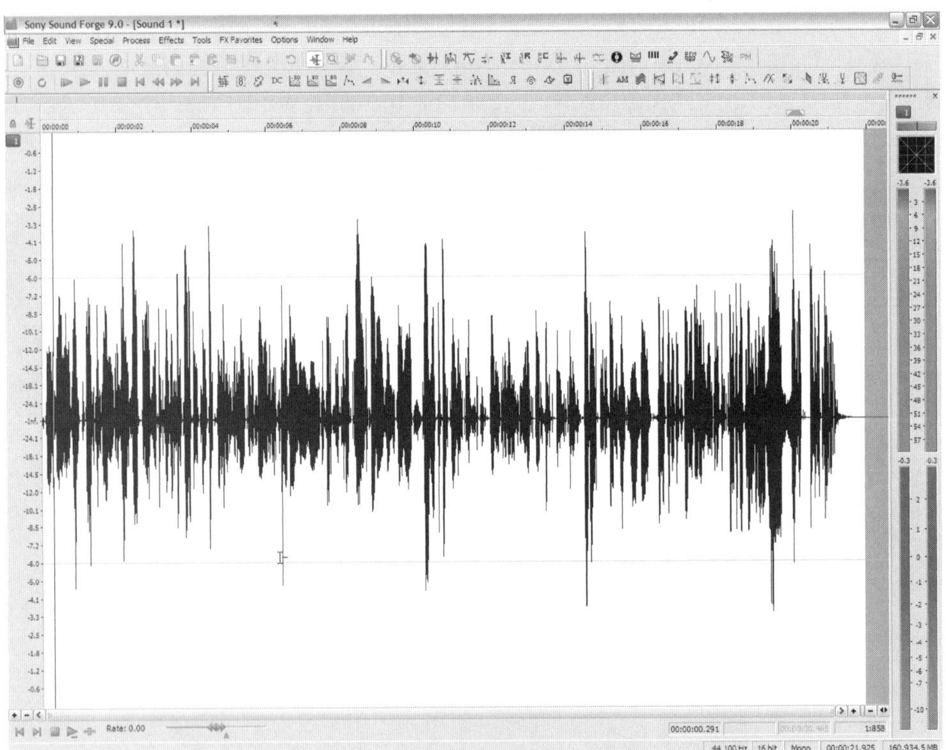

Figure 8.13 Test file.

You're looking at a two-dimensional (2D) representation of sound digitized by the computer. Pretty darn cool, huh? Alright, maybe it's not that cool, but it's interesting in a "Can you visualize an alien planet" kind of way. Play back the recording, watch, and listen. Do you see how the screen waveform changes depending on the words? Later, you'll be editing these little waveforms just like you do words in a word processing program.

Make sure you save and name your recording at this point. In Windows, use the WAV file format; Macs use the AIFF format (though both OSs save in either or both formats). So MyFirstRecording.wav or MyFirstRecording.aiff are not just catchy titles, but quite appropriate naming conventions. Both of these formats are uncompressed, full-quality digital files. That also means they are *big* files. A single minute of mono CD-quality sound takes up 5MB on the hard drive. Naturally, files this large are unwieldy to e-mail. Thankfully, there are ways to significantly reduce the size of these digital wave files, by saving to a smaller, lesser-quality format like the popular MP3.

Some software programs save the "project" file and not the single file as in our example. You need to understand that, in this case, the real recording is hidden on the hard drive. To get it out of the project, you may need to render or export it to the single file. Refer to your software instructions in this case.

Can't I Just Record and Save My Auditions as MP3s?
A Point/Counterpoint Debate with Harlan and Jeffrey

H2: I'm all for saving audio files to the highest level you can—except for auditions. It wastes a lot of time and simply isn't necessary. Everybody I know just saves in MP3 and sends them off.

JPF: But what if that audition proves to be dead-on for the client? The client may want the higher-quality version later. I've seen that happen with nonbroadcast work.

H2: Any talent worthy of being called that should easily be able to re-create the audition. More importantly, the *last* thing I want to do is send a track good enough to actually use to a client. It's possible the client would use it and you would not get paid! Many VOs and agents "watermark" auditions with a tone or purposely change a line or two in the copy to avoid being ripped off.

JPF: I'm not saying to send the big file. I'm suggesting just recording and saving in the better format and doing any editing or other processing on the high-quality file. Then, after you're sure it's perfect, you can do a Save As and dumb it down as an MP3. E-mail that one.

H2: I don't disagree with the concept. I question the possible value given the time it takes and possible confusion for our newly home-studio-equipped readers. I don't want them to be intimidated by all this extra work just for auditions. Final spots and nonbroadcast, fine, but in my opinion, you should simply record auditions at 44.1/48kHz and 16 or 24 bits and save them as MP3s using the sometimes complicated naming conventions requested by the client or your agent—exactly. Right or wrong, that's what everybody does.

JPF: If everybody jumped off a bridge into the Chicago River, would you do it, too?

H2: Absolutely. Especially if it was St. Patrick's Day and the river was dyed green.

JPF: Okay, forget that. Let's just agree to disagree slightly on this one. I still feel it's best to record *and* save initially at a higher-level format and then make a separate MP3 for distribution …

H2: And I think you are an audio geek worrying too much about zeros and ones … but my very good friend audio geek whose opinion I respect and whose generous offer to buy lunch if I said those words exactly is accepted.

JPF: Done. But the pocket protector stays where it is.

H2: Not again! How many times are we going to go through this parking lot drill, Jeffrey? There are three simple rules when eating lunch with Harlan:

- All your laptops stay in your car.
- Both Bluetooth ear dongles stay in your car.
- The omnipresent pocket protector stays in your car.

(*Perhaps you both should just stay in your cars. —Prunella*)

Recognizing Correct Onscreen Levels

A good recording level should look like the basic digital waveform shown previously in Figure 8.13. The overall level will be consistent, with a few peaks that don't or barely exceed –6. If you set the level too low, it might look like Figure 8.14.

Now, recording tracks at too low a level is not as bad as recording them too loud (too *hot* in studio parlance—see Figure 8.15). However, when you record at too low a level (that is, gain), you are then forced to increase the volume when editing. And as you make the recording louder, you also boost any noise. Background sounds that were hardly noticeable before now become painfully obvious.

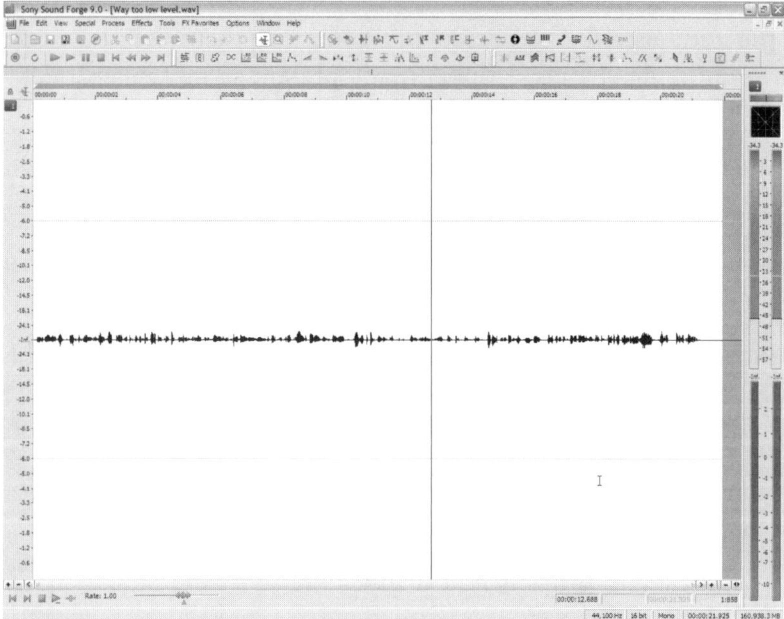

Figure 8.14 Too low.

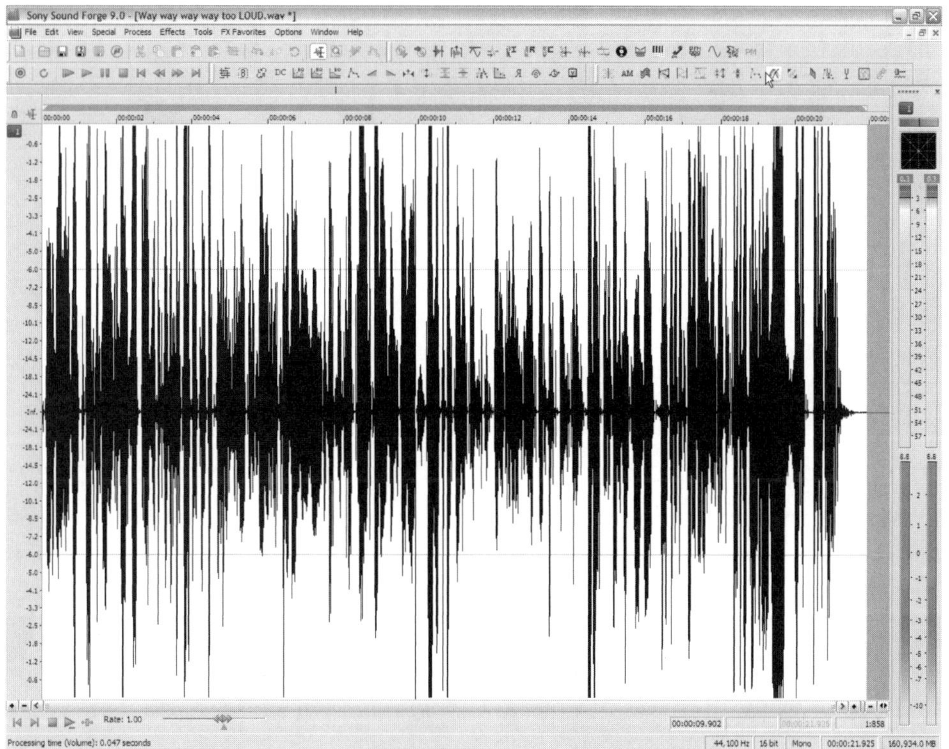

Figure 8.15 Too loud.

Louder levels maximize the good signal (your voice) and minimize the noise you don't want (the inherent room sound, aka the noise floor) that's present in any recording.

Plus, recording a higher level means that an audio engineer who might mix your performance later on with other sounds (like music or sound effects) can always turn down your voice if needed, and that would further reduce any background noise.

However, if the level is way too high, your recording will look something like Figure 8.15.

Notice that the really loud parts are squared off as if somebody came in and clipped the top of the waveform with a pair of scissors. If you zoom in, they look something like Figure 8.16. This kind of distortion, called clipping, sounds like sandpaper rubbing on your ear. Also, notice the meters on the far right. Remember that anything above 0 is bad, and this is B-A-D. On your computer screen, you'll see this level in red, versus black and white here in the book. We got real tired of hand-coloring each copy of this book after the first half-dozen, so please use your imagination.

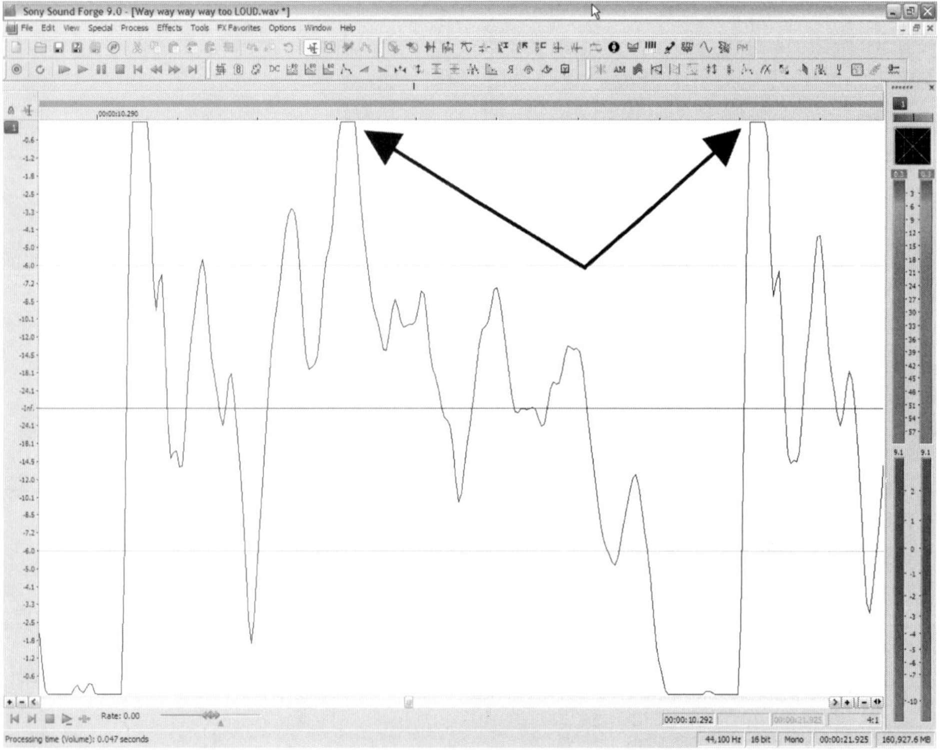

Figure 8.16 Clipping.

We mentioned zooming. Your audio software will have controls for zooming in and out. Just look for a little magnifying glass. It's often easier to work on your sound files when you zoom in a bit. You can more clearly see what you're doing, so you can make better edits. Unfortunately, you may occasionally zoom in too far and get lost in zoom hell. If that happens, just zoom out to regain your perspective. You might want to invest a few extra dollars in a mouse with a scroll wheel so you can seamlessly zoom in and out on the waveform; it will save you tons of time compared to constantly clicking on those magnifying glasses.

THE Most Critical Rule in Digital Recording

We know we've said this twice already, but it's extremely important that you never, *ever* exceed 0dB with a digital recording program that uses digital peak meters, like those found in *Audition, Sound Forge, GarageBand,* and others.

This is one rule you cannot break!

Keep your loudest peaks below 0, with the overall level even lower. Try peaking at between 6 and 12dB below digital 0. Digital is a low-noise recording medium, so your levels don't have to be as "hot" as they did in the old analog recording days. Trust us—don't hit or exceed 0. Promise? If you do exceed digital 0, we suggest recording another take at a lower level because the clipping distortion on that first pass will sound terrible (and flags you as a flagrant amateur).

Now make some more recordings, adjusting and tweaking the controls until you get consistent levels. Use your mic technique, moving closer or farther away, to deal with performance situations where you need to shout or whisper. Luckily, recording at home is low risk, because you can always rerecord a bit that didn't turn out quite right. Once you've made a few recordings, you'll get the hang of it.

VU for Vous? In the analog world, measuring the volume or level of an audio signal, whether coming from a microphone, guitar, or other sound source, required a volume unit, or VU meter. A good level kept the meter between –3 and 0dB, and it was okay to jump past the 0 occasionally. There was space, called headroom, to handle a quick peak without distorting.

In the digital world, there is also a 0dB maximum, but unlike its analog counterpart, *it is not acceptable* to exceed it. When you do, the resulting sound is distorted. It looks as if the sound waveform was clipped off with scissors, and it sounds strident, muffled, and nasty.

It's important to note that 0dB analog (as shown on the analog VU meter to the left in Figure 8.17) is the equivalent to –20dB on a digital meter (as shown on the peak meter to the right in the same figure). Run a steady tone through an analog mixer, and set the levels so the meter stays at 0dB VU. Connect this output to the computer, and then set levels so that the steady tone reads –20dB on the digital peak meter. This is the only way to make sure you've matched the output of your analog gear to the digital domain.

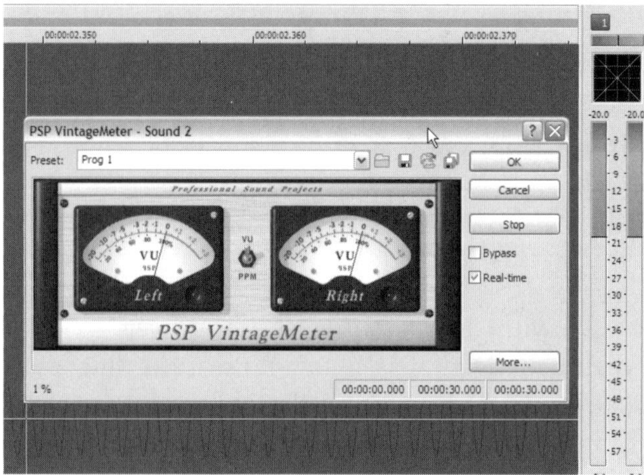

Figure 8.17 VU versus peak meter.

You can download the test tone from this book's companion Web site: http://www.audiosmartactors.com.

Getting Up Close and Personal with Your Microphone

Alright, now it's time to fine-tune microphone placement. Minor changes can greatly affect the resulting sound. Don't be afraid to experiment, but the following basic suggestions should work for almost all the work you do. Remember to make additional level tests after moving a microphone's location.

First, double-check that you have positioned the mic capsule—where the wire mesh and the diaphragm is—correctly. Talking into the back of a mic provides an interesting but unusable recording. Make sure the capsule is centered and even with the front of your mouth. Don't use the center of the mic housing as your reference point. Make sure you center the diaphragm capsule. You can usually see it through the mesh grill that covers and protects it, especially on large diaphragm condenser mics.

The easiest way to keep recording room noise out of your recordings is to get close to the mic, roughly 4 to 6 inches away. If you use a shotgun mic, back up to about 6 to 10 inches for starters, as pictured in Figure 8.18.

Figure 8.18 Shotgun mic position.

If you're a particularly quiet speaker or you're trying for that breathy, sensual sound, get even a little more up close and personal. Remember: there is an increase in the low-frequency bass content to your voice as you get closer to a cardioid mic (called the proximity effect). This can add fullness to thin voices, but it can make deep voices overly heavy or boomy. So let your ears judge what's best for your particular voice. Do some test recordings, play them back, and evaluate what you hear.

If you're a strong, loud speaker, back off a little, but not too much. You don't want your voice swimming around the room, making the recording sound like it was done in a tunnel. Instead, readjust your recording levels to accommodate your loud mouth, which was a rather nice metaphor if we do say ourselves. You'll sound drier, closer, and more intimate. It will give you that "in-your-face" sound.

Be aware that the closer you are to the mic, the more mouth noises you'll pick up in your recording. Lips smacks, tongue clicks, denture clatter, and other gross-out noises have no place in polished performances. A little technique here can go a long way toward reducing unwanted sounds. Alternatively, you can edit out those sounds later, which is one of the beauties of digital recording; removing vocal mistakes is fast and easy.

You also run a much greater risk of popping Ps and Bs as you work a mic closely, so position a pop filter halfway between your lips and the mic. If you don't have a pop screen (yet!), you can try taping a pencil across the outside of the mic, centered right over the capsule. The pencil keeps the puff of air from a P, B, or T from striking the diaphragm. Another antipop technique is to position the mic so it's between 20 and 30 degrees to the left, right, or above your mouth (so the bottom of the capsule is even with your upper lip (as seen in Figure 8.19). Be sure to aim the mic capsule directly at your lips, though. This strategy keeps the mic out of your direct field of vision—and breath—making it easier to see the script and helping reduce plosives and some sibilance.

Figure 8.19 Large diaphragm position.

Sibilance, by the way, has nothing to do with your irritating brothers and sisters. Sibilance is excessive S sounds in a recording. Record "Susie sells seashells by the seashore" and hit those Ss hard, and you'll recognize what we mean. Even at a proper recording level, they sound strident, harsh, distorted, and almost as irritating as your siblings. In general, women tend to have a more sibilant quality to their voices, but men are not immune. To fix this in your recordings, invest time with positioning the mic until you find the best—least sibilant—sound. Also, "auditioning" a number of different microphones and preamps until you find the combination that diminishes sibilance on your particular voice is well worth the effort. Of course, practicing and perfecting a cleaner, clearer delivery can really cut down on those S sounds.

You can also reduce sibilance by applying some frequency-dependent compression or EQ after recording, but we'll get to that advanced technique in Chapter 12, "Advanced Production Techniques." Meanwhile, you can impress your friends by memorizing this phrase, "Yeah, the sibilance was destroying the vibe, so I ran the DC Offset, applied some frequency-dependent compression, EQed out the lows, normalized the output, rendered a 128kbps MP3, and FTPd it to the client." The client won't know what the hell you're talking about. And right now, odds are you might not know what the hell you're talking about. But you soon will!

Keep on Tracking

Enough preparation. It's time to get down to business and do some serious recording. You've set up the gear, placed the microphone where it makes you sound your best, and checked and double-checked your levels. And you're ready...

Basic recording is called tracking in the trade. It's where you record your various takes of the script. Each take is a separate performance or part of a performance. What are the characteristics of a good spoken-work recording? Number one is clarity, and a natural, pleasant quality to the voice comes in a close second. We need to hear what you say clearly and in a way that makes the listener interested but without sounding phony or overenunciated. It's a delicate balancing act. Keeping your recordings free of distracting noises will go a long way toward that goal.

As an actor, the last thing you want to worry about while performing is technology. That's why we've insisted you do all this preparation work up front. You can't be a computer or recording technician and a good performer at the same time. But if you've taken the time to get all basics set *before* recording, you can now simply turn everything on, press Record, step up to the mic, and perform your butt off.

Harlan has this down to an art because he took the time to make everything ready to go on a moment's notice. He doesn't need to tweak at all. Jeffrey has seen him rip copy from his fax machine, take a step to his desk, start a new file recording with a mouse click or two, walk three more steps into his Whisper Room, pull the door closed, take a brief moment to make sure the mic is positioned, pull on headphones, reset his stopwatch, and begin speaking. A couple of takes later (and often just one!), and he's back at the desk, stopping the recording. Then it's a quick trimming off of the chit chat at the head and tail of the recording, saving the file, and attaching it to an e-mail or posting to FTP. Literally 3–5 minutes have elapsed, and often far, far less.

So with everything preset in your home studio, you can let the technical details of recording take care of themselves. You can—and should—relax and simply perform. Enter what the founder of the method school of acting Constatin Stanislavski described as a state of inspiration: "When an actor is completely absorbed by some profoundly moving objective so that he throws his whole being passionately into its execution, he reaches a state we call inspiration."

Have some fun now recording one of the sample scripts included here, or choose something of your own that takes about a minute. A brief soliloquy is a good first project.

Grab a copy of your favorite magazine to read aloud. Start your software and get into record mode. Run through and record the piece a couple of times and then listen back. If you need to redo a few lines, do that now. Don't feel the need to necessarily complete your performance in one take. The beauty of digital recording is how easily you can edit bits and pieces from several takes into one seamless and polished performance.

We do suggest you do whole sentences as opposed to parts of one. Even though digital editing makes piecing together many disparate elements into a composite take easy, usually the performance suffers. And performance is king. So work on delivering more complete sentences and paragraphs.

Sample Script: Bright Ideas

Here's a bright idea.

If everybody replaced just one incandescent light bulb with an Energy Star qualified Compact Fluorescent, America would save over $600 million in annual energy costs. That's enough energy to light over 3 million homes for a year. And we'd prevent greenhouse gases equivalent to the emissions from more than 800,000 cars.

All that by replacing just one bulb.

Visit www.energystar.gov and help change the world, one light at a time.

Sample Script: Water Ballet :60

This Labor Day weekend the best ballet in town won't be in a theater...

The most precise choreography, the most demanding ensemble work, won't be on one of Chicago's stages. No, this drama and spectacle will be played out on the waters of Lake Michigan, to an audience gasping and applauding on Navy Pier... as the tall ships return to Chicago.

From the pier's resident tall ship, the schooner "Windy," to the 154-foot-long "Highlander" of Canada, you'll be transported back to a time when canvass was king and the tall ships were masters of the seas.

You can climb on board, witness an old-fashioned tug-of-war, and enjoy fireworks on the water, as only Navy Pier can do them.

Tickets are available at the Navy Pier box office. Don't miss this chance to see the tall ships at Navy Pier.

Sample Script: Navy Pier Dinosaur Giants

SFX: Traffic noise

Mindy: Ladies and gentlemen, welcome aboard. On your right is Navy Pier, home of...

Kid: The Ferris wheel!

Mindy: Yes, and dinosaurs.

Kid: That's the museum. What kind of guide are you?

Mindy: The one in charge, Mr. Smarty Pants. And right now Navy Pier is the home of a giant dinosaur—60 feet long and 130 million years old...

Kid: That's bigger than T-Rex!

Mindy: And recently discovered, it's called Jobaria...

Kid: I don't believe it!

Anncr: Believe it. Chicago paleontologist Paul Sereno has discovered a new species of dinosaur, and now's your chance to see it as dinosaur giants invade Navy Pier daily, now through March 19. For details, call 595-PIER.

Mindy: And why aren't you in school?

Kid: Teachers Institute Day?

Mindy: I don't believe it.

When you're satisfied with your raw performances, save your files to the high-quality format of WAV or AIFF. Even though you may send them later as an MP3 file, do *not* use that format for storing these takes or for editing. You want to keep the quality intact at this point. You can always save to an alternate format later. (Reread the sidebar, "Can't I Just Record and Save My Auditions as MP3s? Yes and No," for Jeffrey's and Harlan's takes on this subject.)

Save your files. Yes, we know we're repeating ourselves because you will be less than human if you don't, at some time, forget to save the file you've just recorded or save it to another format accidentally. Usually you'll make this mistake only once, but it will inevitably be on something that was just perfect. If only you'd saved it.

Create a folder for each project on your hard drive, and keep all the files related to the project in the folder. Harlan has folders for each of his agents, and he saves auditions for a specific agent only in that folder. You can store other information in the folder, too, such as scripts and notes. For big audio projects, you may need to create subfolders within the main folder. For example, Jeffrey creates separate folders for voice, sound effects, music, and final mixes on his more complicated projects. Avoid meaningless or cryptic file names; you might be looking for that file a year from now, and "Second_try_louder" isn't going to ring a bell. For versions, consider using a number extension. Use the 001, 002, and so on format to keep the files in proper numerical order.

Before you move on to the editing stage, make a backup and take a break. You need to rest your mind and ears and make the mental switch from performer to technician.

Important Reminder It's good practice to back up your work after a fruitful tracking session. Don't risk losing the best performance of your life due to some error on your part or the machinations of a malicious computer. After reviewing your takes to make sure there's enough raw material there, save the files to an alternate place. We suggest using the Save As command and choosing an alternate save to location, such as a different hard drive, flash drive, Internet-based file storage, or a CD (data or audio).

With this strategy, you can always return to these original files no matter what happens later. We speak from experience; you'll never regret making an extra backup. The time it takes to make a backup is far less than the time it would take to do an extensive piece all over again.

Make a point of backing up the final versions, too. For critical masters, make another copy and save it offsite with a friend or relative or in a safe deposit box. Or you might even upload it to Internet-based storage.

Get Set to Edit

Listen to your raw tracks first on headphones. You need to do two things simultaneously:

- Judge your performance and choose the best parts.
- Listen for recording problems like distortion, background sounds, and other glitches.

Some people prefer to make notes on the script while assessing their recordings. Most recording software lets you put markers on the waveform to denote certain parts of a file, which can be an efficient method for indicating stuff to keep (or lose).

Use headphones at this point for another reason. If you record and edit in the same room, even with a booth, there may be noise on the recording that you'll miss on speakers. Your brain is rather adept at tuning out the general racket of your room (cars whizzing by outside, computer fan, heater kicking in and out, TV down the hall, and so on). You can easily ignore (as in not hear) the noise around you. Microphones aren't so smart; they hear *everything*. The noise of your surroundings may be part of your recording, too, but you won't hear it on speakers because of the noise being also in your room. The background noises are in *both* the recording and the room.

A few years back, Harlan was booked by a video production house to record a lengthy narration for Komatsu earthmoving equipment. When he arrived, he was surprised to see there was no audio booth—just a microphone on a stand smack-dab in the middle of the editing suite. All the whirling video drive noises, hard drive fans, and clients fidgeting in their seats were dutifully recorded. In his headphones, he could hear that the whole recording was going to be unusable but hesitated to say anything and figured the moment the clients listened to a playback, the obvious mistake would be heard and corrected. But when the track was played back—in the same noisy room—it sounded just fine! Not surprisingly, he was rebooked the following day at a proper recording studio to rerecord the whole script, once the client heard the tracks outside the video suite. Headphones help you at this stage by isolating your recording—warts and all.

If the sound checks out on headphones, switch to speakers for further evaluation and to make your editing choices. Turn off or mute your microphone before bringing up the speakers to avoid the howl of feedback.

Caution: Before you do another thing, make a copy of the file you are going to edit. In the *Sound Forge* software, simply choose File, Save As and rename the file. If you named your original file Voice_001.wav, name the copy Copy_Voice_001.wav. Then work on the file copy from now on. Leave the original as a backup in case you really make a mistake. Plus, you made another backup as we suggested earlier, so you have a double safety net.

If that sounds overly cautious or paranoid to you, ignore our advice. Go ahead. We won't mind. However, don't come a-complainin' to us when you lose everythin' in a power outage, to a virus, because of criminal or other malicious malcontent, or whatever conspires to wipe your work off the face of Mother Earth. If you have all the time and enthusiasm to redo and otherwise re-create your best work, rock on. The rest of us rest better knowing we have backups to cover just such an eventuality.

For example, Jeffrey recently suffered a major computer setback, but he's fastidious when it comes to backups. (*In contrast to his table manners! —Prunella*) He did lose some works in progress, though. And he blamed himself for not taking an extra few seconds to back those up the evening before the crash. A few seconds then would have saved him hours of valuable time. Despite all the backups, he spent almost 20 hours getting back on track—and he didn't have 20 hours to spare. Without backups, he'd probably still be trying to get up and running, but then he wouldn't have completed this book, so you wouldn't be holding it now. And in that case this story wouldn't matter at all. (*What? —Prunella*) So our advice is back up everything. Always!

When you are working on the copy of your file, be sure to run a little utility called DC Offset. Harlan is convinced that DC Offset refers to Interstate 495, but Jeffrey refuses to even comment on that. In truth, sound cards/audio interfaces sometimes add direct current (DC) to the audio being recorded when doing the digital conversion. This might result in the waveform not being positioned correctly around the center line. A DC Offset utility such as what's shown in Figure 8.20 automatically corrects this problem if it occurs. If you don't run this, you might hear clicks, pops, or other unwanted noises after editing or applying effects to your recording. As a rule, run the utility on every file you record *before* you start editing. Save it again. Then start to edit.

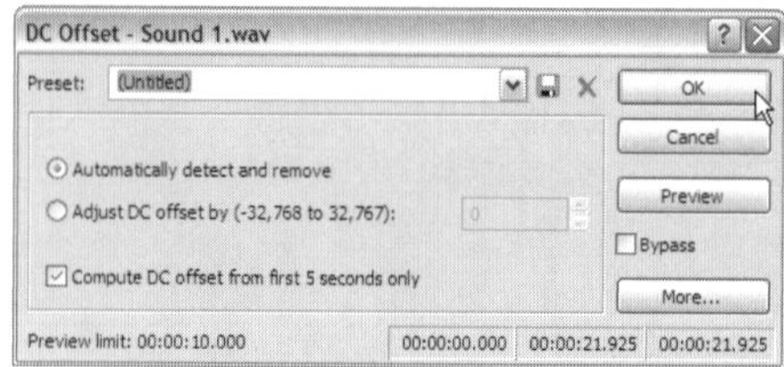

Figure 8.20 DC Offset.

Use the notes you took when listening to your raw tracks and begin to assemble a complete recording. You have two choices for working in an audio recording and editing program:

- You can edit the file directly. If you recorded everything in one file—several takes and line fixes—it's easier to simply edit out the mistakes and compile the best bits within that single file.
- You can edit in a blank file. If you recorded in several files, it's best to start with a blank file and copy and paste the best parts from those raw files into a complete version.

Both techniques are valid, and we select the best approach based on the project. You need to find the workflow that makes sense for your brain.

In either case, get rid of all the unwanted parts and save the best performance. Cut out all the background noises, clearing of your throat, paper rustles, and so on from before you started recording in earnest and in between takes. Listen for lips smacks and other mouth noises and cut them out, too.

Every Breath You Take There is great division in the sound world about breathing. Specifically, some people cut out breaths, and others leave them in. If you cut out every breath in a recording, your delivery will sound unnatural (unless that's what you're trying to achieve). If you leave the breaths in, they sometimes start to annoy listeners. Part of this is the unfortunate side effect of positioning the mic so close to your mouth. The mic hears every breath, up close, and accentuates them. In normal conversation, other people don't typically hear you breathe (the exception being in the closeness shared between two consenting adults). Unfortunately, recorded voice can sometimes sound unnaturally breathy.

What's our advice? Work on your breathing so you're not gasping for breath. Catch breaths, those quick inhales you take between long phrases, almost always sound horrible. Mark up the script by indicating natural breathing points to avoid these gasps for air. When you really feel the need for a large inhale, turn away from the mic slightly, take the big breath, turn back, and start speaking.

During editing, you can cut out the breaths that add nothing to your performance, along with most catch breaths. You can tighten your performance by dumping these breaths and moving the adjacent words in their place. However, do leave the more natural-sounding breaths in place, even if they sound particularly pronounced. You can always reduce their volume level a little when editing.

Editing on Your Computer

Editing audio is really no different from editing a word processing document. You can even "see" the words, although they're not in any alphabet you'd recognize. Instead, you see a 2D waveform representation of the sound you recorded. Best of all, you can actually hear the words, too.

You just need to use your basic computer commands, like select, delete, cut, copy, and paste. You select parts of the digital waveform by holding down the left mouse button and dragging it along the waveform, as you see in Figure 8.21. Then you can delete, cut, or copy the selection. It's easy to get rid of unwanted sections and even rearrange them.

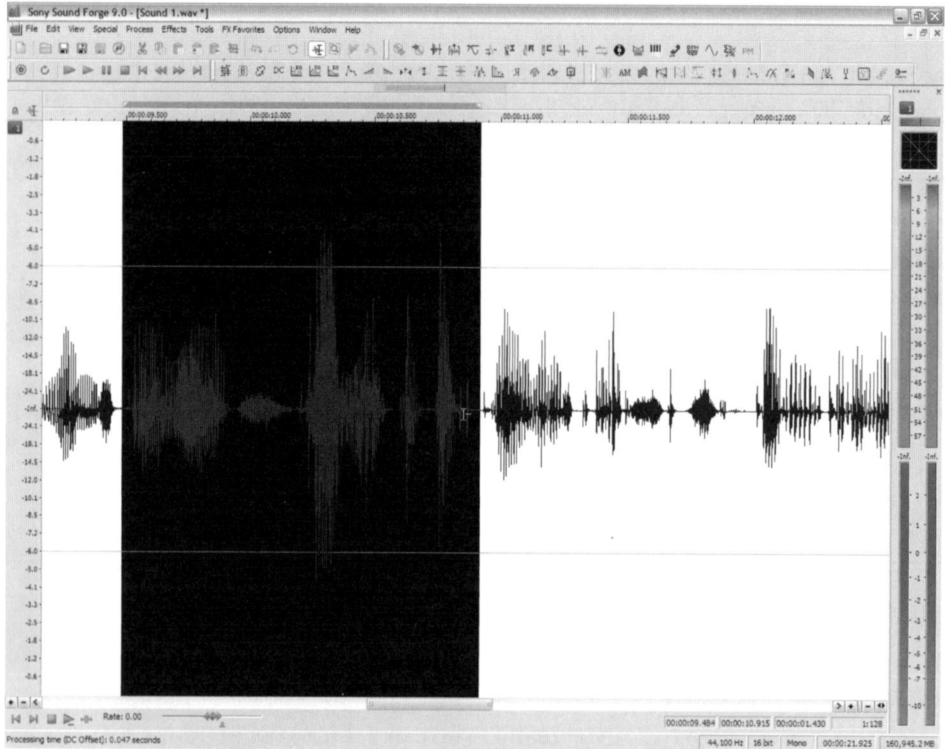

Figure 8.21 Make selection.

When editing a sound file, you just need to remember to make edits where the waveform crosses the center line. Why is there a center line? Audio is a wave, and just like its water counterpart, it has crests and troughs. The center line in audio is like the still pond. Throw a stone into it, and you get waves that move both *above* and *below* the water surface.

Another analogy is to think of the center line as the space between words in a word processor. You wouldn't cut in the mid...dle of a word, would you? As you make selections in the audio editor software, check that both ends are at points where the waveform crosses the center line. Zoom in to be sure and adjust as needed.

Notice in Figure 8.22 how cutting (or deleting) the selection from the preceding waveform in Figure 8.21 moved the adjacent sections closer together.

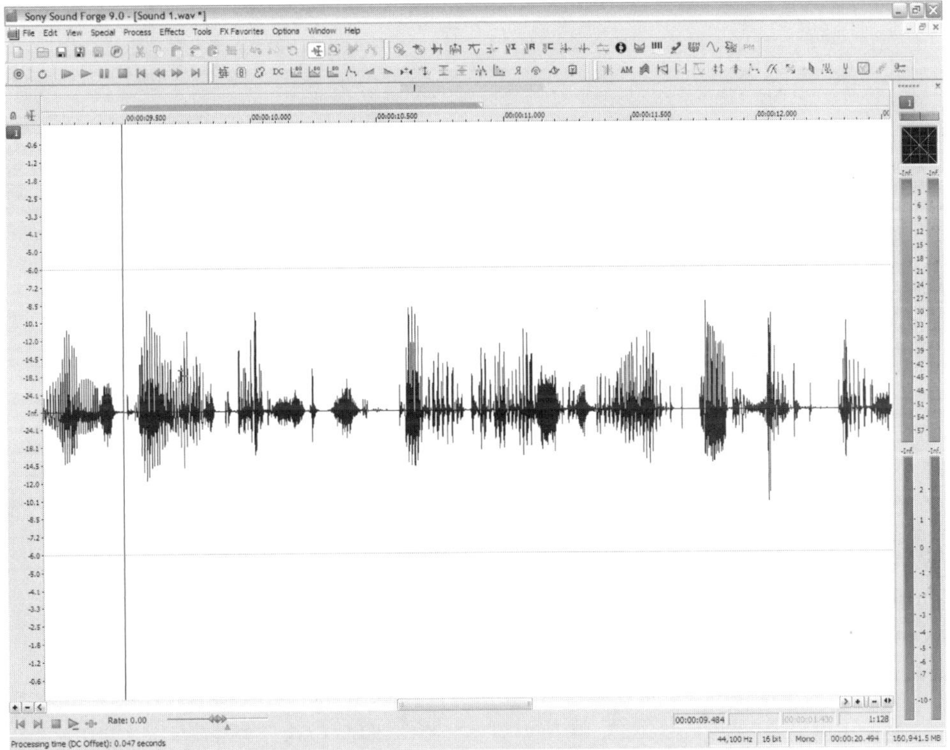

Figure 8.22 Delete selection.

If you need to move a section from one place within the file to another (or from one file window to another), make the selection and cut it. This places the data in a temporary computer memory area called the Clipboard. Next, position the cursor where you want to put the cut section by clicking your mouse. Paste the cut section in place like you see in Figure 8.23. Take some time to work on your file until you're satisfied with how it sounds. When you've finished, save it.

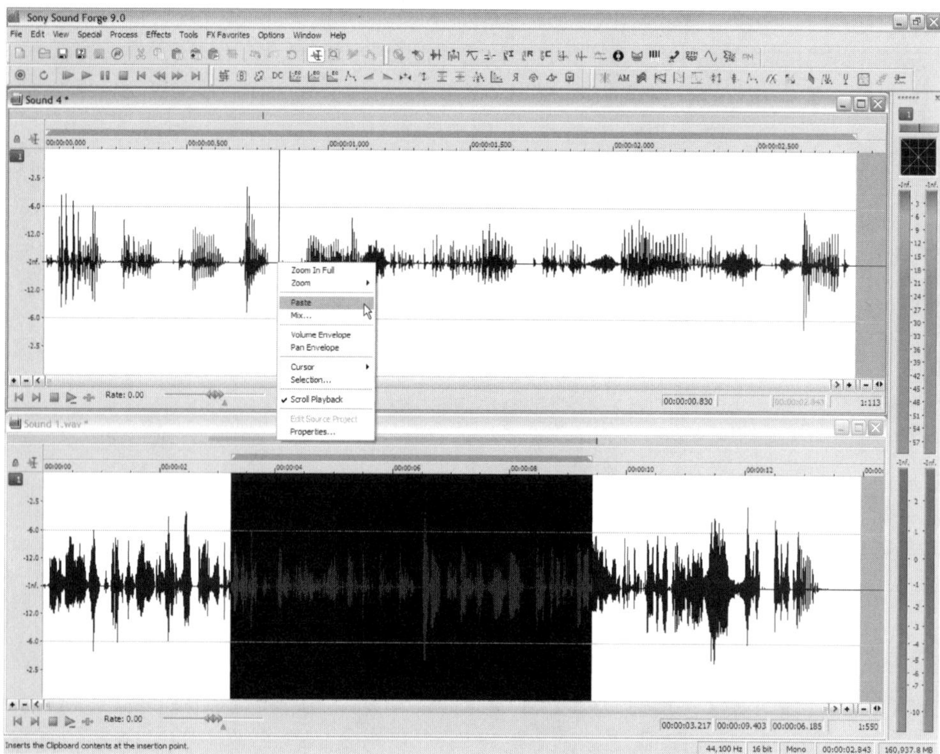

Figure 8.23 Paste.

If there are other issues with your voice recording, check out Chapter 12 for tips on how to fix most common problems.

Hooray! You've recorded, edited, saved, and finished your first voice-over performance. You deserve a standing ovation, roses, and great reviews. Or at least a stiff drink.

9 Teleportation—Long-Distance Direction

"I'm working on something that will change the world and human life as we know it."

—Jeff Goldblum as Seth Brundle, *The Fly*, 1985, Brooksfilms

Well ... we know just how well that teleportation-twisted-science-scheme worked out in all the various permutations of *The Fly* motion pictures. For voice actors, though, telephony teleportation has made it possible for us (at least our voices) to travel—with broadcast-quality sound—all around the globe. Instantly. However, when discussing telephony-based recording with people feigning interest, do not—under any circumstances—pronounce Telephony (*tuh*-lef-*uh-nee*]) as *Tell-ah-Phony*. If you do, they'll quickly realize you are one.

For many years, producers have relied on the most basic form of long-distance recording: the so-called phone patch. Many sessions today are still conducted using this kind of teleportation. Phone patch sessions have a few drawbacks, though, because the bandwidth of "regular" telephone lines—POTS, or Plain Old Telephone Service—can't send and receive audio at the level of quality needed for broadcasting. Instead, the producer and talent use the telephone to hear each other for direction and performance. Air-quality files are delivered *after* the session is over, usually on recorded media like a CD or via the Internet.

Because time was—and is—almost always of the essence with audio projects, other technologies emerged over the years. For a brief period, many long-distance sessions were produced using satellites. Quality audio flowed in both directions, and the recorded tracks were ready to go on the air. The downsides were the limited satellite time available, the complicated scheduling since most sessions used PBS's satellites, sunspots (really!) that sometimes garbled the audio, and the cost—astronomical isn't just a metaphor here.

A better solution, ISDN digital telephone lines, appeared in the late 1980s. You can win a few bets in nerd-frequented bars (*where you'll likely find Mr. Fisher —H2*) or a free

VO baseball cap at one of Harlan's Long Haul workshops by knowing that ISDN stands for Integrated Services Digital Network. In the unlikely event you find it equally fascinating that ISDN was originally called Integriertes Sprach und Datennetz, please close the cover of the book quietly and leave the room—now.

Basically, two or more phone lines are used to send and receive data (our voices in this case) digitally on the ISDN lines. And, like satellite transmission, the high-quality audio is instantly available. From a talent standpoint, recording via ISDN was, and is, a dream come true. No commuting, no parking, no dress code. Harlan calls 'em Boxer Shorts Sessions. *(Now that's disgusting! —Prunella)* Unlike phone patch sessions, there's nothing to record and send on later—other than your invoice. However, ISDN for a home studio comes at a serious cost in gear and ongoing telephone line fees.

The very good news is that Internet-based solutions have been developed that are less expensive and can—in many cases—deliver as good a quality as dedicated ISDN lines.

You may also want to be able to do long-distance sessions on the road. Most of the equipment we'll discus for phone patches is small enough to take along, and you can plug into the nearest telephone line and even your cell phone (with some additional gear). Although there are portable ISDN units made, it's rare to find the requisite ISDN digital phone lines installed in your hotel room or rented beachfront condo. However, we know talent who had had a local phone company do precisely that rather than miss a full-week's worth of station imaging sessions. Internet programs will generally work just fine provided there is a reliable high-speed connection available. A wise road warrior carries both a traditional POTS phone patch device and an Internet program so that in a worst-case scenario, he can at least record with telephone direction and then send the tracks moments later via the Internet.

Bottom line: As soon as you have the equipment and confidence to be doing going-on-the-air-tomorrow sessions from home, your producer will want to direct you, and for that you'll need a "patch," which is in reality just a long-distance studio talkback.

Phone Patches

This is long-distance direction at its simplest. The person directing the talent listens on a regular telephone line to your reading and gives direction. Sometimes the director will be in a recording studio hearing you over a professional phone interface and studio speakers, but other times the director will listen in on a regular, cellular or speaker phone. It's basic, inexpensive, and works well. There are a few tricky parts, though, and some additional equipment you'll need to make this work smoothly.

In lieu of the proper phone patch equipment, or in an emergency, you can just record while holding the telephone near your mouth, but we don't recommend it. The producer will hear your reading, but not, of course, the actual sounds you are recording. And depending on the quality of the telephone handset, he may not hear you clearly enough to make good judgments about the sound and interpretation.

A bit better idea is to use a telephone headset. The headset is easier to deal with than trying to hold the phone up to your mouth without blocking the microphone. The best choice would be one that allows you to talk on the phone hands free. You'll be able to hear the other parties on the line, and they'll hear you speak. At the same time, you will, of course, be recording yourself properly through your regular microphone/recording setup. The earpiece is just for communicating with people outside the session. There is one giant problem with either of these low-tech approaches, though. If your client utters the following five words, you are screwed:

> *"Can I hear that take back?"*

And the likelihood of the client asking to hear a take played back? In our experience, about 89.658 percent. Do you really want to take that chance?

So you'll invest a few bucks on a professional phone patch device that sends audio to and from the telephone. The good news is that phone patch interfaces are not prohibitively expensive, and many are quite portable, too.

The MicTel in Figure 9.1 made by CircuitWerkes (http://www.broadcastboxes.com) packs everything you need into a blue box about 5 inches long, 2 inches high, and 3 inches wide, weighing in at 1 1/2 pounds.

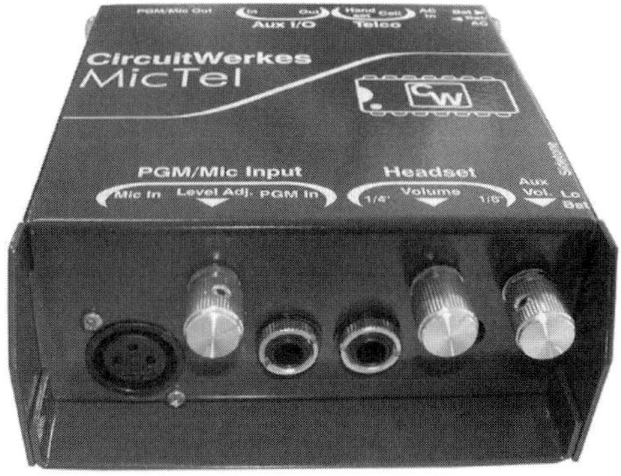

Figure 9.1 MicTel.

The MicTel, and the other phone patch boxes we'll talk about in a minute, are built for broadcasters, so they are remarkably rugged and reliable. (*More alliteration! —Prunella*) The MicTel runs on two 9-volt batteries for 20–35 hours. If your session takes more than that length of time, consider other means of employment, or perhaps never working for that producer again! In addition to professional connections (XLR), the MicTel functions as a mini-mixer. The latest version even features a jack that lets you connect to your cell phone. You'll need a male-to-male 2.5mm plug to connect to your phone, and the longer the better so you don't pick up annoying cell phone buzz during the recording. Hosa makes a 10-foot-long cord that is just perfect.

The MicTel uses your telephone's electronics to work. When you are ready to record, unplug the handset from the telephone and plug it in to the interface. Don't try to use a telephone that has the keypad on the handset, because that means the electronics are located there rather than in the base. If you do, as you've probably guessed, the moment you unplug the handset, the interface doesn't have the telephone electronic "guts" to work with and will just sit there looking up at you as sweat drips from your brow.

Besides the possibility of saving money by using your cell phone instead of a pricey per-minute telephone in your even pricier hotel suite, a cell phone can solve a problem you may encounter on the road. Some hotel switchboards and systems are digital and are incompatible with "regular" phone patch devices. Harlan only ran into this problem once, but it does happen. Using a cell phone patch or the JK Innkeeper PBX, described later, solves that problem. Two really compact and convenient cell phone patch devices to consider are the JK Audio (http://www.jkaudio.com) Daptor Two and Daptor Three (pictured in Figures 9.2 and 9.3).

Figure 9.2 Daptor Two.

Figure 9.3 Daptor three.

The JK Audio Daptor Two works like the MicroTel but has fewer inputs and outputs and is smaller and less expensive. Daptor Two also uses the 2.5mm headset jack to connect to your phone.

The JK Audio Daptor Three—the latest JK innovation—connects using Bluetooth Wireless Technology to your cell phone and your Bluetooth-enabled laptop.

JK Audio also makes an elegant solution for your home studio that is small enough to travel with and will work with every telephone line you'll ever run into.

As shown in Figure 9.4, the Innkeeper lets you plug in a professional microphone to capture studio-quality audio of your own voice and have your producer/director's voice digitally separated to its own output. Plus, the Innkeeper will operate over digital multi-line PBX, ISDN, and analog telephone lines like those you have at home.

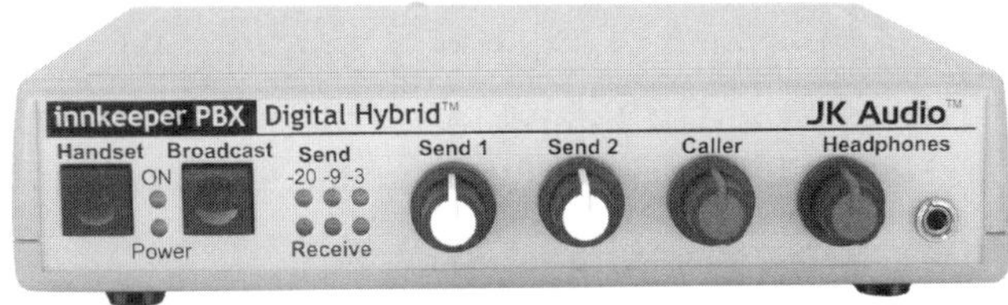

Figure 9.4 JK Innkeeper PBX.

Comrex Corporation (http://www.comrex.com) makes a number of even less-expensive phone patch products, as do several other companies. You can also find rack-mounted phone patch units designed for heavy-duty studio and broadcast stations, but frankly, these are overkill in terms of cost and complexity for most home studios. If you are electronically inclined, you could no doubt manage to create your own phone patch with a few connectors, a transformer, and a capacitor, but if you can actually do that, we have to wonder why in the world you're reading this book.

Okay, for the rest of us, we'll need to figure out how to use the handy device we just bought. How are we going to "plumb" it into the system? Exactly how you'll set up your patch will depend on what kind of mixer you have and how it's been wired. You can save some time and energy by asking—*and paying*—a professional to set up your phone, ISDN, or Internet audio patch. Once it's up and running, make a cheat sheet, such as the one in Figure 9.5, to remind you how things work, or place reminders to make life easier in the future. Two months from now, you might forget how everything worked when the engineer was in-house.

Figure 9.5 Mixer patches.

Basically, patches of all types require what's called a mix minus. That simply means that, as you're recording, you'll hear yourself and the producer in your headphones, and they'll hear what you're recording on their end. *But*, and this is obviously critical, you *won't* be recording them, only you. Hence, the moniker "mix minus"—it's you that gets recorded, minus the conversation on the phone.

Call Mario Brothers! We Gotta Figure Out da Plumbing!

When using phone, ISDN, or an Internet audio patch, you obviously need to hear yourself, and you need to hear the client on the other end of the line, no matter what kind of "line" that happens to be. However, not only don't you want to record what the client says, but you don't want to send their voice back to them, so you need *two* independent mixes. Otherwise, you'll get an annoying feedback loop that sounds like a repeating echo.

The best solution is to use a mixer that has an auxiliary bus—essentially a mixer within a mixer. The slang word *bus* simply refers to a way to route or move signals around. Auxiliary busses may also be called monitor or effects depending on your mixer brand. Many auxiliary (Aux) busses have a pre button, too, sometimes abbreviated PFL. This simply means that the auxiliary bus gets its signal *pre*-fader—*before* the main channel fader affects the volume level up or down.

With the setup shown in Figure 9.6, you'll be able to hear both the remote conversation and your performance in your headphones while simultaneously sending just your voice to the client.

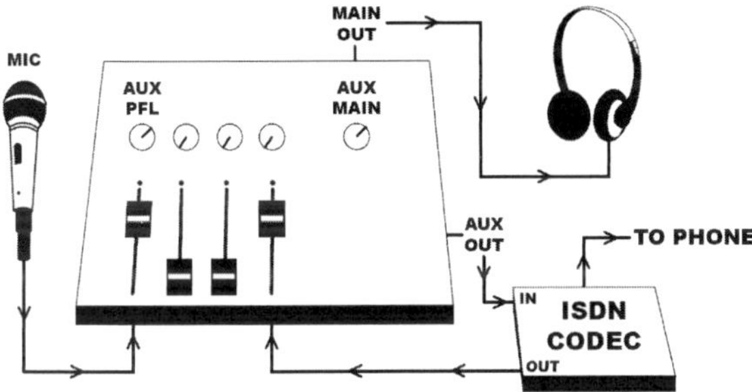

Figure 9.6 Mix minus.

Plug your mic into the mixer as you normally would, and set the levels with the channel fader. Now take the output of the phone patch or ISDN codec, and bring it into another channel at the mixer.

Set a comfortable level for this audio using its channel fader so you can hear the remote site clearly.

Plug the output of the auxiliary bus into the input of the phone patch or ISDN codec. On the auxiliary bus, use the knob that corresponds to your microphone channel *only*. Turn it all the way up. If you have a pre button, engage it. Keep all other auxiliary knobs off. Next, slowly increase the volume on the auxiliary bus main knob until you're sending the correct level to the phone patch or ISDN codec.

If, however, you do not have (or want) a mixer, there's an alternative. Plug a cable into the headphone jack of your external audio interface and plug the other end into the phone patch input jack. This sends the mic audio to your client. Next, plug your headphones into the headphone jack on your phone patch so that you can hear both yourself and your client's direction. Since what you record and play back can always be heard on your audio interface headphone out, this same signal now goes through to the phone patch for your client to hear. He or she can listen in on your live recording and any files you play back. And since you're plugged into the phone patch with your headphones, you'll also hear yourself and your client's comments and direction—the client's talking won't be recorded at all!!

You can balance the audio levels of what you send to the client (using the audio interface's headphone volume control) and what you hear back over the phone with the phone patch interface headphone volume control. When you are done with the patch session, unplug your headphones from the audio interface and replug them back into your audio interface or mixer. Now, there are a few drawbacks to a traditional phone patch.

Audio Quality

Because the bandwidth on a telephone is pretty limited, the first problem is that the producer won't be able to hear every nuance of your stellar performance as clearly as if he or she were actually in the studio with you. Even worse are the sessions when 12 people gather in the conference room and try to listen and direct you via a speaker phone—it's like listening in a canyon.

Delivery Delay

The second problem is one of time. Now that you've recorded—and the clients have agreed on—which takes you are going to provide, your clients have to sit back and wait. The wait is short if you can quickly send your audio via the Internet, but it's much longer if you burn a CD and overnight or snail-mail it. For long narrations and documentaries or a session with hundreds of takes, it's sometime just not practical to use the Internet for delivery, especially when the client wants uncompressed audio in WAV or AIFF format.

Responsibility

The third drawback to traditional phone patches may sound a little esoteric, but believe us it's not. When you, the talent, are recording in your home studio, even with direction and ultimate approval from the client, you are playing engineer, producer, *and* talent. You are guaranteeing that the audio will be useable and of top quality. This is a lot of responsibility—far more than in a "normal" studio setting where the producer, director, and engineer hear all your takes and decide they are happy with your interpretation and the audio's quality and suitability. All you have to do is read the script in time as directed, sign your contract, and leave. Because of the limitations of regular POTS telephone lines, you are serving as the production team's "ears" and ensuring the takes are air quality.

Happily, there are other ways to work from your home studio without the drawbacks of a traditional phone patch: ISDN and Internet Audio delivery using VoIP—Voice over Internet Protocol.

ISDN Patches

ISDN is the digital way studios, broadcasters, and actors "send" their voices and images around the world instantly, but at a price. Aside from the cost of lines and gear, you will be subjected to more techno-jargon—like SPIDS, CODECS, LAYERS, and BRIs. Have faith, friends, it's not nearly as complicated as it sounds, as you'll see.

First off, ISDN has a big established infrastructure and is very reliable. We believe it will remain the "mainstay" for real-time professional audio production (especially among broadcasters who are loath to change anything!) for at least another five years, although slowly but surely, the use of Internet-delivered audio will come into its own. ISDN lines were created to send data, and when we send out voices, it's in the form of data. Faster ways to deliver data are continually being developed, and ISDN is now considered "slow" by many standards, so in some areas of the country, it is not being supported. When Harlan moved a few years ago, it was a struggle to convince his local telco (geek-speak—telephone company = telco) that he didn't want DSL or a T-One line or anything other than ISDN.

Generally, though, here's what happens. Your local phone company will install special ISDN lines to your home, for a fee around $150. Then you'll be charged an additional monthly fee of around $40 to $50. You'll get two, not one, ISDN phone numbers because this digital connection uses two physical and three logical lines. Why extra lines? To get the bandwidth necessary to deliver your voice with on-the-air quality! When you finish an ISDN session, it's exactly as if you were face-to-face with a producer in the studio. The producer has the broadcast-quality takes he needs, and you are free to move on to (or dial up to) your next session.

Once you've got your numbers (your SPIDS in ISDN-speak), you'll have to invest in a codec (an encoder/decoder), which is like a very sophisticated computer modem. Suffice to say, this device takes your voice, crams it down the phone lines, to be uncrammed at the other end by the other locations. Okay, okay, it's called compression—but we like the cramming, stuffing, shoving imagery. *(Figures. I've seen you boys at lunch. —Prunella)*

Just to complicate things a bit, you need to know that there are different types of codecs, and they are not compatible. The most popular units use the MPEG compression algorithm, which stands for Motion Picture Experts Group (yeah, we know we weren't going to get into definitions, but we find this one amusing—sounds more like a movie critics club, doesn't it?) and APT, or Audio Processing Technology. Many studios have both of these kinds of codecs, as do some performers. In general, most voice-overs use MPEG codecs, which send files similar to MP3 audio. If you need to "talk" to a studio that has only APT, it's very simple to arrange a "bridge" connecting the two devices at another location. Companies like Digifon and Ednet provide bridging services for a modest fee. These same companies can bridge ISDN codecs to Internet audio programs, but more on that subject in a moment.

Buying an ISDN codec isn't cheap; even used models are generally well over $1,000, and new units can cost thousands depending on features. CDQ Prima's made by Musicam USA (http://www.musicamusa.com) and Telos Zephyr's (http://www.telos-systems.com) are the most popular with voice-overs (see Figure 9.7). Both companies make portable units as well, so if you have a vacation home and have had ISDN lines installed, you can just take the "box" along, and you're ready to go to work.

Figure 9.7 Telos Zephyr ISDN codec.

Luckily, there are experts you can talk to about installing your codec, like Dave Immer at Digifon. His Web site (http://www.digifon.com) provides a wealth of help and advice as well as products and services to many studios and voice actors across the country. He even offers prepackaged voice-over packages with everything you need and has complete ISDN line-ordering instructions on his Web site. Dave is our hero and can personally help you order service.

EDnet (http://www.ednet.net) can also provide help with lines, equipment, and services. If you really want an in-depth education in ISDN resources, check out Dan Kegel's ISDN Web pages (http://www.alumni.caltech.edu/~dank/isdn/index.html)—yeah, we know, just typing in the Web address is intimidating, but this resource is worth the keystrokes.

All right, the lines are installed, and the codec is plumbed into your recording system with a mix-minus setup (see earlier section). Now what? Well, here are two very important tips for any ISDN session if you haven't communicated with a particular studio before:

- Always test the lines and the setup—*before* the session.
- Remember that the caller pays, and it's pretty much standard operating procedure that the studio will initiate the call to the talent.

Setting Up the Dial-Up

For two ISDN codecs to communicate with each other, you have to set them up the same way. Unlike a regular telephone, where you have no control over how your voice is sent, in a digital world, you have way too much control over bits per seconds and scary stuff like that. This could be, but isn't, a problem for voice actors because 99.9999 percent of the time, you'll send your voice with both codecs set at Layer 2, Mono 128.

That's the mantra for virtually every session you'll do. When you and the engineer at the other location test the lines (in advance), the engineer will almost always say, "Hi, I'm set at L2, (Layer 2) Mono 128," and you'll reply, "Me too." You really don't need to know anything else, and if the remote engineer wants some other setting (highly unlikely), he or she will talk you through changing the setup. Despite all the ways you *could* send data via ISDN, for voice work, it's almost always Layer 2 (L2) mono. When the connection is made, you'll hear two little digital-sounding "bleeps" and marvel at the clarity of the producer's voice in your headphones.

As we said, who places the call matters when it comes to ISDN; the caller foots the bill. Other than your monthly service fee, if you don't call out, you don't pay anything additional. If you need a bridge because you and the studio don't have compatible ISDN codecs, make sure you discuss in advance who will pay the freight.

Cost, not technical ability, is the biggest reason many voice talents resist having an ISDN-equipped studio. Performers who do any amount of promo work for radio or TV must have ISDN available to compete in that market, but we've found that, as a rule, the performers who tell you that you don't really need ISDN or Internet audio are the folks who don't have ISDN or an Internet audio solution themselves.

Is the investment worth it? We think so. And an ISDN-equipped studio indicates a higher level of professionalism. Believe it or not, many clients will actually insist on paying you a fee for using your ISDN home studio facilities. Many talents have found their studios becoming a profit center by making their capabilities available to other actors to do ISDN sessions.

Is the Future on the Net?

Yes.

But not quite yet.

Making the investment in ISDN is a big decision, and you can't help but wonder if this technology—like so many others—might suddenly disappear and your expensive codec become a "boat anchor," now that Internet programs mirroring ISDN connectivity are available.

The Internet and VoIP, coupled with a reliable high-speed connection and a software program, does allow you to send and receive air-quality audio via the Internet—with a few caveats.

Source-Connect (http://www.source-elements.com/Source-Connect/), for example, is a plug-in program, shown in Figure 9.8, that runs with *Pro Tools* or any audio program supporting VST plug-ins, such as *Audition* and *Sound Forge*. The cost of the basic program (all that a voice talent would need) is less than $400 and—that's it. No additional telephone lines to install, no monthly telephone line fees. You just purchase the program and, separately, a little plastic "key" called a *dongle* that holds your license information and plugs into any USB port on your home computer or your laptop when you are on the road and—voilà! You are "on the air," with another *Source-Connect* user.

Ah. Reread that last sentence again. There's the potential rub. At the other end, the studio you are connecting with needs to have *Source-Connect* as well. In practicality, most studios already have the program, and many have embraced its use because it saves so much money in line charges. But even if your connection point has only ISDN, you can still bridge to it for a small fee, and you are all set.

Audio TX (http://www.audiotx.com) is a similar VoIP solution, although it's more expensive. *Audio TX* talks to another *Internet* audio TX user, much the same way as *Source-Connect*, but *this* program also has the capability to emulate any ISDN codec, so it can hook up directly to any ISDN installation! Accomplishing this trick will require the purchase of a special ISDN adapter card for your computer(s) so you can plug in your existing ISDN lines. See the screenshot in Figure 9.9.

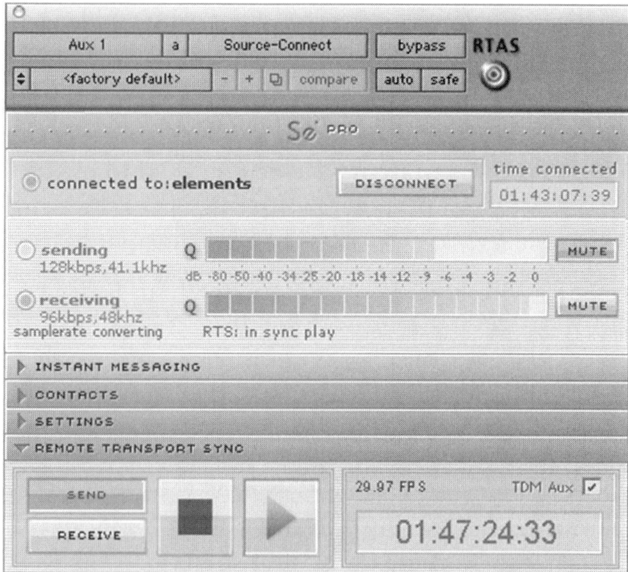

Figure 9.8 *Source-Connect.*

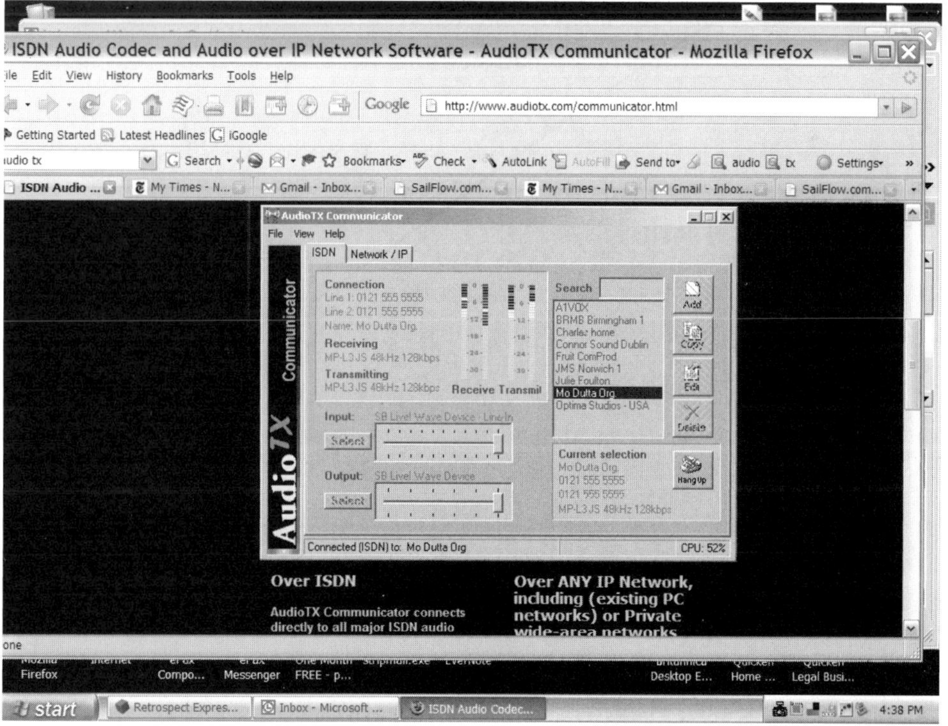

Figure 9.9 *Audio TX.*

One VoIP program called *SoundStreak* (http://www.soundstreak.com) allows talent to see and read to video. *SoundStreak*, unlike the other programs we mentioned, does not compress files and deliver them "live." Instead, it allows you to record the tracks on your computer and send lower-quality audio to the producer. The producer chooses the best full-bandwidth tracks and sends them to a *SoundStreak* server and then to the end studio. The delay involved—although not huge—may be a problem in the get-this-on-the-air-now world of TV and radio. As of this writing, the software was being provided free to performers, with the end studio paying a fee to *SoundStreak* for the service. We're not yet convinced that the ability to read to picture for most voice-overs will outweigh the necessity of installing either a video monitor or a noisy computer in their recording booth. On the other hand, the audio, once received by the studio, is of the highest quality, which may be reason enough for *SoundStreak* to become a success.

One more "rub" with Internet VoIP. Because of the way data is sent via the Internet today (disparate packets of data are sent in bursts) versus the streaming of contiguous audio, Internet audio can sometimes be choppy and create audio artifacts. In fairness, ISDN can get a little goofy from time to time, too, but it's fairly rare. When the Internet changes protocol (which it will), these minor hiccups will disappear, and we'll be putting the ISDN codec up on the shelf next to the DAT machine. To solve these problems in the meantime, *Source-Connect* unveiled a new version of its software that automatically detects any "dropped" out-of-order packets and restores the audio seamlessly! Quite amazing.

Right now, Harlan uses both ISDN and VoIP software. At home, ISDN is his primary connection, with *Source-Connect* as the backup. On the road, he uses *Source-Connect*, often with a bridge to ISDN clients. While speaking at the National Association of Broadcasters in Las Vegas with his coauthor (*Hey, that's me! —JPF*), Harlan did a problem-free session from the 50th floor of the Wynn hotel on his laptop using *Source-Connect*—wirelessly!

There is no doubt in our minds that real-time Internet-based audio delivery is making a big impact, and as the user base grows, it will *in time* most likely become the primary way we "teleport" our voices.

Regardless of the technology you use—telephone, ISDN, VoIP—long-distance direction can be a little daunting. It's much harder to direct and be directed when people can't see each other and their expressions. As a talent, you really have to listen and listen closely. Often, the producer will be far off-mic and difficult to hear. In that case, ask the engineer to turn up the volume on the talkback mic or repeat the direction for you; if you can't hear the direction clearly, there is no way you can deliver what the producer/

writer/director wants. It's obvious perhaps, but since you can't see the other people in the end studio—beware. No off-color jokes or snide comments about the product, the copy, or politics. Listen closely, be silent while they discuss the next take, and be a pleasure to work with.

In closing, although we promised not to speak in ISDN techno-babble, here's a phrase from an ISDN manual we just couldn't resist tossing around: "Digital telephone CODECS use Psycho Acoustic Masking to send audio."

Now, one of us, who shall remain unnamed, says that means the computer inside your codec analyzes sound and automatically eliminates any audio data not absolutely necessary.

The other of us, equally unnamed, claims Psycho Acoustic Masking is a patented makeup technique developed by Max Factor for that Jim Carry flick where he was dancing around with a green face—but you decide.

Yeah, we know, that gag was in the first edition of this book, but both of us liked it so much it's been reprieved. After all, it's *our* book, and we're nothing if not redundant. (*Finally! A statement I can agree with! —Prunella*)

10 Profitable Promotion

"With the right advertising, this thing could be bigger than Hula-Hoops."

—Jim Belushi as Patrick Martin, *Little Shop of Horrors,* 1986,

The Geffen Company

Or maybe even bigger than Pet Rocks, or Bell Bottoms, or Beanie Babies, or... not? You are now in a position to offer two new features to your clients and agent(s): a great-sounding home *and* portable studio. The benefits? Your agent and your clients have almost instant turnaround for auditions and sessions, even when you are AWOL. Having something new to promote—in addition to your voice talent—is exciting and worthy of some good old-fashioned ballyhoo. However, the corridors of commerce (*Now that's nice alteration. Who did you steal it from? —Prunella*) are littered with failed fads, foolish fashions, and freakish foibles foisted fervently, frequently, feverishly, upon an oft-fawning, fractious, formidably frenetic fellowship. (*Enough already! I have another F-word for the two of you. —Prunella*)

The point is that now you've got to let everybody know about your new facilities and abilities, in addition to the normal day-in and day-out job of promoting your voice work.

Unfortunately, in our combined 52 years of experience in the audio/voice-over business (*That's 50 for Harlan and 2 for me. —JPF*), we've seen an awful lot of talented voice actors come and go almost as fast as this weeks's new miracle diet or instant weight-loss pill. One minute she's the go-to voice in town, and suddenly it's "Whatwashername?" Of course, voice trends change and people change, but by and large, there's no mystery to these vanishing voices. Those otherwise-talented performers failed to sustain their careers because of ineffectiveness, inconsistency, or—all too often—a total lack of advertising and promotion. If that sounds a little familiar, and you've felt uncomfortable telling the world about your talent, your home and on-the-road studio just might provide not only the motivation but a damn fine excuse to finally start promoting!

But, like your Web site—the one you agonized over—and the "killer" voice demo that cost you the equivalent of two months' rent, your home studio abilities aren't going to sell themselves.

We need to repeat that.

Nothing sells itself.

And selling is not a dirty word or something that's beneath the dignity of a serious voice artiste.

Like it or not, you are a commodity, a service. You are selling your talent and your recording facilities. None of us can foist this job off onto our agents, our Webmaster, or our demo producer. None of us can simply rely on good luck and blind faith. Instead, we all have to build and grow our careers using constant, consistent promotion—what Jeffrey calls "Ruthless Self-Promotion" (from his book of the same name).

Of course, you'll want to let your clients know, especially the cash-strapped ones, that you've invested in home recording facilities. Many times, particularly for nonbroadcast, "industrial" clients, being able to "toss in" the studio will mean the difference between demanding the professional fee you deserve and losing the gig to a discount voice-over. Having your own studio adds value to your voice services, but you need to promote that added value to potential and repeat clients.

The Anatomy of Success

Those of you who play sports competitively know the value of getting your head into the game. Along with immense physical preparation comes intense mental concentration. To be a success with your career—and your promotion—you need to bring the same physical and emotional power to the table. Specifically, you need your head, heart, and stomach at their peak performance.

Head = Brains

There are two sides to your head: creative and logical. You need your creativity to serve you well in your acting and performing pursuits. But don't ignore the logic either. To make it in the crazy world of VOs, learn all that you can about how the business works. The more you know, the better off you'll be.

Heart = Passion

Desire comes from your heart. It's the love you have for yourself, your friends and family, and your creative work. Is there a fire inside of you that won't burn out unless you achieve your dreams? If there is, channel that passion into everything you do. If you don't have the passion inside of you, ask yourself why. And then take steps to stoke the fire.

When you feel passionate about what you do, that positive energy works in your favor. Your enthusiasm rubs off on others, creating a good experience for everyone you associate with.

Stomach = Guts

You have to take risks—whether you have the stomach for them or not. There are two key issues to address.

- It's okay to make mistakes. That's how you learn and grow as a person and as a professional. Vow not to repeat errors, and try to limit the downside to every venture you take on.
- Give yourself a challenge. Don't rest on your laurels. Always push yourself to do and be better. It is this constant pursuit of bigger, better, brighter that drives the most successful artistic temperament.

Spread the Word

You might also want to let other talent (even competitors!) know about your recording facilities and turn them into studio clients for sessions, auditions, and demo production. Be very cautious about promoting to recording studio owners. They'll be glad to know you have a home studio that can connect via the Internet or ISDN with them. They won't want to get the impression you're their competition, though.

How do you get the word out? In addition to calling and "talking up" your new facility, write a brief blurb that promotes it. Use this blurb on everything you have printed: business cards, demo CD labels, ads, postcards, your Web site, e-mail signature, and so forth.

Caution: There's no reason to include a laundry list of all the geeky-gear we convinced you to buy! Just print up some business cards listing your new services and facilities. You can easily make these on your home computer using Avery's Clean-Edge Business Card stock (http://www.avery.com). A better alternative may be, especially for color cards, to use an online printer, such as PrintingForLess.com (http://www.printingforless.com).

Okay. We agree that we have some sales work to do, so let's take a brief look at the five ways we'll be promoting our home studio capabilities and our voice-over skills at the same time.

Five Relatively Painless Ways to Promote

Here are some time-tested techniques that consistently prove their worth for businesses.

(1) Direct Contact

Most of us don't think of certain activities as sales calls. You know, those everyday occurrences that are part and parcel of the VO trade, such as talking to our agent on the phone, taking direction over talkback in a recording session, telling a recording engineer you are now available via ISDN, playing our new demo for a friendly producer, or chatting at a cocktail party with an aspiring young moviemaker. The truth of the matter is that all of these activities are most definitely sales calls and sales opportunities. Direct (sales) contact is how business gets done in just about every business, and we're no different. Our direct one-on-one and often face-to-face contact sells our talent, abilities, and personalities as we, in turn, help our clients create (and sell) *their* product or service—from a new animation series, to a healthy new snack for kids created in an organic, environmentally green factory with a low, low, carbon footprint.

(2) Publicity/Public Relations

PR usually involves articles or mentions in industry and general-interest publications—both in print and the Web—about you, your recent work, or accounts. Many actors, and in particular celebrities, have publicists who make sure the press is constantly aware of every accolade and spinning every bad review into oblivion.

The wonderful and powerful thing about publicity is that it is (or at least appears to be) "third party." Someone else, not you, is trumpeting your brilliant voice-over career and its recent triumphs. Well-crafted public relations publicity is usually regarded by readers as news, and it's estimated that 80 percent of news articles about people and products are actually planted by the PR industry. So don't fight 'em—join 'em with "news" about you! You can hire PR professionals, of course, but you may be surprised how easy it is to write a brief story about a recent success and send it to a trade periodical, your alumni magazine, or a local newspaper or radio/TV station. All these outlets are constantly looking for *interesting* material.

Your publicity can't be blatantly self-promotional; that would be an advertisement, and you'd pay for it. But any article that has an intriguing news worthy twist to it can reap tons of publicity—virtually free! Perhaps a story of how you managed to still record a TV promo while on your honeymoon in Maui while your wife was getting a pedicure might capture an editor's interest. "You know, Ms. Reporter, I owe it all to my laptop, *Source-Connect,* and the swell gear recommended in a book called... ahem... *Voice Actor's Guide to Recording at Home and on the Road.*"

Sometimes good publicity finds you. When the Broadway revival of *Talk Radio* debuted, Harlan was surprised and flattered when a reporter from the *New York Times* contacted and interviewed him. The director had hired voice-over performers instead of stage actors to portray the off-stage characters that call the show's acerbic host played by Liev Schreiber. The *Times* asked Harlan to comment on the art of voice-over and how it differs from film and stage work, and he was only too happy to oblige.

But don't feel only the *big* media is what counts. Highly targeted media that reach exactly the people you want to reach are worth more of your resources and constant attention than a single hit in a mega media outlet. So find those places—magazines, Web sites, blogs, radio/TV, and so forth—that reach your clients and potential clients, and then pursue those outlets with great story ideas.

(3) General Advertising

Advertising—unlike publicity—is directly purchased, and in ads, we can sell more directly. For voice-over actors, advertising generally means "print advertising." You might buy an ad—called space—in a production periodical like *Backstage, Advertising Age, Screen, Post,* and so on. Your investment in advertising will hopefully result in an increase in sessions, but it has the extra benefit of helping establish and maintain an image of you as a successful performer. The downside to buying ads is that they reach many nonprospects as well. So general advertising is almost always much more expensive than highly focused and targeted direct response advertising. Space advertising is also harder to "track" than direct response. People rarely tell you they saw your particular ad (unless you ask when they call). Most experts advise that strategic general advertising partnered with judicious direct response is a good long-term promotional strategy.

We also see a lot of Web-based advertising in the form of banner ads and a great many Google ads (http://adwords.google.com) where you pay per click. While this may be working for some voice talent we feel there are better ways to invest your money, such as aligning yourself with the right Web sites where people actually go to find talent. We suspect that most of the people who type "voice over" into Google are aspiring VOs looking for work, not producers looking for talent!

(4) Direct Response

When you send a promotion directly to clients and selected prospects, such as postcards, letters, your latest voice demo, and even e-mails, these are all part of direct response advertising. You are contacting individuals that you know or have very good reason to believe might hire you. Direct response is effective but can also be dangerous. Because it is a very personal form of advertising, you need to be sure your message is appropriate and welcomed by the recipient. In other words, the last thing you want to become is SPAM!

To market directly, you need to develop and maintain a good prospecting list with both snail mail and e-mail addresses. Most agents invest considerable time compiling and maintaining a list of potential employers that they will share with their exclusive talent, but you also need to keep your own list. Your list will most likely start with your present clients and then expand by contacting advertising agencies and production houses that hire voice talent.

From a cost-effectiveness standpoint, it's hard to beat good old-fashioned post-cards. And Internet-based e-cards are even less expensive since you save a bundle on postage. Take a look at Modern Postcard (http://www.modernpostcard.com). Its quality and service are tough to beat, as are its prices. It prints your full-color postcard along with hundreds of others on huge presses. Another inexpensive source is VistaPrint (http://www.vistaprint.com). Both companies can also mail your cards for you, a service called "fulfillment." You only need to supply a computer-created address list.

If you have artistic talent or a designer you work with, you can send digital artwork to be printed. You can also design cards yourself on either company's Web site. There are stock photos and various typefaces available to choose from as well. You can also get inexpensive photos and illustrations from other sources, such as iStockphoto (http://www.istockphoto.com).

If you do decide to use e-mail for promotion, just be sure to include a way for prospects to opt out or unsubscribe so that your promotion doesn't turn into an annoyance.

Vertical Response (http://www.verticalresponse.com) is one of hundreds of companies that can help you design an e-card and send it to your list of clients and prospects. Using e-cards assumes you have the e-mail addresses you need, of course. Because there is no postage or physical printing expenses, your cost is less than one-tenth of that of traditional postcards.

One of the biggest bonuses of using direct response advertising is that you can easily see the effectiveness of your promotion by the response you get back. If your prospects respond by requesting a demo, auditioning, visiting your Web site to check out the new studio, or—best of all—actually booking you, you'll know your promotion was a resounding success.

(5) Advertising Specialties

Many actors find that giveaways such as stopwatches, mouse pads, coffee cups, pencils, and pens are an effective way to thank a producer for hiring them and serve as a gentle reminder for future bookings. There are literally thousands of items that can be customized with your name and contact information to leave behind after a session or send out as direct response promotions. The yellow pages and the Internet list thousands of companies that offer what some derisively call "Trash and Trinkets." The important thing is that the giveaway be useful to the recipient and have your contact information permanently and prominently displayed.

What about the Web?

Surely, the Web is important, isn't it? Of course, it is. The Web opens promotional and pragmatic doors for your talent and home studio. The Web is so important, in fact, that we're giving it its very own chapter, next.

Seven Questions to Promotion Success To promote your VO and recording services effectively and make more sales, ask and answer these seven questions. They apply whether you are approaching a media outlet with a story idea or directly approaching a client or company. They'll help you develop suitable copy for any ads you put together, too.

- What do you sell?
- What job/client do you want to land?
- What does it take to get the sale?
- Are there any obstacles or drawbacks?
- Who is responsible for buying?
- How do you make contact?
- What will your pitch or offer be?

When you answer these questions, you'll be better prepared to promote and close the sale.

A Few Words on Word of Mouth

Many people cite "word of mouth" as the main way they get business. This magical, mystical promotional strategy seems to bring in sales with little or no effort. People just contact you or buy your stuff with little intervention on your part.

Well, that's not entirely true.

Real, effective word of mouth needs nurturing to work properly. Your effectiveness will come partly from reputation and partly from perspiration.

Earning a reputation helps you perpetuate your word of mouth. Those people who are satisfied with what you did in the past will likely purchase from you again.

With that rep in hand, it's time to push it a little harder by encouraging satisfied customers to spread the word *for* you. Here's how to get your word-of-mouth work working:

1. Decide what it is you need to promote. Get specific.
2. Make a detailed list of all the people you know. Include past clients, prospects who never bought anything, relatives, media contacts, business associates, and so forth. Put anybody who knows your work and reputation on this list.

3. Develop a promotion package that highlights what you need to promote. Include all the appropriate and suitable materials, such as postcard, flyer, business card, CD—whatever makes sense for you. Also, make sure your complete contact information is on everything that leaves your office/studio.
4. Send this promotional material to each person on your list. Make sure in the cover letter you are *not* asking for their business. Instead, you want them to pass on this information to someone they know who would be a candidate for your work. Again, don't ask them for business. Ask them for their help in letting other people know about you and how they can benefit from what you offer.
5. Of course, you can bypass step 4 and simply ask your clients for referrals to other people. Make sure you thank them for helping you spread the word. Additionally, you might consider offering incentives to those who help. Either give them a discount toward a future purchase or kick back a commission for a sale (or suitable gift) that comes as a direct result of their recommendation.

Word of mouth can be a highly effective promotional tool. But only when *you* start spreading the word first.

Other Home Studio Revenue Streams

We have a buddy with a nice home studio who landed a regular gig recording an actress at his place. Their mutual agent had casually mentioned to him that the actress was going to lose a monthly narration job for an out-of-town client because of the high costs of a full-fledged Chicago studio.

> "What do they need?" he asked the agent.
>
> "Just straight tracks," the agent replied. "They edit and assemble them at their AV department."
>
> "I can do that."
>
> "Yeah, but they direct over a phone patch."
>
> "I can do that."

And so he did, and he's making a nice monthly fee from his home studio, without even opening his mouth, other than to say, "We're rolling on track one."

Other home studio revenue streams include recording and sending in auditions for actors who haven't yet set up their own studio. And, of course, every voice actor needs a really good and really current demo. Who knows? Maybe you'll decide to help other performers create their demos. New to demo creation? Keep in mind a very simple structure as you create these demos. Like a play or a movie, a demo needs a dramatic arc, complete with a beginning, middle, and end.

- **Act One.** It doesn't matter if the talent is a working pro with hundreds of produced spots to choose from or a newbie—young and green—forced to create voice samples. Begin with the "signature" or "money" voice. Always start with the sound the actors are usually, or most likely, to be hired for. Producers often listen to only the first few seconds of a voice talent demo, so you have to put the most likely-to-be-hired sound right up front and in their face. Lead with a wallop that grabs the not-so-easily-impressed and doesn't let go.
- **Act Two.** Relax just a little after the thundering overture of the first act. Throw in a character voice or a nice, crisp bit of dialogue to add a little drama to the demo. Don't go too far astray, because you have to keep this section brief. Soon it'll be time for Act Three.
- **Act Three.** This is the end of the arc, the finale. You want to leave the client remembering that sound that people buy over and over, so end with another example of the signature voice.

This basic form works not only when producing a demo for a fellow actor, but for your own demo as well!

No Copy? No Problem!

Years ago, voice-over demos were three or more minutes long and were—in fact—audio resumes. It was considered bad form to put any "created" spots on your "reel." Well, times have changed. Voice actors realized that too often the actual spots we did—particularly television commercials—weren't really the right medium to showcase our voices. So, little by little, "created" demos have become the norm, which is fine, as long as you don't pretend to have been the voice on a commercial that someone else actually did.

So where do you get good copy for your or your actor clients' demo? There is a treasure-trove of great copy lurking right there in your home. Really? Don't see it? It's underfoot, piled in the bathroom, stacked on your nightstand, and stuffed daily in your mailbox. We're talking about magazines and catalogs. They provide a veritable cornucopia of great voice-over demo copy. With just a touch of rewriting, this material provides fabulous spots for your or your client's demo. Don't just plagiarize the whole thing;

be creative with the copy you find, and certainly change it to the first person. Just think of this as another form of recycling.

As for length, short and simple should be your guidelines. Better still, have multiple demos on various types that showcase your particular strengths. You can send hard copies to prospects, but most people have their demos available for listening and downloading on their Web site and their agent's. Don't worry about making a "killer" or "breakthrough" demo. Always remember that your goal as a demo producer is to present the product—you or your client—in the best possible light. Make sure the demo gives an accurate representation of the talent in a way that works. And that means—it sells!

Avoid the temptation to overproduce your demo with sound effects, music, and slick production values. And don't overprocess your voice with echo, compression, or EQ. Keep it simple and straightforward, and present your voice in the best way possible. You are not selling your ability to make radio-ready spots. You are trying to get your voice heard and hired!

Home Studio Legal and Logistic Concerns

If you are having people come to your home or apartment to record sessions, auditions, or demos, check your homeowner's or apartment-dweller's insurance policy. Should someone get injured in your home, you want to be sure you have insurance. Your home studio, in this instance, would be considered a place of business. The good news is that basic business insurance is very reasonable, and you will probably be able to purchase a rider to your normal insurance policy. Call your insurance agent and explain the situation.

Also, be mindful that your apartment building, condo, homeowners association, or town may have strict zoning laws about conducting business in a residential area. So do a bit of homework before you begin your home work.

If your home studio is now producing revenue, be sure to keep good records of your deductible business expenses and all the income it makes. At some point, you may want to consider incorporating your studio business and perhaps your voice business. There are Web sites like LegalZoom.com that can help you incorporate very reasonably.

Finally, if you have a significant other or some rug rats, cats, or dogs, consider the impact of having strangers trooping into your home or apartment to record with you. Make sure they all agree with this new possible invasion of their privacy.

Now That You've Built It, They Will Come!

Like so many things in life, and in particular the life we've chosen as performers, we have to trust that good things will happen to us if we prepare well, hone our craft, invest in the right tools and training, and simply hang in there.

Building your own home and on-the-road studio and learning the basic art of recording will—believe us—pay huge dividends in the long run, but it does take a giant leap of faith to buy the equipment necessary and spend the time necessary to learn to use it well. Before long, however, you'll wonder, "How did I ever get along without it?"

11 Working the World Wide Web

> "I love this Internet. It's part fantasy, part community, and you get to pay your bills naked."
>
> —Stockard Channing as Dolly in *Must Love Dogs,* 2005, Warner Brothers

Pay bills?! Shoot, if you keep your Webcam turned off, you could even do a session *au naturel,* although the authors do not recommend it. We prefer to keep a tidy, fashionably attired mental picture of you surfing the Web, happily discovering the employment opportunities it offers to voice actors with home studios. Now, judging by that grin on your face, we suspect you are reasonably Web savvy. But if we're wrong about that, wipe off that silly smile and go invest some time really learning how to use the Internet, and then come back to this chapter.

Seriously.

Still here? Good.

Just back? That's good, too.

The Internet lets us voice actors do lots of cool things:

- Inexpensively promote our talent on our own Web sites to our agents and on free and fee-based casting sites
- Send our auditions and session audio tracks to anywhere in the world and use voice over IP (VoIP) to perform "live"
- Seek and get worldwide employment
- Obtain talent agent representation, far from our physical location
- Control and promote our careers better

We love the Internet!

Then again, sometimes we hate it.

Why this love/hate relationship? Because even with all the benefits the Web provides, there are some undeniable downsides. We now compete with talent from all around the world for every single job. We audition constantly because it's so easy for creatives to e-mail scripts to agents everywhere demanding—and getting—quick turnaround. We get not just spam, but voice-over-specific spam. We've become isolated, too, rarely seeing or working with other performers. We get carpal tunnel syndrome from too much mousing around, and we find ourselves staring at a video monitor most of the day instead of talking into a microphone.

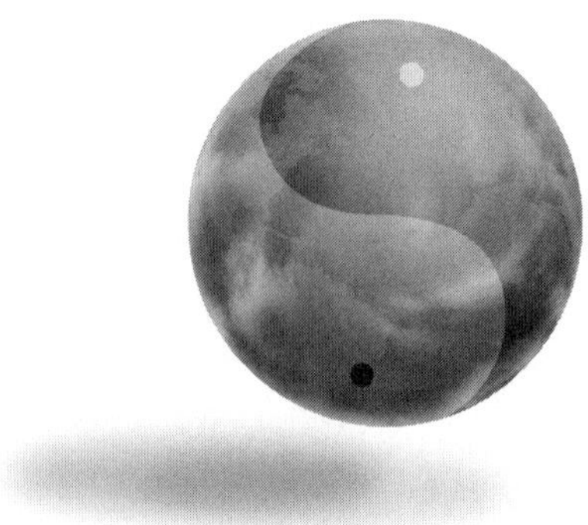

So, A Practically Perfect Partner

Acknowledging the yin and yang of the Web leaves no doubt that the Internet has changed the world of voice actors in profound ways. We can live or visit just about anyplace there's a reasonably high-speed Internet connection available and then e-mail or FTP our work to our employers. The Web itself offers monetary opportunities, as our commercials, industrials, games, and documentaries pop up on the Internet and we get additional use payments. And, of course, a great many Internet sites speak, and we can easily provide that talk—for a fee.

More importantly, the Internet offers us a solution to one of the most costly and time-consuming tasks we faced in our never-ending quest to find work: distribution of our voice demos.

No matter how great your voice demo was, there was always the daunting job of getting it into the hands of potential employers. Although professionally duplicated CDs are quite reasonably priced from suppliers like Disc Makers (http://www.discmakers.com) or Evatone (http://www.eva-tone.com), even the best deal for 1,000 CDs in full-color cardboard jackets is pricey compared to simply uploading your demos to a Web site.

Then factor in the additional costs of traditional distribution, like labels, jewel cases, padded envelopes, and the biggie—postage—and the old method becomes astronomically expensive. And let's not forget the environmental impact of making and distributing discs that all too often end up in a landfill.

So simply uploading audio to various Web sites is a huge Internet benefit for everyone.

Your Audio Web Site Opportunities

There are several ways you can connect via the Web with people and places important to your career.

Your Agent(s)

Every agent today has an Internet Web site where prospective employers can hear your audio samples. Some agents charge talent a small fee to help cover the costs, and it's well worth it. Many agents still do create a physical "house CD" with a compilation of their exclusive talents' demos for those talent buyers who prefer them.

Generally speaking, you'll have around a minute for your demo and need to create several different ones depending on the kind of voice work you do best. So you may be assembling separate commercial, narration, station imaging, trailers, animation/ character demos, and so on. The great thing is that now you can put these together in your home studio at zero cost.

However—and this is a big caveat—you'll be well served (especially considering how miniscule the cost is to distribute your demos this way) to invest a little money and have your favorite pro audio engineer tweak and finalize your demos, preparing them for the Web in the format requested by your agent. Those formats will usually be MP3s, Real Audio, or QuickTime. Of course, we'll show you how you can prepare your own files for the Web in this chapter, but consider the benefit of having another set of ears fine-tune your work. Some agents require a CD of your various demos so they can have their own Webmaster prepare your samples for their site.

Independent Sites

A number of independent voice-casting audio sites also will host your demo. Most charge a fee. Some are somewhat free—listing you and even sending along audition descriptions. The catch is that to actually *submit* an audition, you need to pay a joining fee. Just a few of the fee-based sites include Voice123 (http://www.voice123.com), Canadian-based Commercial Voices.com (http://www.commercialvoices.com), and Voices.com (http://www.voices.com). Voicehunter.com (http://www.voicehunter.com) charges for listing you and posting your demos and charges a commission on the jobs they cast. An agent will most likely post your demo to Voicebank (http://www.voicebank.net). You cannot post to this site on your own, however. Some new pros-only sites like http://www.elearningvoices.com are not only fee based, but membership is by invitation only.

You could end up spending a lot of money to be on all these and other talent sites on the Web. Our advice? Go slow. Since most of these sites list their talent roster, talk to at least a few of their clients to see if they are happy with the service. No site can guarantee that you'll get work, but you're betting that the exposure will at least result in some additional bookings.

Also, consider the amount of time you have in your day to audition and the priority you'll have to assign to auditions received from your personal agent versus auditions from these group-based sites. Some sites have hundreds of people auditioning for each job and, let's face it, if your audition isn't among the first 10 or 20 received, the odds of anyone actually listening to it are greatly reduced. If you are auditionee number 450, forget it. So do you have the time and, more to the point, are you willing to sit by your computer all day watching for an audition to pop up so you can instantly turn it around?

Your Personal Site

Nice as it is to be on your agent's site and on selected group casting services, there's nothing like your own space to really showcase your talents. Best of all, none of your voice-over competition will be there! The first step is to buy a domain name like myname.com. Now, we don't mean that literally. Myname.com is for sale at the moment, and it's a measly $10,000,000.00. And no, we didn't go zero crazy—that's a cool 10 million! Some people pick a more obtuse Web presence name like varietyvoice.com or perfectvoice.com. You may find that your name or your great site name dot-com is already taken. Not to worry though. In the past few years, many other extensions have become available, so you may be able to get yourname.*tv* or perfectvoice.*biz*.

Wonder if your favorite name is available? The easiest way to find out is to type an appealing name into your Internet browser. For example, http://www.perfectvoice.com is taken as is, but http://www.perfectvoice.tv is (was!) available as of this writing for $17.99 a year at Go Daddy.com (http://www.godaddy.com.), and we could have grabbed it instantly with a credit card. There are many domain name companies, like Go Daddy and the largest, VeriSign (http://www.networksolutions.com). So for a very reasonable yearly fee, you can establish your own presence on the World Wide Web.

And you should. Right now. You can't go wrong grabbing a Web domain of your own name. Of course, if your name is Jeffrey P. Fisher (http://www.jeffreypfisher.com),

Harlan Hogan (http://www.harlanhogan.com), or Audio Smart Actors (http://www.audiosmartactors.com), you're out of luck. But we'll sell you all three for $9,999,999.00. (That's cheaper than myname.com.)

Here's a serious tip: If you know that people frequently misspell your name, you might want to buy similar domain names. For example, in addition to harlanhogan.com, Harlan owns harlinhogan.com, harlandhogan.com, and harlenhogan.com just to be on the safe side. The misspelled Harlans just automatically forward to his actual Web site. Your domain name is an inexpensive and—assuming you pay the annual fee—permanent address on the Internet. It's a domain all your own.

Okay. You've got a great domain name, and you're ready to carve out your piece of cyberspace. To do that, somebody has to host the party: a Web-hosting service.

These services are in the business of maintaining Web pages like yours. Yes, this will be an additional cost, but worth it. The fees are reasonable, and you're never at the mercy of a particular company because you can easily take your business elsewhere if you're unhappy or it goes out of business. Your domain name (and even your Web site content) is fully portable. A few years back, Jeffrey's Web host went belly up, but he simply transferred his domain and content to a new host—in just a few minutes—and voilà, all was well again at http://www.jeffreypfisher.com.

VeriSign, Go Daddy, Pair Networks (http://www.pair.com), Addr.com (http://www.addr.com), and many other companies can provide Web hosting for you at competitive rates, based on your specific needs. HostIndex (http://www.hostindex.com) ranks the top Web-hosting companies each month as a free service to help you choose the service that's right for you. You can also check Web Hosting Ratings (http://www.webhostingratings.com) for help in choosing your provider.

Your Web-hosting service will also provide an amazing ability that lets you walk on water.

Okay, that's a slight exaggeration.

But it *will* provide the ability to use FTP!

Yep! You get a never-ending stream of first-rate oil additives that will make your car run smoother and longer.

Okay, that's a flat-out lie.

FTP (File Transfer Protocol in geek-speak) is sort of a mini-Internet of your own that lets you send and receive those huge, uncompressed audio files you recorded but are way too big to just e-mail.

You can send most auditions and short audio selections to clients, prospects, and your agent via e-mail, but most e-mail programs have limits on the size of files you can send and receive. A single minute of CD-quality audio (5MB/minute mono) may be too big for many users' Inboxes. Even MP3s are large (about 1MB/minute), so a long narration or several commercial takes sent directly to a client may end up being rejected.

With FTP, you simply upload large files to your Web site and tell your clients (in an e-mail) where to go to download the files at their leisure as shown in Figure 11.1. You can usually password-protect your FTP files so that only your client has access to them. As an added bonus, your client will be visiting your Web site again, which is a nice reminder of your professionalism and abilities.

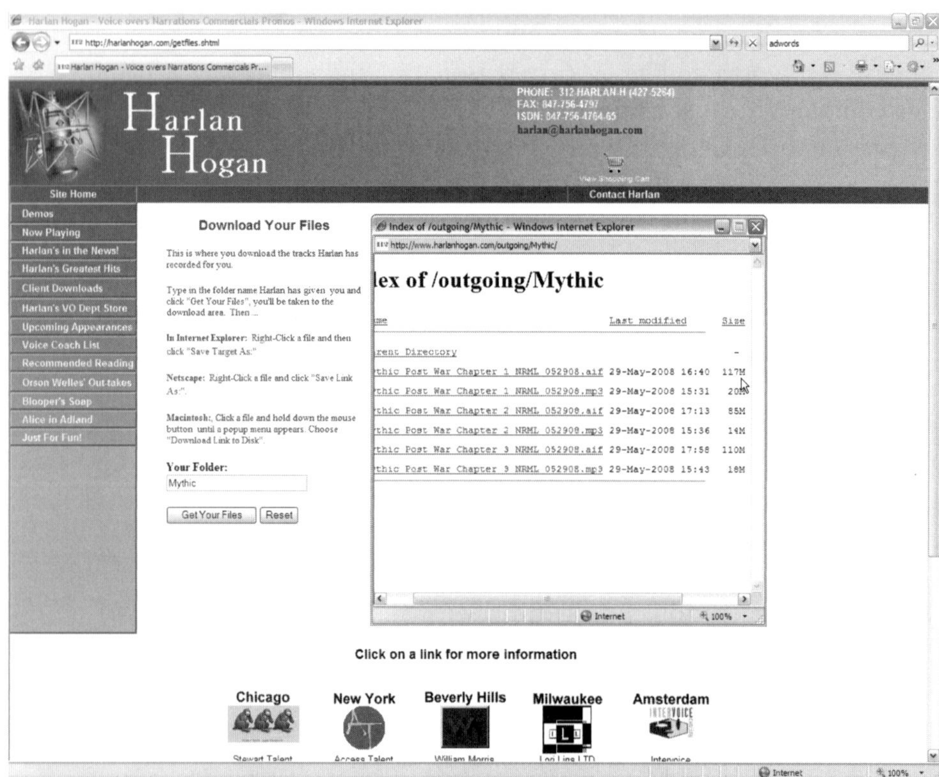

Figure 11.1 FTP example.

By the way, using a dedicated FTP uploading program is far faster than adding files to your FTP area just using your standard Web browser. Jeffrey likes the inexpensive Coffee Cup (http://www.coffeecup.com/direct-ftp/).

Web Design: Can You Do It Yourself?

Now that you have your domain name ready, great audio prepared, and a Web-hosting company set up, how are you going to design a good-looking, practical, and useful Web site? Is it possible to do it yourself? Before we answer those questions, let's think about what a good voice talent Web site needs to have.

First, your Web site is in fact a cyberstore that sells your services (and products, if they apply). So you'll need your best promotional material, your full contact information, your demos, a short list of projects and clients, and perhaps their testimonials and recommendations, articles by and about you, perhaps some pictures, and anything else you feel is important. You might want to provide some added value to your site by including voice-related information (blog, anyone?), samples, useful tips, links, even humor. This works for you in two ways. First, you're freely giving interesting information to visitors to your site (rather than just an endless commercial about you), and that information will make people anxious to revisit regularly to see what's new. Of course, that means you'll have to regularly update your site! Second, you have a reason to promote your site each time you do add new content, and that further drives traffic to your little corner of cyberspace.

Do some homework by visiting a few other voice-actor Web sites and seeing how the ones you like are using the Internet to their advantage. There will be plenty of bad examples, too; learn from their mistakes. After your research, plan out your Web pages on paper, and use these ideas to rough-design your site or to offer input to a Web designer you've hired. Gather all the content for the site, and plug it into the rough design to see how everything flows. Then make changes as you see fit.

After all this preparation and testing, you'll need to physically put your site together. If you're lucky, you have friends or relatives conversant with otherworldly languages like HyperText Markup Language (HTML), the language of the Web. If not, and you feel fairly comfortable with computers and basic design, programs like Microsoft FrontPage, Adobe PageMill, SoftQuad HoTMetaL Pro, or Macromedia Dreamweaver can help you design and set up your site.

All these programs use a nontechnical approach called WYSIWYG. "Wizzywig" sounds impressively weird, but the letters W-Y-S-I-W-Y-G just stand for "what you see is what you get." Simply put, as you lay out your Web pages in these programs, you design something that looks good to you, and violà: What you *see* on your computer is what others will *get* when they visit your site once you've uploaded your files to your Web-hosting service.

Alternatively, you can buy ready-made templates (go ahead and Google "Web templates") that let you plug in your own content and go. These templates can be edited with a simple text editor or one of the software programs we just mentioned. And places like MySpace and Facebook have built-in, online design and layout tools.

But assuming you just don't have the time or inclination to learn yet another new skill, or you want a state-of-the-art-whiz-bang Web site, it may be time to hire a professional, like our friend Warren King.

Your E-Mail John Hancock Make sure you include an e-mail signature that accompanies all your outgoing messages. This tagline should include your name, phone number, e-mail address, and Web site address. Consider also adding a short promotional message. This is a nonintrusive, nonobnoxious little ad for you and your services. Perhaps: "Heard my latest promos for CNN? No? Visit http://www.mydomainnamehere.com." You'll want to make that link clickable, so type its *full* URL address. Check your own e-mail program's documentation for exact details on setting up an electronic signature.

Jeffrey uses a freeware program called Pegasus Mail (http://www.pmail.com) that accommodates multiple signatures. You can write different versions for specific situations and choose the appropriate signature to accompany your message. Pegasus also supports mailing lists, where you can send the same e-mail to hundreds of people at once. Microsoft Outlook also offers a mailing list feature.

Professional Web Design

Warren King, Harlan's Webmaster, is a soft-spoken man usually found surrounded by a number of different computers. Warren is spending this evening, like many others, on quality control, checking the Web sites he's designed to see that they look and sound right on every kind of "box," from the slowest to the fastest, regardless of their make, model, color, or condition. It's this attention to detail that keeps Warren and other Web designers like him in demand. He's the consummate Web design professional, and one you'd be lucky to have working for you.

We asked Warren what advice he has for the average voice-over performer who feels comfortable using his home studio to record auditions, save tracks as WAV files and convert them to MP3, and now wants a Web presence.

Warren:

> Well, you can do many amazing things on a Web site today, but those things only make sense if they *sell* your product—in this case, you. Luckily, the cost of

your own Web site itself is not terribly expensive, and you can do your own design if all you want to do is create a basic informational page and put a link to your voice demos. The question is always whether you have the time or desire to learn how to do that. If not, or if your needs are more complicated, then it's best to hire a professional.

You should ask [Web designers] for reference sites you can look at that they've designed and make sure they understand how to integrate audio into their design. Once you've decided who is going to design your Web site, the next issue is what that site will look like, and that's the most important thing. Your site has to look professional because it is, after all, a reflection of you. You want any prospective voice clients visiting your site to instantly see that you are the real thing, that it's not risky to book this [with] you because you are obviously a pro, based on the quality look of your site and, of course, the great sound of your demos. Your design and the words and phrases you use on your site also [have] to take into consideration the search engines of the Web and the key words that make [your] site show up when someone searches—what most people now call Googling even when they may be searching with Yahoo, MSN, or any number of other search engines.

There are some simple, basic things you can do to get good rankings in the various search engines. First, make your pages relevant to what you are doing, concentrate on what you do best, and keep the pages short, as they rank better. Second, submit your pages to the top search companies whenever you make changes to them. On the major search engine sites, you'll find instructions on how to submit your pages. Once you are on the important search engines, they will automatically send their Web bots out to your site regularly and register any changes. Third, try to choose the right key words, which is both an art and science. You need to not only discover the exact words your potential clients are using to find talent like you, you also need to find out what words your prospects are using to find you that your competition is *not* using!

You can use the keyword tools found at Google AdWords (https://adwords.google.com/select/KeywordToolExternal).

Having said that, don't get too hung up on ranking highly in the search engines, because the fact is, most of the traffic that arrives at your site will come from traditional promotion like word of mouth, e-mail, links on other sites, postcards, publicity, public relations, and ads rather than Internet searches. With that fact in mind, put your Web site address on everything: business cards, demo CDs, blog and forum postings, and every e-mail you send.

Web Promotion

With your site up and running, it's time to brag a bit about your state-of-the-art recording facilities and all the fun and interesting things instantly available for those who visit your domain. A simple way to constantly promote your site is with banner ads. For example, to promote his book *VO: Tales and Techniques of a Voice-Over Actor,* Harlan had an animated banner ad created (shown in Figure 11.2). There were three rotating messages: "Finally a book about voice-overs that's almost as much fun as performing them!" "Great Stories, Great Advice," and "Wanna-bee, Newcomer or Old Pro, You'll love it." Clicking the banner took you to Harlan's Web site with complete ordering instructions for the book and, of course, all his voice demos. (*You sly OLD fox, you. —Prunella*)

Figure 11.2 Web banner.

You may find, as Harlan did, that owners of other Web sites were willing to put up his banner ad for a little cash or to "trade space." For example, Harlan put a link to Canada's CommercialVoices.com site, where he is a member. They in turn included his banner ad on their site. Many people were happy to post Harlan's banner ad as a professional courtesy, and he returned the favor with an autographed copy of the book and one of his VO: As Heard on TV baseball caps.

Getting Your Voice Demos "Web-Ready"

Here's how to get your demos up and sounding great on the Internet using the most popular Web formats.

As we've already discussed, digital audio files are large—about 5MB per minute in mono. Since that's too big to e-mail effectively, we need to reduce the file size while keeping the relative quality high. For auditions, the universal standard that voice actors use is MP3. Most choose the typical 128kbps setting (about 1MB per minute), which gives a small enough file to send but maintains decent audio quality. Most MP3s you download from music sites use this same setting (see Figure 11.3).

MP3s, along with Real Media and Windows Media, are lossy formats. That means they use special encoders to make the file size smaller while maintaining reasonable fidelity by eliminating (losing, hence lossy) frequencies that other sounds cover up, or "mask."

Figure 11.3 MP3 setting.

This process is called *psycho-acoustic masking*. When you put your demos on a Web site, you'll use one of these formats and select the best quality encoding you can. Usually it'll be called "CD quality" even though it's not really. You don't want to have huge files that take forever to download, but you don't want to make the files so small that you lose all the nice audio details you worked so hard on. So you need to strike a balance between performance and file size. For Real Media, choose 100 Kbps Audio as a minimum. For Windows Media and your MP3s, the 128 Kbps setting is ideal.

Flash

This is not a format, per se, but rather a method of delivering audio to Web site visitors. The actual audio that plays is in MP3 format. (See the next section.) The Flash player, such as the one shown in Figure 11.4, makes it easier for people to play your demo, or you can embed the sound directly into the page so it starts as soon as people reach the page. This requires the viewer/listener to have the free Flash player installed on the computer, because the demo runs inside their Web browser. Most Web browsers support this, but occasionally a client may not have this and may need to upgrade. One added benefit to the Flash delivery is that people can't actually download your demo; they can just listen to it online in real time. Alternatively, your file can play automatically when people visit your home page. Go to http://www.audiosmartactors.com and hear an example of this as Harlan and Jeffrey greet you when you arrive.

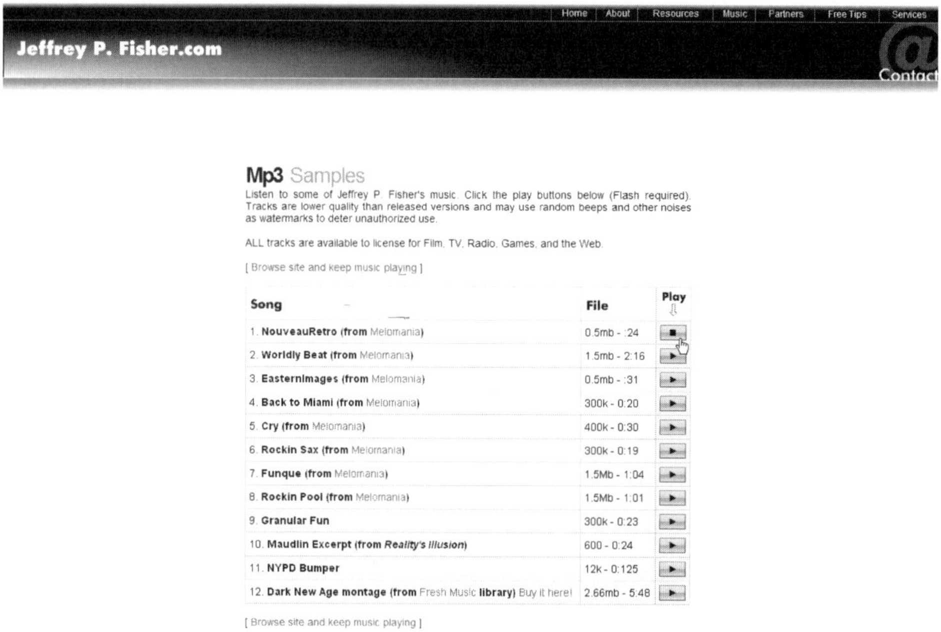

Home | About | Resources | Music | Partners | Free Tips | Services

Jeffrey P. Fisher.com

Contact

Mp3 Samples

Listen to some of Jeffrey P. Fisher's music. Click the play buttons below (Flash required). Tracks are lower quality than released versions and may use random beeps and other noises as watermarks to deter unauthorized use.

ALL tracks are available to license for Film, TV, Radio, Games, and the Web.

[Browse site and keep music playing]

Song	File	Play
1. NouveauRetro (from Melomania)	0.5mb - :24	■
2. Worldly Beat (from Melomania)	1.5mb - 2:16	►
3. EasternImages (from Melomania)	0.5mb - :31	►
4. Back to Miami (from Melomania)	300k - 0:20	►
5. Cry (from Melomania)	400k - 0:30	►
6. Rockin Sax (from Melomania)	300k - 0:19	►
7. Funque (from Melomania)	1.5Mb - 1:04	►
8. Rockin Pool (from Melomania)	1.5Mb - 1:01	►
9. Granular Fun	300k - 0:23	►
10. Maudlin Excerpt (from *Reality's Illusion*)	600 - 0:24	►
11. NYPD Bumper	12k - 0:125	►
12. Dark New Age montage (from Fresh Music library) Buy it here!	2.66mb - 5:48	►

[Browse site and keep music playing]

Figure 11.4 Flash player.

MP3

This popular format finds its roots in the video compact disc (VCD), the precursor to the DVD. The name designation MP3 stands for MPEG-1 Audio Layer 3, which is the audio portion of the VCD. DVDs use a different format from Dolby called AC-3. Anyway, these files sound very good and are much smaller than regular WAV/AIFF files, which is why MP3 became the most popular audio format for use on the Web. It's an ideal solution for your online demos and for sending auditions to your agents and sometimes even finished files to certain clients. (Many radio commercials are directly distributed to stations as MP3s.) Thanks to these MP3s, you can trot around with a couple gazillion tunes on your iPod. Most audio software programs can save audio files directly to MP3, but you can surf the Internet for other shareware or freeware encoders.

Real Media

As one of the original Web audio formats, Real Media compression algorithms are impressive, especially for audio. And you can stream the audio from your Web site easily. Encoding your file to the Real Media format requires using their production tools, called Real Media Producer (http://www.real.com). Alternatively, some audio software, such as Sound Forge, lets you save your uncompressed files in the Real

Media format, ready for Web posting. This format is slowly being replaced by Flash players using the MP3 format. Also, this format requires your listeners to have the Real software on their computer. It's a free download, but they must initiate the installation.

Windows Media

Microsoft goes head to head with Real Media and MP3 to offer outstanding quality even at high compression with its Windows Media. You can download a free encoder (http://www.microsoft.com) or use the encoding tools found in your audio software. The other advantage to this format is that every computer that runs the Windows operating system has this player already built in. However, Macs may have trouble playing these files.

Streaming versus Downloaded Audio Files

There are two ways to access sound files from the Internet: streaming or download.

When an audio file *streams*, it plays in real time, such as the Flash example we talked about. After buffering a little of the file, it starts to play, while grabbing the next portion of the file in the background. Depending on the file, the encoder used, and the Internet connection, you can hear the file play with little or no interruption, almost instantly. Typical streaming files include Real Media, Windows Media, and Flash.

In contrast, with a *downloaded* sound file, you save the entire file to your hard drive before you can start playing it. The wait can be worth it, though; because the file is downloaded, it plays seamlessly with no "hiccups." That is why most downloadable demos on the Web are around a minute or so in length; the wait to download is only a few seconds, and the audio sounds and plays great.

Preparing Your Files for the Web

After you've cleaned up, edited, and polished your performance, save the file as an uncompressed, CD-quality file. This is your master file. From it you can burn a high-quality CD to send out. However, this file is not yet ready for the Web. You need to treat it before encoding it. Why? Because if you follow our advice, your files will sound better. Period.

Open the master file in your audio editor—in this example, Sound Forge. Use EQ to carefully shape the sound you will encode. EQ, short for equalization, lets you affect the tonal qualities of a sound file. You can emphasize certain frequencies, such as bringing out more highs or eliminating some low-end rumble. To prepare your file for the Web, roll off all the frequencies below 80–100Hz and above 10,000Hz (10kHz) rather sharply (see Figure 11.5). These EQ tools may be called low- and high-shelf or, more commonly, high- and low-pass filters. Not all the compression encoders respond well to extremely low- or high-frequency content. This EQ trick eliminates these frequencies, leaving a sound file that sounds better after final encoding.

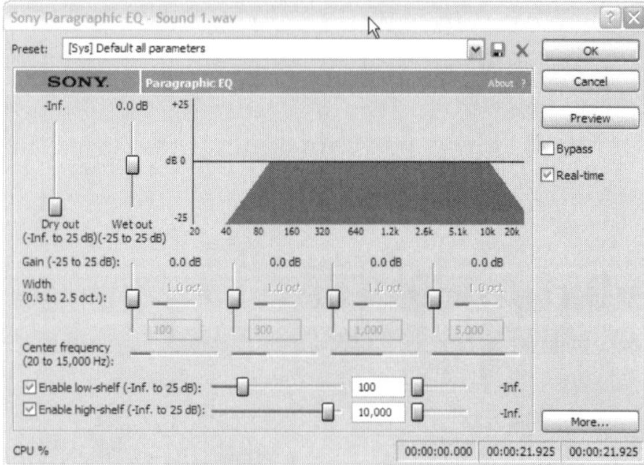

Figure 11.5 Web EQ.

After processing the file with EQ, consider reducing its dynamic range. The difference between the loudest and softest parts of a sound file comprises its dynamic range. For MP3 and other Web encoding, it's better to limit that dynamic range to about 12dB. This means you need to squeeze a larger amount of sound energy down a smaller pipe. Compression is the only way to squeeze those dynamics; it's the funnel you use to do this. By decreasing the volume of louder sounds, moving them closer to softer sounds, the compressor works to level the overall volume. See Chapter 12, "Advanced Production Techniques," for more details.

For voice tracks, set the threshold level about 3 to 6dB below the loudest peak level. In other words, if your loudest peak in your recording is at –3dB on the digital meters, set your threshold to about –9 dB. Try a 4:1 ratio. Set the attack medium fast, about 10ms, and set the release to a long setting, about 500ms (such as what's in Figure 11.6). This setting will smooth out your recording by only compressing the loudest sounds. Note that your file may be a little softer when applying the compression. To compensate for this, raise the level or output gain a little. (Keep an eye out for clipping, though.) If you feel you still need a little more compression, experiment with the threshold and ratio settings.

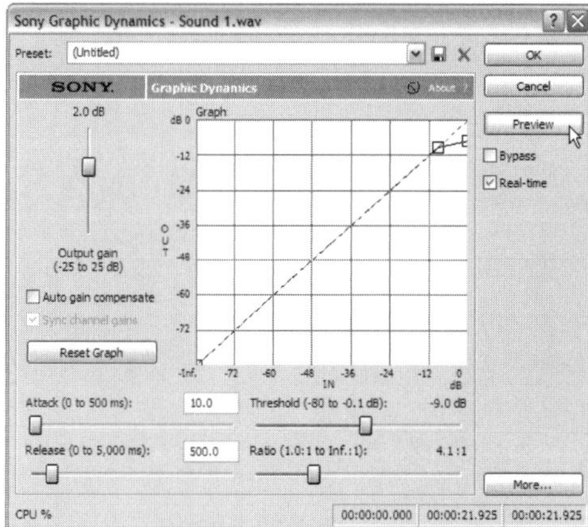

Figure 11.6 Compression example.

Note: A little compression goes a long way. Don't be tempted to slam the compressor to make a really loud file; it'll sound horrible. Too many demos we hear—not to mention some on-air work—is way too compressed and "funky" sounding. All you are trying to do here is tighten things up a bit, not blow your clients' ears out!

With your file EQd and compressed, you need to maximize its overall level through a process called normalization. Essentially, *normalization* raises the volume of a sound file. You have two choices: peak and RMS. With peak normalizing, you set a maximum volume level. The software then takes the loudest peak in your sound file and moves it to the level you picked. The software also raises the level of the rest of the waveform by the same amount it boosted the peak. If you set the peak normalization to –1dB—a great idea for MP3s—and the current highest peak level is –6dB, the software will boost the volume 5dB for the whole file.

This is handy because it automatically raises your volume without your having to guess and risk going over the dreaded digital zero, which, as you know, results in a horribly distorted file.

Using the peak normalization tools provided by your audio software, peak normalize to –1.0 or .5dB. That's plenty loud for Internet compression encoding (see Figure 11.7).

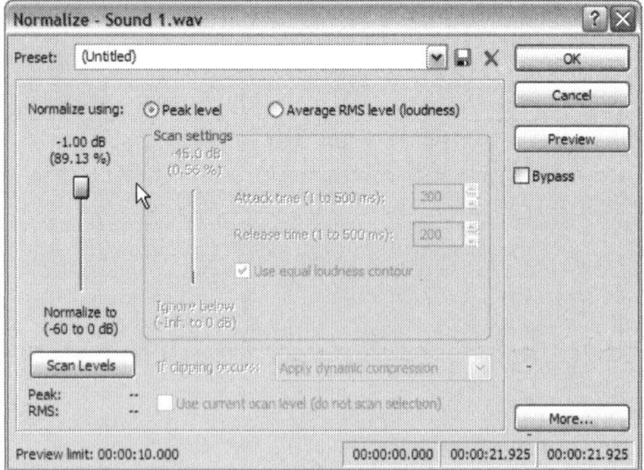

Figure 11.7 Normalize.

RMS normalizing raises the average volume of the file, what might be called *perceived loudness*. Normalizing using RMS settings is often unpredictable for the novice. Stick to peak normalization.

Normalization helps maximize the volume of your sound file. Note the difference in the amplitude (volume) between the before (see Figure 11.8) and after examples (see Figure 11.9).

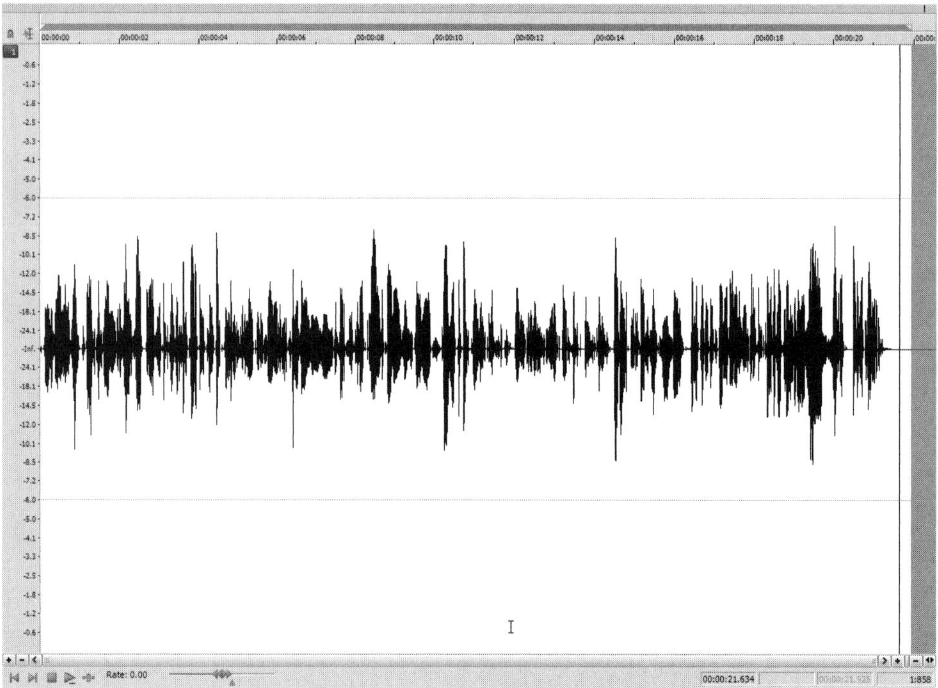

Figure 11.8 Before normalize.

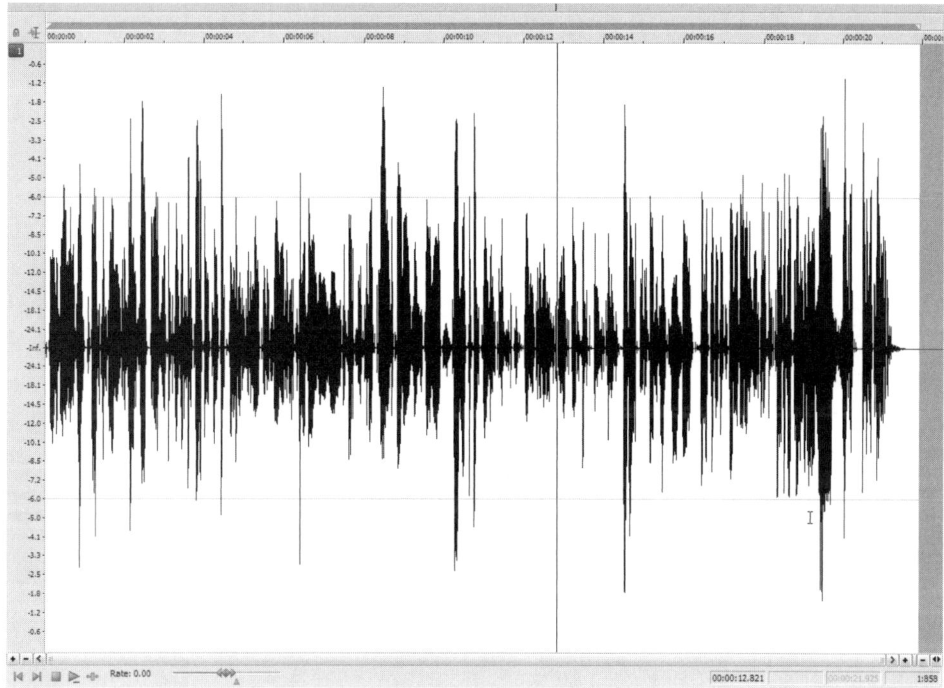

Figure 11.9 After normalize.

Now your file is ready to encode to Real Media, Windows Media, or MP3. Make sure you save this file with a different name than your master file. Simply add "Web" to the file name to help you remember which file is which.

Sony Wave Hammer

The full-featured version of Sound Forge includes a special plug-in called Wave Hammer. As its name implies, it helps you maximize the volume of your sound files through a combination of compression and normalization. The software automatically applies some gentle compression to your sound file and then maximizes that output to a setting you indicate.

This tool is ideal for preparing your files for Web encoding. First apply the EQ as indicated in the text, and then use the Wave Hammer tool to apply final compression and normalization in one operation.

The Wave Hammer includes a preset called Master for 16-Bit that is perfect for this operation, as you can see in Figure 11.10. You may get better results if you alter that preset slightly to be the threshold at –10dB, ratio to 4.5:1, output gain to –0.3dB. (That's negative *point* three dB.) Also, check the Peak Scan Mode, Auto Gain Compensate, and

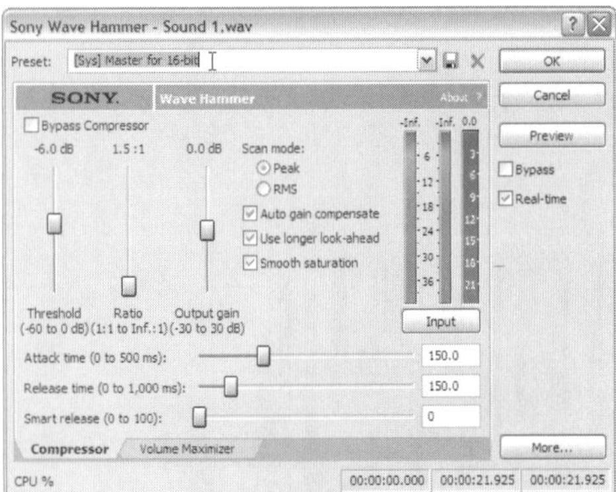

Figure 11.10 Wave Hammer.

Use Longer Look Ahead boxes. For the volume maximizer setting on the other tab, choose –0.5dB. (Again, that's negative *point* five.) The result is a loud, in-your-face sound perfect for preparing the file prior to Web encoding.

We Are Virtual Voice-Overs

Many of us started out to be actors, treading the boards, to the appreciative applause of theater goers. Soon we found ourselves waiting tables, even when we had successful theatrical careers. So we discovered voice-over work as the way to pay the bills and use our acting talent in what the business folks call a niche market.

Some of us voice-over performers started in broadcasting. As station after station was gobbled up by corporate America, we found ourselves in a dying profession dominated by only a handful of performers. We, too, looked to voice-over work as a way of using our skills and paying the bills.

Regardless of our backgrounds, smart voice performers are embracing the Web and mining its new opportunities without spending time and energy bemoaning the fact that clients rarely call a local talent agent and say, "Book 'em" like they once did.

This is a virtual, international world, and we can be part of it by welcoming new technology and getting ourselves—actually our voices—into cyberspace for a waiting and appreciative audience. The smart money's on becoming a virtual voice-over.

The Virtual Voice-Over and the Home Studio Auditions

One of the biggest—if not the biggest—changes the Internet has brought is a major change in *where* voice actors audition. Fewer and fewer auditions are held at casting directors' or even in your agent's office, although this isn't always a good thing because you have to "self-direct" and miss the opportunity to demonstrate your versatility and personality. And the sheer volume of auditioning makes the home studio "rip, read, and send" audition model practical and prevalent. Obviously, the advantage of not having to spend hours commuting for a chance at work that you might not even get is a big mitigating factor, as is the opportunity—thanks to the Internet—to audition for work nowhere near your physical location. In addition, many voice actors have found they can get talent agency representation in markets far from home, providing even more casting opportunities.

The scripts that your agent or a direct contact e-mails to you to record at home are not just easier and quicker than physically going to your agent's for a session. There are also some psychological benefits to recording at home. The waiting room at most agents' and casting directors' is wall to wall with actors. This can be a bit intimidating if you're relatively new to the world of cattle calls. More importantly, everyone is in a hurry to get you in and out, and all too often you just don't get a chance to experiment with your reading. Nine times out of ten you're halfway home when the right reading dawns on you. But by then it's too late. Auditioning in your home studio provides a quiet oasis in which you can record as many takes as you like, listen to them, and then choose the one or two you feel are your strongest.

Another advantage is that you have more control over the sound of your audition. More than likely, the equipment you own now (or soon will) is as good as, and frequently far better than, your agent's. Using your computer, you can clean up your takes, perhaps adding a touch of EQ or compression so they stand out. Don't go overboard with these tricks. Your tracks will be sent along with all the other actors' takes, so it can't sound *too* different. But, life being life, the absolute best take will inevitably have a tiny mouth noise in it or a big-honking breath sound. Those flaws would stay in the audition if recorded at your agent's or a casting director's studio. But when you record and edit at home or on the road, you can zoom in on the waveform and surgically remove the mouth noise and delete that big-honking breath!

Watermarking If you are auditioning directly for people you don't know, here's a word of warning. The audio quality of even a basic home studio today is often good enough to go right on the air, be used in a narration, or be posted on a Web site. That has happened to more than a few actors. Imagine their shock, surprise, and outrage when they discover their audition actually being used—*with no payment*. So, here are a couple of little tricks you can use to *watermark* the audition. (You probably won't need to watermark anything sent to you through your agent or clients you already know and work for.) One technique is to alter the copy. Intentionally transpose a few words or even mispronounce them so the audition can't become the real thing. Harlan often changes the phone number in a spot to his own of 312-427-5264, particularly when the copy reads—as it often does—"Call 1-800 XXX-XXXX." Another trick used by a Hollywood agent who represents celebrity voice-overs is to insert a beep or a 60Hz hum tone very faintly in the background during a few random sentences. You can easily do the same thing with your computer-based recording software.

There's a free audio effects plug-in that runs in any host audio software that supports VST. (That includes *Sound Forge* and *Audition*.) It's called the Beeper, and it automatically adds beeps to your sound file. Get it from Voxengo (http://www.voxengo.com/product/beeper/).

The Virtual Voice-Over and the Future

We don't know what the future will be. That frank admission is why neither of us has run for political office. That and several unfortunate incidents in young Jeffery's adolescence that we'll just ignore and try to forget. (*Thankfully! —Prunella*)

However.

Now that sounded more politically correct!

Today's global economy and globally connected virtual world are here to stay. Even with their drawbacks, the Internet and home studios have empowered voice talent, enabling voice actors to send auditions and session audio tracks instantly, perform live via the Internet, pursue employment and representation worldwide, and create and post demos inexpensively. The Web—coupled with your home studio—is a critical tool for success for every virtual voice-over.

It's our profound hope that these tools will eventually net you the voice agent equivalent of Jerry Maguire and that you'll send a small pittance of your multibillion dollar earnings each month to us in simple gratitude. Jeffrey's check can be sent to The Center for Aging Audiophiles and Harlan's c/o The Rockford Rehabilitation and Retraining Home, where he is reinventing himself as a mime. Both accept PayPal, money orders, and cold hard cash.

> "I will not rest until I have you holding a Coke, wearing your own shoe, playing a Sega game featuring you, while singing your own song in a new commercial, starring you, broadcast during the Super Bowl, in a game that you are winning, and I will not sleep until that happens."
>
> —Tom Cruise as Jerry Maguire, *Jerry Maguire,* 1996

12 Advanced Production Techniques

"Eddie, we're in show biz. It's all about razzle-dazzle. Appearances. If you look good and you talk well, people will swallow anything . . ."

—Jeffrey Jones as Criswell in *Ed Wood,* 1994, Buena Vista Pictures

Well, almost anything. B-movie (C? D?) writer/director Edward D. Wood's clothing choices and his homemade film effects that were anything but special might not have cemented his reputation as a world-class film director, but teenagers watched his budget movies in drive-ins across the country. At least we assume they were watching the film. Ed kept things simple—like the flying saucer that was actually a spinning aluminum pie plate dangling from a thread. His technique and vocabulary didn't include the word *advanced.*

So in the spirit of Ed Wood, let's start this chapter on advanced techniques by reminding you of two simple things you need to do every time you record yourself:

- Always record at a correct volume level.
- Minimize unwanted noise in your recordings whenever possible.

That's all you'll need to do to most of your work in addition to a bit of editing to generally clean up your tracks, such as deleting mistakes, page turns, and unwanted audio at the beginning and end.

Sometimes, though, you'll need to use more advanced techniques, usually to fix or hide imperfections or to take your voice recordings to a higher, more creative level. We divide these into two categories: fixing and sweetening. Fixing means just that: using audio tools and techniques to minimize mistakes and repair problems. Sweetening involves audio processes that can make your voice recordings sound extraordinary. Sweetening techniques include compression, equalization (EQ), reverberation (reverb), and adding music and sound effects to your finished pieces.

Your Essential Post-Production Workflow

Before we get into the nitty-gritty of fixing and sweetening, it's important to lay out an essential finishing workflow for all your recordings.

(1) Edit Out the Obvious Garbage

Eliminate noises, blown lines, lip smacks, loud breaths, and other gremlins. Deleting the unwanted parts and rearranging sections is straightforward once you get the hang of it.

Editing your recordings is both aural and visual. You can hear and *see* all the changes you make. It's just like word processing. You select, delete, copy, paste, rearrange, and otherwise revise your audio the same way your edit a text document. Though the audio waveforms you see onscreen look a little strange at first, they are just as easy to manipulate as the letters, words, phrases, sentences, and paragraphs on this page.

Over time, you may even begin to recognize certain audio waveforms by sight for what they really are without having to hear them. Jeffrey claims he can spot a breath or a lip smack in a file from a dozen paces away. (*And he's* proud *of that for some reason? —Prunella*) Harlan claims he can recognize Jeffrey from a dozen paces away as well. (*And he's proud of* that *for some reason? —Prunella*)

Don't forget that you must make all edits where the waveform crosses the center line. This prevents clicks and glitches in your edits. Your software may do this automatically or have an option to turn this feature on (or off), but check to be sure.

If you have large gaps in your recordings—like between takes or the dead air as you step up to the mic when starting and after finishing—you can quickly eliminate them. Just highlight the area you want eliminated and press the Delete key on your keyboard. A faster way in *Sound Forge* is to use the Process, Auto Trim function, as shown in Figure 12.1.

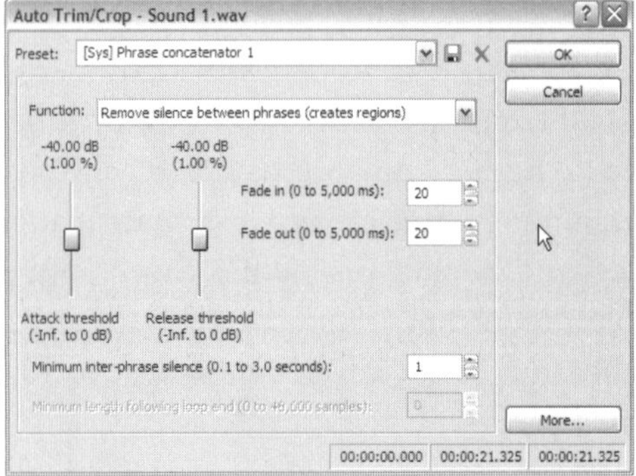

Figure 12.1 Auto Trim.

(2) Use EQ to Do a Little Noise Reduction

We know you've been careful to keep as much noise as possible out of your recordings, but extremely low- and extremely high-frequency noise is present on every recording, no matter how careful you are. Using EQ properly allows you to remove these sounds without affecting the sound quality of your voice.

EQ adjusts the tonal quality of your recordings. If you've ever adjusted the treble or bass control on your home or car audio player, you've already used EQ. Turn up the bass and make the music go thump, thump, thump. This is especially useful for annoying crabby neighbors. Turn up the treble, and the recording sounds brittle and shrill. Excessive treble is perfect to freak out your crabby neighbor's mangy cat and snarling dog.

You may have seen something like Figure 12.2, which is called a graphic EQ. There are other styles of EQ, but whatever one you use, try the following settings.

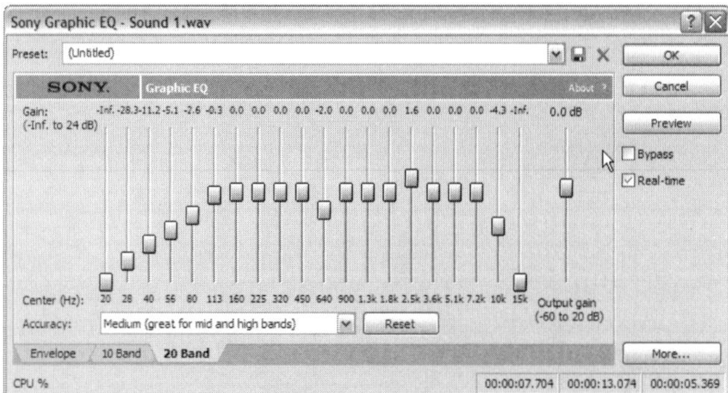

Figure 12.2 Graphic EQ.

Gradually reduce the frequencies below 100Hz using a high-pass/low-cut filter (so called because it lets the high frequencies pass through and cuts the lows). If you have a particularly deep, low voice, you might start at 80Hz instead. On the other hand, people with a higher register may be able to go up to as much as 160Hz. We don't want to affect *your* tonal sound, just the noise around it. When you lightly EQ this way, it generally sounds as if something heavy were lifted from the recording. If the application of EQ starts to make your voice sound a little thin, try a lower starting frequency.

Next, do the same at 10,000 or 12,000Hz (aka 10kHz–12kHz), gradually reducing the high frequencies using a low-pass/high-cut filter (the opposite of the high-pass/low-cut filter) that lets low frequencies pass and cuts the highs.

If you feel that the clarity and diction on the recording isn't as clear and crisp as it could be, you may need to bring out the sound of consonants a bit for the listener. Enhancing consonants contributes to better speech intelligibility. The best setting to "pop" those B, C, D, F, G, H, J, K, L, M, N, P, Q, R, S, T, V, W, X, Z, and sometimes Y sounds is a slight increase at 2,500Hz (2.5kHz); try 1–3dB.

Now remove the troublesome "mud" frequencies by using a slight 1–3dB cut around 650Hz. When you're done, your EQ will look like Figure 12.2 or 12.3.

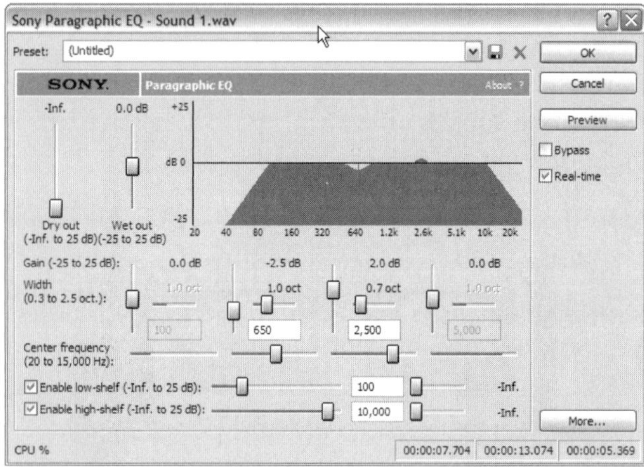

Figure 12.3 EQ in action.

Be careful when using EQ; keep an eye on your level meters. Using EQ can change the volume of your sound file—even when you cut out frequencies as suggested here—so check that the level doesn't get too loud and clip.

As you adjust these settings, listen carefully. Trust your ears. If it sounds better, it is; if not, either omit or adjust the settings to taste. We're giving you general guidelines that may not work as well on your particular voice.

High Pass, Low Pass, and Do Not Pass Go! Sometimes EQ settings are referred to as high-pass or low-pass filters. As the name implies, a high-pass filter lets the high frequencies, or treble, pass through while cutting out the low bass frequencies. A low-pass filter lets the bass pass through, cutting out the high frequencies in the process. Many professional mics have a high-pass switch on them that effectively cuts out the extreme low frequencies. We suggest you experiment using that switch if your mic has one. Some mixers and audio interfaces have a similar switch. This filter doesn't usually affect the sound or the quality of your voice (test to be sure), but it improves the quality of your recordings by keeping out those nasty low bass frequencies (some of which you may not even hear).

---

(3) Even Out the Volume

You want to reduce any obviously too-loud sections, bringing them closer to the average level. You do this via editing—highlighting selections and then lowering the volume accordingly. Now, don't go crazy on this step. You don't want everything at the same level. Just adjust those words or phrases that really stand out. Figure 12.4 shows an example where one phrase is a bit too loud. Using a volume tool, you can bring it more in line with the surrounding phrases.

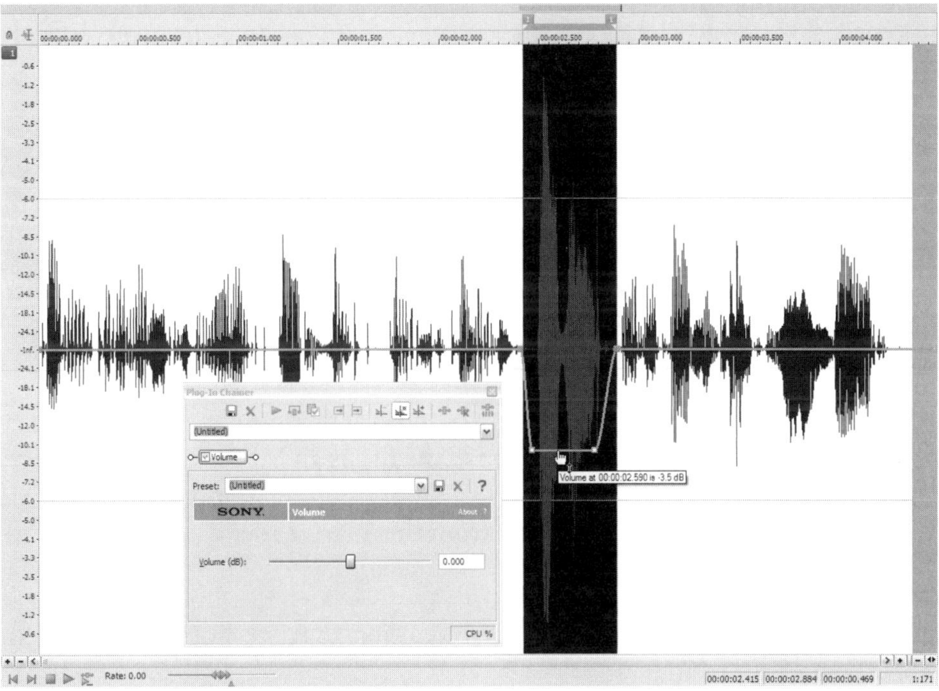

Figure 12.4 Volume fixing.

There is a good chance that you'll skip this step entirely on many of your recordings. But when you need to tame a loud peak in your performance, highlight it and lower its level a bit. If it visually matches the surrounding waveforms, you're on the right track.

(4) Raise the Overall Volume

Now that you have a nice even volume level, you'll want to raise the overall level. While you can simply boost the overall volume, you do run the risk of getting too loud, with inevitable clipping and distortion ruining your recording. Instead, we suggest using a "smart" volume adjustment known as normalization. Normalizing a track boosts the loudest parts to be as loud as they can be (without going over 0) and raises the quieter sounds at the same time. So if the loud parts get boosted 5dB, so do the quiet parts.

Always use peak normalization. We suggest you set that to –1.0 as the loudest limit, as shown in Figure 12.5.

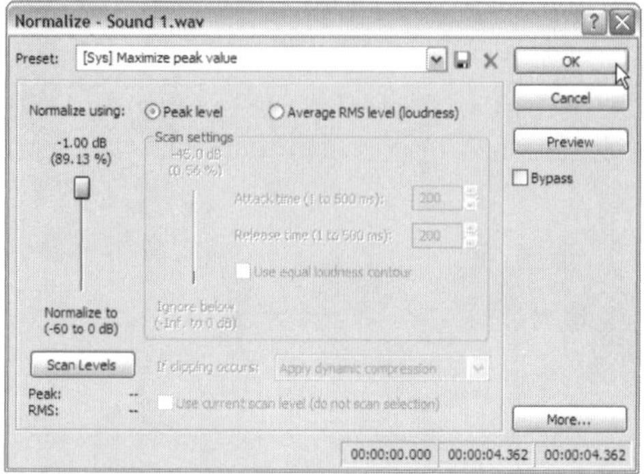

Figure 12.5 Peak normalization.

(5) Create the Master File

Save the file with a meaningful project name and the extension Master, such as Voice Intro MASTER.wav. Make this master the highest-quality digital file you can. In other words, if you recorded at CD quality, 16 bit, 44.1kHz, save it that way.

Use this master to create any other file formats you need. For example, if the producer wants you to e-mail an MP3, save another version of the file as an MP3. For Web delivery, use the techniques we showed you in Chapter 11, "Working the World Wide Web." If you need the file on a CD, simply burn the CD from this master file.

(6) Celebrate

You've recorded, edited, and finished a master recording that we hope will result in large checks, fame, and adoration.

Fixing Common Problems

Here are some common recording problems and ways to fix them. Of course, the best thing is to get good, clean sounds recorded in the first place so you won't need these tricks, but stuff really does happen!

Lip Smacks

Have you ever really listened to a kiss? It's a sound that, out of context, is positively gross. This is especially icky when you're receiving the kiss-off or the kiss of death or if some French person sends some spittle a-flyin' with that weird air kiss thing they do. Our brains are actually pretty adept at ignoring many unpleasant sounds in daily life, but recordings have a way of magnifying and amplifying those sounds. And few things sound more obnoxious than an annoying smack every time you open your mouth.

These lip smacks usually occur at sentence starts and occasionally on certain words. Reduce them—and other mouth noises—at the source. Keep your mouth and throat lubricated. Avoid cold and hot liquids. Instead, have some room-temperature water nearby when recording. Also, moisten those lips with some saliva or lip balm.

When a lip smack or two slips through, however, you can eliminate them using your audio editing software. Lip smacks usually stick out as a small bump in the waveform just before a word begins. See the thin, sharp waveform just before the bigger one in Figure 12.6? That's a lip smack that begs to be cut out. If you can't see a lip smack but you can hear it, try zooming in for a closer look. Find the smack, select it, and either mute or delete it. Please.

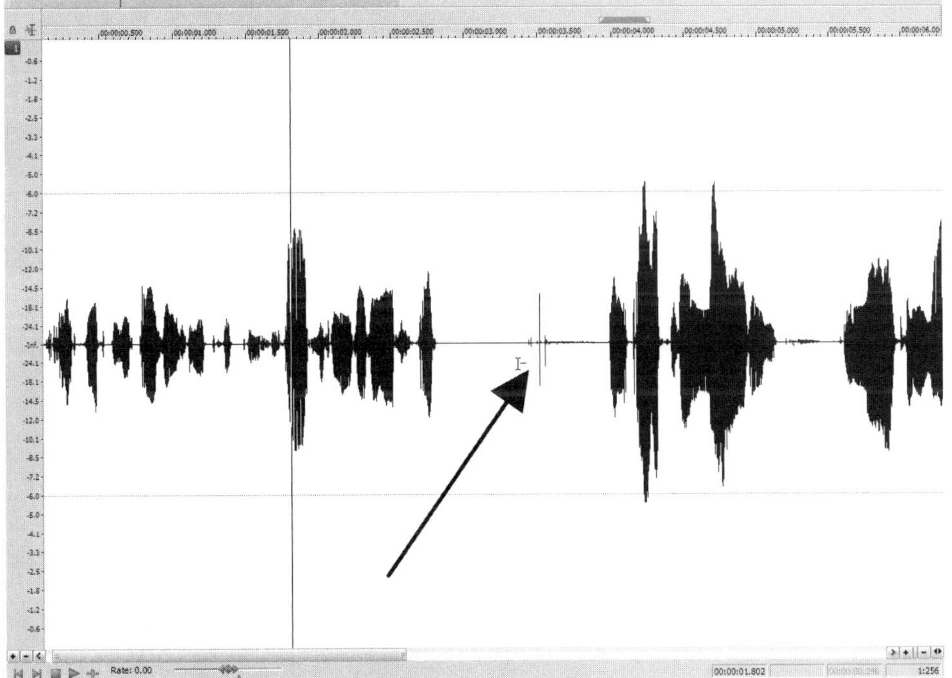

Figure 12.6 Lip smack.

To Mute or Not to Mute? Ah, that is the question. When you select/highlight a sound (or a portion of it) and mute it, the sound volume is reduced to nothing—just silence. When you delete a sound, however, that section is removed completely. Obviously, deletion also affects the length of the take. Generally speaking then, if you need the time of your performance to remain the same but you want to eliminate something nasty sounding, use mute. If the timing isn't critical, go ahead and use delete.

Another nauseating noise that can slip into recordings comes from dentures. Make sure they're firmly in place before a session. You don't want them clicking around during a take like castanets!

Breaths

Audible gasps at the beginning of sentences are the mark of an amateur. Eliminate bad breathing while recording through good mic technique. But if you need to, you can cut bad breaths in editing. Cutting bad breaths won't help with bad breath, so keep some Altoids nearby if that's the real problem. Alternatively, you might be able to use a noise gate to automatically eliminate some breathing sounds. See the "General Background Noise" section later in this chapter.

Remember that you can delete or mute a breath. Sometimes simply lowering the volume of the breath a bit as in Figure 12.7 sounds more natural, though. It's still there, but it's less pronounced. To do this, select/highlight the breath sound and lower its level using an envelope-based level tool.

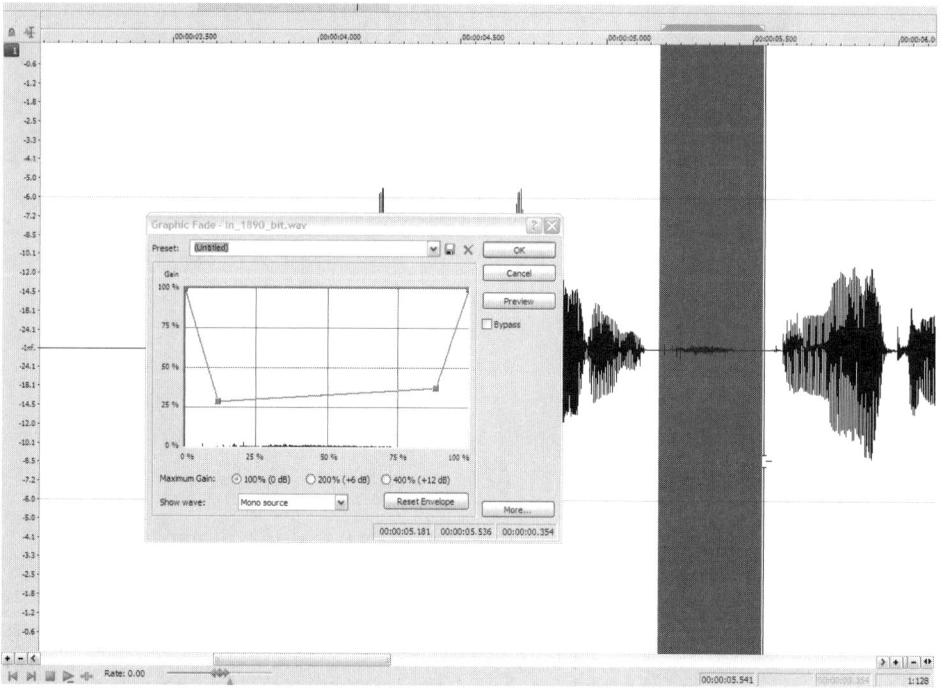

Figure 12.7 Breath volume lower.

Extraneous Noise(s)

"To be - - [*beep beep*] - - or not - - [*honk*] - - to be - - [*screeeeeeeeech*] - - that is the - - [*CRASH!*] - - . . ." If this is what your typical session sounds like, you might want to consider recording someplace else. Getting the most noise-free recording that you can in the first place makes your post-production life so much easier. However, even in professional studios with tens of thousands of dollars of soundproofing, an unwanted sound sometimes manages to sneak in.

The simplest thing to do if you hear noises while recording is just to redo the line. Oftentimes, though, performers are so focused on delivery that they don't notice these noises until they listen back. Still, you are better off rerecording the problem section rather than jumping through hoops to try to salvage it.

But if your schedule and real life precludes you from recording a new alternate take, you can try to save the day with editing. Eliminating or reducing errant sounds can be very easy or extremely hard. It's a snap when the noise falls between words or phrases; just select/highlight the errant sound and remove it. However, if the noise happens *simultaneously* with your speaking, you have a much harder job ahead.

One trick is to add another sound element, such as music or a sound effect to mask extraneous noises, but that's not always a viable solution. Some audio programs like Adobe *Audition* and the iZotope RX plug-in let you look at waveforms in a different way, called a spectral view. This lets you see the offending sounds across words or phrases and allows you to edit out only those frequencies, not any of the audio you want to keep.

Another solution is to use EQ since it lets you control the tonal characteristics of a sound. You can zero in on the audio trouble spot and boost or reduce it to make the recording sound better. Most inexperienced users of EQ tend to boost EQ to overcome deficiencies. Professional EQ users reduce the offending frequencies instead.

Listen carefully to the sound you're trying to minimize. Is it a low sound, such as a thump? Or is it a high sound, such as a squeaky chair? In either case, EQ is quite likely to help (a little anyway). If the sound falls more in the middle, EQ will be less effective because your voice occupies those midrange frequencies, and trying an EQ fix here will adversely affect the quality of your voice.

Here's how to see if the EQ will work. Using your audio editing software, highlight just the section of your recording where the noise resides. Open up the EQ tool such as what's pictured in Figure 12.8 and try boosting one of the bands, sweeping it through the frequencies as the section plays. When you find the spot where the noise is, it'll usually pop out very loud.

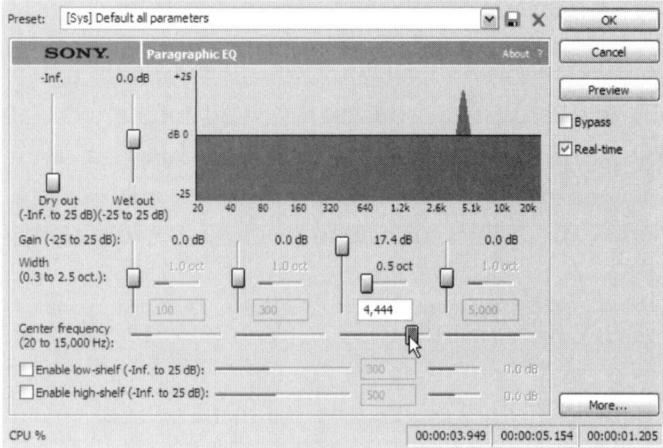

Figure 12.8 EQ noise search.

Now reduce the EQ level at that magic frequency shown in Figure 12.9. The noise should be greatly reduced, but it'll never be gone completely. It will take some trial and error before you find the right setting. Let your ears help you judge whether the sound gets better or worse or stays the same as you adjust the settings. Unfortunately, in some cases EQ won't work at all, and you'll have to live with the noise, or rerecord.

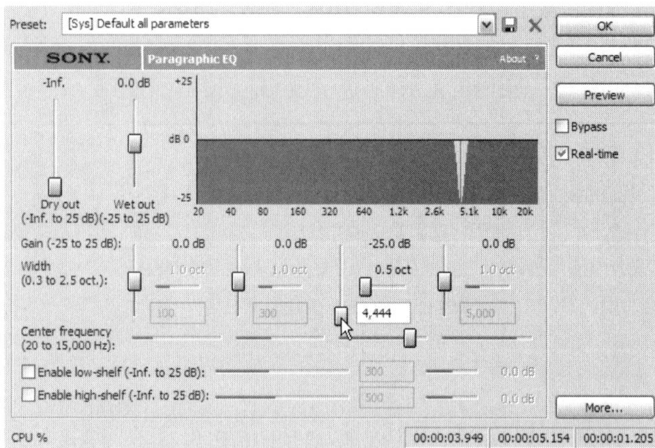

Figure 12.9 EQ destroy.

General Background Noise

Instead of a single distinct noise like a doorbell in your recording, you might have an overall and continuous noisy din. Air conditioners, computer fans, distant traffic, and the like can add a much-unwanted sound element that you need to eliminate.

Applying a noise gate to the finished recording can be an effective way to deal with background noise. As the name implies, a noise "gate" lets the good sounds through when open and shuts out hum, hiss, and other heinous background junk when closed. Noise gates typically have three settings: threshold, attack, and release. Threshold adjusts how strong a sound must be before the gate will open. When the volume falls below the threshold setting, the gate closes. Attack determines how fast the gate will open once the volume exceeds the threshold. Release determines how long it will take for the gate to close after the signal falls below the threshold setting. Short release times abruptly chop off the sound, while longer release times offer smoother sound reduction but with the risk of keeping more noise on the recording.

Setting the noise gate threshold is easy. Start with the gate fully open (infinity), and play the file. Slowly increase the threshold (as shown in Figure 12.10) until you continue to hear your voice but the noise disappears between phrases. Be careful not to accidentally chop off the start and end of words. Either lower the threshold a little or increase the release (or a little of both) if this happens.

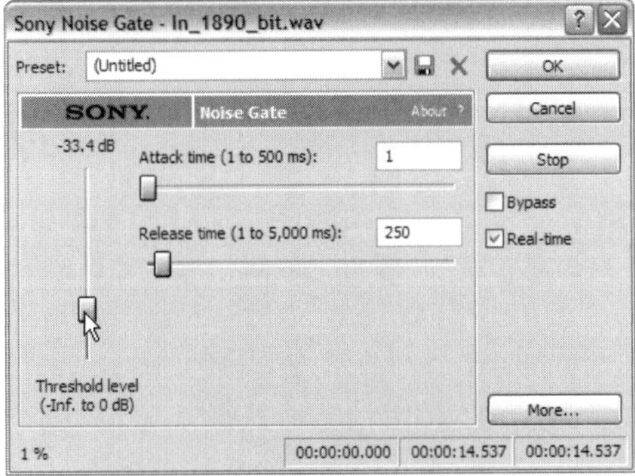

Figure 12.10 Noise gate.

Always listen to your entire recording after applying the noise gate to be extra sure you didn't chop off something. If you did, undo the noise gate, readjust the settings, and try again. We are, of course, assuming you have adhered to our earlier advice and made copies of the original file, so you'll always be able to undo any accidental damage you may have done while experimenting with the gate.

The downside to using a noise gate is that it only shuts out the noise *between* words and phrases when no other sound is present. Obviously, the noise will continue when you're speaking. You're counting on your voice covering up that noise, effectively masking it. Unfortunately, you might hear the noise gate working because the background noise holds steady under your talking but then disappears completely when you pause. This can actually sound worse than just leaving the noise in if the listener becomes aware of the "jumps" of noise and silence. Our ear/brain combination is better suited to tuning out constant noise than noise that disappears and reappears regularly. So adjust the noise gate controls until the recording sounds smoother, or scrap the idea entirely. Leaving the noise in, if it's constant and not totally distracting, often is the better solution.

Another tool to consider is an expander (see Figure 12.11), which is really a kind of noise gate that doesn't quite close. In Chapter 11, we described how compressors turn down loud sounds. Well, expanders work just the opposite way and turn down *soft* sounds. Instead of eliminating the noise entirely, like a noise gate, an expander just lowers the noise volume between phrases and can sound far, far smoother. Expanders are usually not included with audio software programs but can be purchased as plug-ins and can make a slightly noisy recording sound phenomenal.

Figure 12.11 Expander.

Using a dedicated noise reduction tool is another method for salvaging some noisy recordings. The full-blown versions of *Sound Forge* and Adobe's *Audition* include some powerful utilities that work wonders on background noise. There are also third-party tools, such as the phenomenally powerful iZotope RX (http://www.izotope.com) pictured in Figure 12.12, that run standalone or plug in to your audio software.

All of these noise reduction processes work by analyzing the waveform and separating the noise from the good stuff. The software then applies filters that eliminate the noise. Unlike a noise gate, the software even eliminates the noise while you're speaking so the tracks sound smoother and transparent.

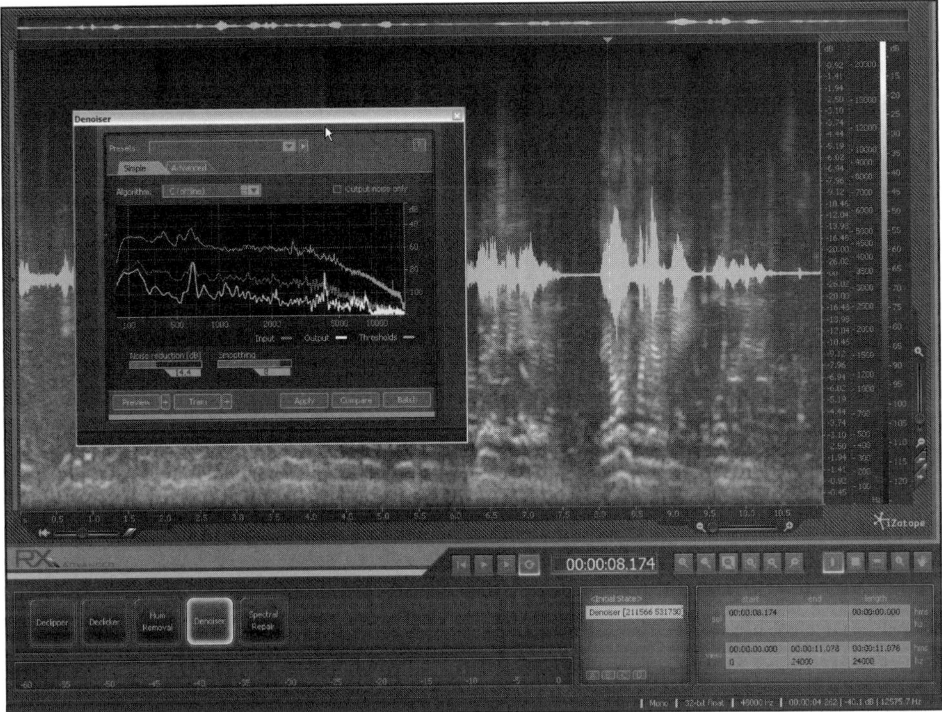

Figure 12.12 iZotope RX.

Unfortunately, applying a noise reduction tool can leave unwanted artifacts behind. While a tiny bit of noise reduction is almost imperceptible, large doses give your voice a watery, swirling, metallic quality that just sounds bad. If your recordings are soooooo noisy that you must resort to such aggressive noise reduction, it's time to rethink how and where you record. But on slightly noisy recordings, where your voice volume is well above the noise, noise reduction tools can save you.

Hum and Hiss

We're not sure which is worse: the annoying zzzzzt of a 60Hz electrical hum or the equally irksome sssss of hiss. (*Oh! You boys are trading your penchant for alliteration to onomatopoeia now? —Prunella*) Both are by-products of using electronic gear and are noises that you should do your best to avoid. Eliminate hum by keeping your cables as short as possible and keeping electrical cords far away from mic cables. If a mic cable must cross an electrical cable, do so at right angles (90 degrees). Running power and mics in parallel is the worst. Also, keep the mic away from the computer monitor because it can introduce noise into your recording.

Hum is often caused by a ground loop, which means—in essence—that there is more than one path for electrical energy to reach ground. This is the result of all the mixers, audio interfaces, etc., we have plugged in to each other usually via those handy power outlet strips. One fix is at your nearest hardware store: one of those three-prong to two-prong adapters (called a ground lift) that we plug the humming device into and listen to hear if the hum has disappeared. Hey, for something that costs under a buck, it's worth a try. Another possible fix is to try plugging all the audio gear into the *same* outlet. (Just be careful not to overload the circuit!)

Hiss comes from using cheap gear (preamps, mixers) or turning up volume settings too high. For example, you might have the faders on your mixer maxed out, introducing hiss. What you really need to do is lower their level and get more gain from the microphone preamp. Proper gain staging, as discussed *ad nauseum* in Chapter 8, "Basic Production Techniques," is vital to making noise-free recordings.

EQ is another way to eliminate hum and hiss. The essential EQ settings from above will do a lot to reduce hum and hiss. The 100Hz low-cut eliminates low-end junk, rumble, and hum, while the 10–12kHz high-cut contains some hiss.

Bad Edits

Always run the DC Offset utility before you change a sound file. This ensures that the center line or zero crossing is correctly aligned. Refer to Chapter 8 for details about DC Offset. Make sure that when you edit the file, you cut where the sound wave crosses that center line. Otherwise, you might introduce a pop or click into the recording. Also, be careful not to accidentally cut off the start and end of words. Listen to *every* edit before continuing.

One simple trick that can really smooth over inadvertent bad edits is to apply a quick fade to them. In Figure 12.13, you can see that all you have to do is highlight from the start of the offending section to the right a tiny amount, say one-third of a second or even less. Apply a quick fade-in if the section is at the start of a word or a fade-out if the section is at the end. Practice this technique until you feel really comfortable with it, because it can really cover up bad edits and other anomalies.

Sentence Pickups

So, you made a mistake. Should you just pick it up from there and move on? No! No! No! Never record sentence pickups where you only redo part of a line. Yes, we know that we mentioned this before, but we felt it was so important that it deserved another strong reminder. Plus, this is a reference chapter and you may have forgotten this important point a year after you first read this. Anyway, no matter how expertly you edit the mistake, we guarantee the sentence pickup will not match the surrounding words. The emotion and delivery will be all wrong, making the sentence fragment stick out like a sore thumb. Always return to the sentence start (and sometimes even farther back than that) when you rerecord the take. Your delivery will sound smoother and more natural, and you'll reduce your editing chores considerably.

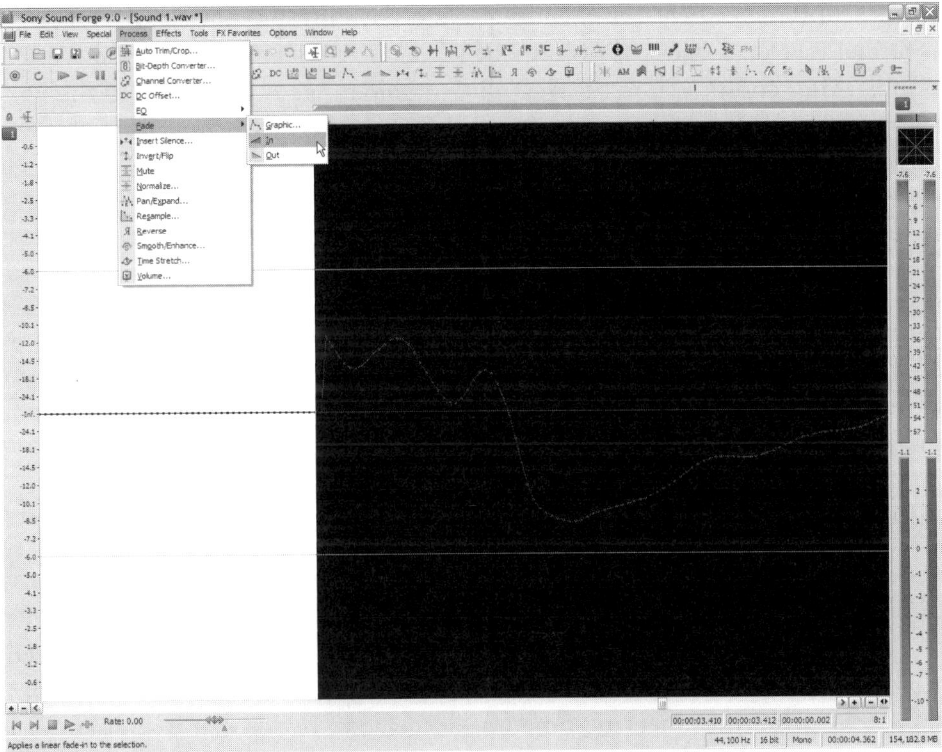

Figure 12.13 Quick fade-in.

Volume Inconsistencies

Several factors can make some parts of your recorded file sound louder than other parts. Your delivery might be inconsistent. You might have turned away from the mic slightly. You also might have set your initial recording levels too low or too high. Thankfully, there are several ways to even out the volume levels.

By far the easiest and best method is to find the parts that are too loud, select them, and decrease their volume by a few decibels. It's best to start with small adjustments and adjust from there. Tweak the amount until everything sounds right. Visually comparing the section you're fixing to the nearby waveforms can show whether your levels are closer and more consistent. A loud peak is easy to spot onscreen. Listen to the surrounding words and make sure the level change sounds natural, too. You can try the same trick on soft sections, increasing the volume a few decibels at a time until it works with the whole file. Remember that changing the volume up or down can affect the background noise making it more (or less) noticeable.

Audio compression lets you even out the volume level, too. This tool squeezes the dynamic range (the difference between the loudest and the softest passages). A compressor acts as a funnel that decreases the volume of louder sounds, moving them closer to the softer sounds. After compression, the overall dynamic range is smaller, and the volume is more even. Then, you can boost the level of the whole track after you compress it, making it sound louder overall. How do you use a compressor? Like a gate, it has several interactive sections.

Threshold

When the recording exceeds a specific threshold volume level set by the controls, the compressor kicks in, reducing audio levels above the setting, depending on the ratio setting. (See the following section.) Any signal below the threshold setting is unaffected, while all signals above the threshold are "squeezed," or compressed.

Ratio

Ratio settings determine how much the audio is compressed. Ratios can be set at unity (1:1) up to infinity to one. In other words, at a 1:1 ratio, a 1dB signal level change results in a 1dB output (no gain or unity gain). At other ratios, the output is reduced by relative amounts. At 4:1, a 4dB increase in input level results in only a 1dB output level gain. That's the powerful squeezing function of the compressor that is so useful for leveling the volume of your recordings.

Attack

Attack sets the time it takes before a recording above the threshold starts being compressed. This important setting ensures that quick transients—fast, almost percussive sounds, such as many hard consonants—remain unaffected before the compression grabs on to the sound. Low settings squeeze signals fast and hard, while higher settings let the punch of the consonants through. If the setting is too low, certain words might sound chopped off. You'll hear a sort of sucking sound, as if the volume were pulled down really fast (which is what is actually happening). If the setting is too high, loud passages might go through without the compressor having a chance to squeeze them, defeating the whole purpose of using the compressor.

Release

Release is like attack, only in reverse. This control determines how long it takes for the compressor to return to unity gain (its original volume level) after the signal has dropped below the threshold. Again, you can vary the time from very short to very long. Short times act on the signal, constantly producing some unnatural staccato effects, while long times are smooth and more forgiving.

Output

The output control helps you return volume to the signal that is often lost during the other processing steps. This extra gain is what makes the compressed file sound louder. Watch those meters when using a compressor, though; you don't want the signal to clip!

Most professional audio programs include compression of some kind and, believe us, a little compression goes a long way. Try a threshold that's just a few decibels below the loudest peak level in your file. For the ratio setting, start with 1.5:1 and consider increasing that to 4:1 if it still sounds good. Keep the attack medium fast (about 15–25 milliseconds), and keep the release long (more than a second).

Figures 12.14 and 12.15 show before and after examples of compression. Notice the more even (and much louder) overall level in the after example.

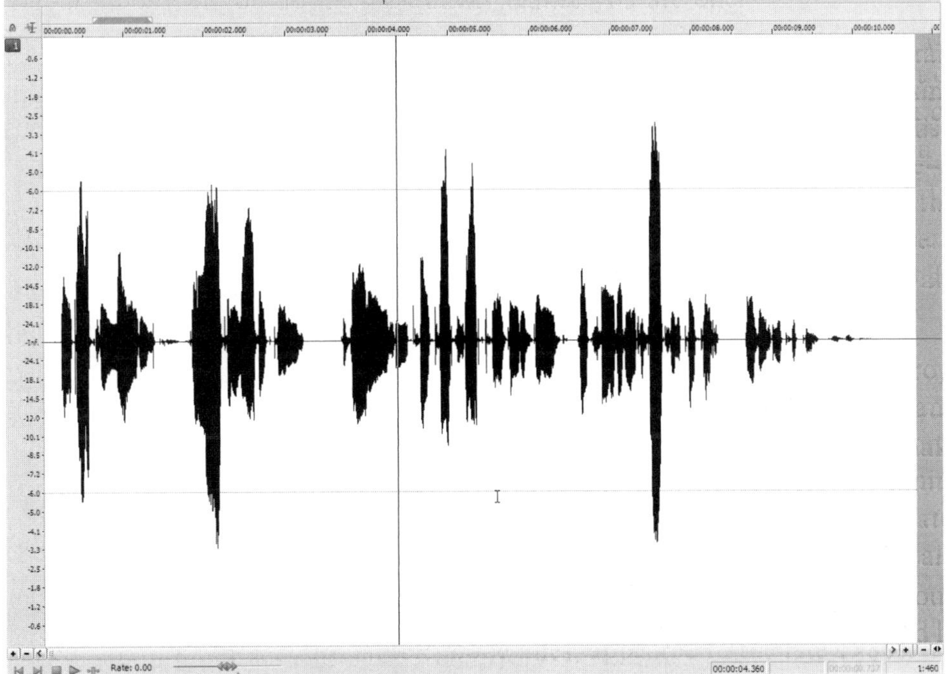

Figure 12.14 Before compression.

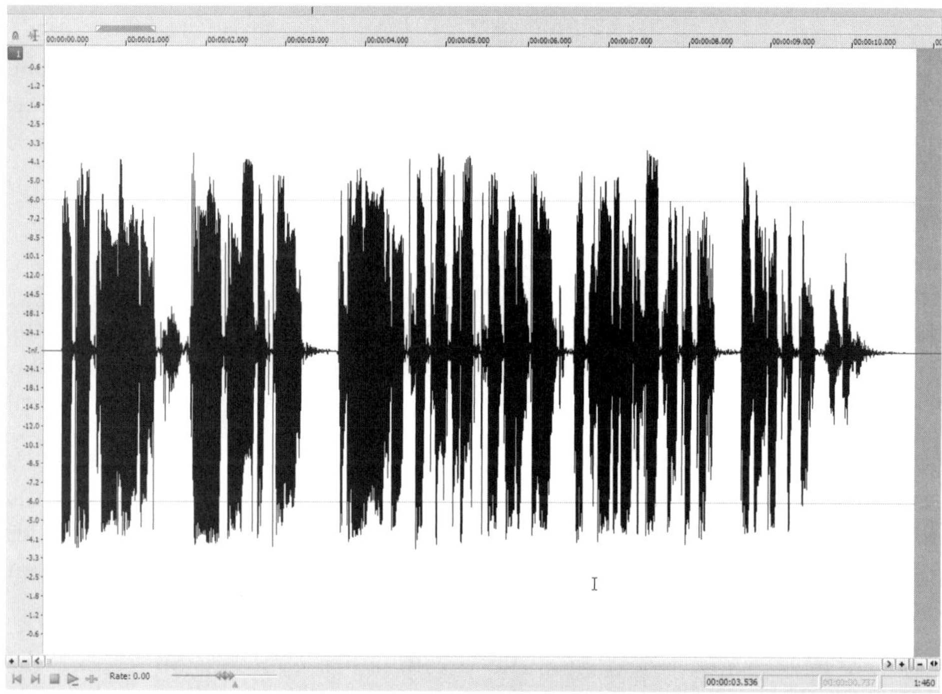

Figure 12.15 After compression.

Clicks and Crackles

There are many things that can put unwanted clicks and crackles in your recordings. In addition to lip smacks and mouth noises, mics and digital errors can create clicking sounds. Microphones can sometimes pop or click if too much moisture gets on the diaphragm. This moisture can come from an overly humid room or from your natural mouth lubricant. (*Please—you're talking about spittle again, aren't you? —Prunella*) Always use a pop filter to keep your spittle where it should be and not on your microphone.

Digital errors can sometimes occur in your software program, and you might hear little digital ticks or clicks in your recording. These sounds appear as spikes, which can be easily seen and quickly edited in your audio editor. However, if the problem is a recurring one, it's likely that you haven't set up the program correctly to play well with your audio interface. Review Chapter 8's section that shows you how to adjust the buffers allocated to your audio software.

Clicks that occur between phrases are easily eliminated while editing. Clicks and glitches that happened while you were performing are harder to fix. Rerecording a new take instead of spending an inordinate amount of time trying to remove these clicks is the best solution, but a Click and Crackle Removal tool—like those used to restore old records—works quite well on these kinds of noises. Essentially, just adjust the controls until the clicks disappear (see Figure 12.16).

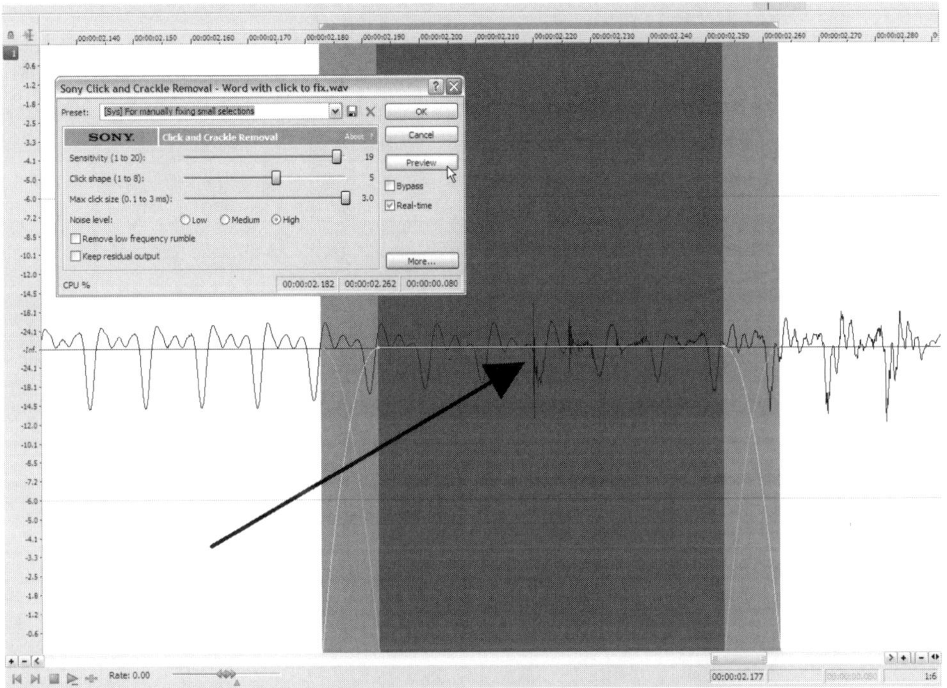

Figure 12.16 Click removal.

Thin Sound

Choosing the right microphone and preamp for your particular voice goes a long way toward making you sound your best. If you're unhappy with the results, concentrate your focus on those two pieces of gear and on your performance and mic technique. EQ can help to beef up a too-thin sound, though.

For a male voice, use EQ to add about 2–4dB at 160Hz. This frequency range boosts the male natural deep resonance, giving depth and authority to it. It won't miraculously make you sound like a deep-throated movie trailer announcer, but it can add nice warmth to your voice. You may need to adjust this frequency slightly between 120 and 200Hz (see Figure 12.17).

To thicken up a female voice, try using an EQ frequency about an octave higher. Add 2–4dB at 320Hz. Again, adjust the frequency as needed, but a little goes a long way.

Dull Recording

Here, too, EQ comes to the rescue. For both male and female talent, add 2–4dB between 10 and 12kHz. Better still is to cut 2–4dB at 650Hz, what Jeffrey affectionately calls the "mud zone." Avoid using EQ in the 4–7kHz range, because that's where sibilance resides, and boosting here can make *S* sounds harsh and distorted. Let your ears judge whether the fix is better than the original. Often, applying these processes, such as what's in Figure 12.17, makes your performance sound different but not necessarily better.

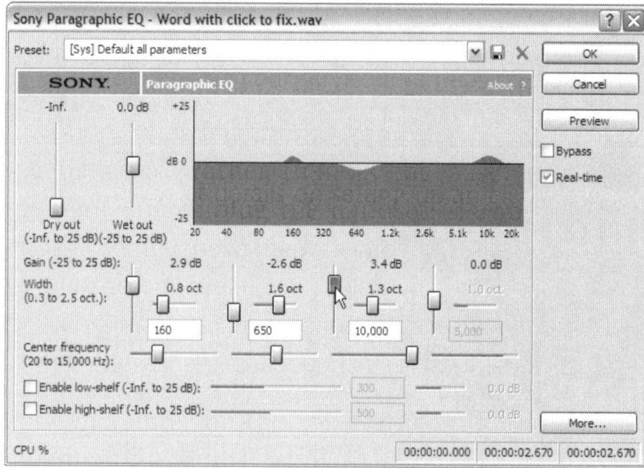

Figure 12.17 Thin and dull fixes.

Louder File

Make sure your levels are reasonably high when recording. You want to get as close to digital zero as possible without exceeding it! As we've mentioned (*a few too many times —Prunella*), digital zero is the brick wall. Digital recording can't and won't handle any volume above zero; it simply clips off the waveform and you hear distortion—ugly, nasty distortion.

Despite your best attempts, you might find your levels are a little too low. As we've seen, you can increase the overall level in several ways: manually, with normalization, compression, or volume maximizers. These are special kinds of compressors that can make your file sound *really* loud. The *Sound Forge* software includes the Wave Hammer utility that can slam your sound files close to digital zero without clipping. You can find more information on this tool in Chapter 11.

Just be sure you realize that boosting the level of quiet sounds can bring up more background noise as well.

Perceived loudness can also be increased by what we might call extreme compression or limiting. Remember the ratio setting described in our discussion about compressors? When the ratio starts to get too high, say 10:1 and above, the compressor turns into a limiter. With a limiter, no matter how loud your recording is, the output volume is kept at a constant level. This may sound ideal, but heavy limiting can squeeze the life out of a performance, making the softest parts as loud as the loudest sections. The volume is now the same throughout the performance and can become just very loud and in your face but lack subtlety.

Harlan loves to apply a little compression (2–3:1) and normalization to his auditions because they make his voice sound louder than the voices of the other actors vying for the part. It's the kind of simple trick that can make your work stand out from the crowd. Jeffrey's favorite tool for this task is a digital emulation of a vintage compressor, the LA-2A pictured in Figure 12.18. It's an expensive purchase (http://www.uaudio.com), but the sound is amazing (*as only a geek like Fisher could appreciate —H2*).

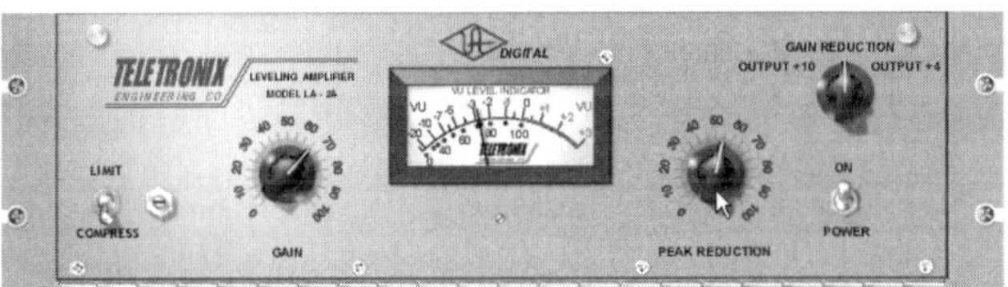

Figure 12.18 LA-2A.

Faster/Slower

In much the same way that Doctor Who travels through time with his TARDIS, you can control time with some software tools. Is your voice track running a little long? Time compress it. Too fast? Spread it out. Time compression works by speeding up the file based on the settings you choose. Now, logic would seem to dictate that speeding up your tracks would make you sound like a Munchkin from the *Wizard of Oz* and slowing them down would bring a certain Sith Lord to mind, right?

Wrong.

The beauty of this software tool is that it simultaneously works on time *and* frequency. You talk faster or slower but at the same pitch. Time expansion slows the file down and shifts the pitch up; time compression speeds the timing up and shifts the pitch down. Both maintain your original voice quality. These effects work, but only up to a point. After about a 10-percent change either way, quality suffers. An odd metallic, swishy sound, called phasing, happens with extreme time compression. And time expansion sounds like, well, like you're stoned. That is, we think it would if we knew what stoned people sounded like (. . . which of course we don't, yer honor). Used judiciously in the 1–5 percent range, either tool works and sounds great.

Another and better tactic for speeding up or slowing down a take involves a little editing. To save time, carefully remove pauses from between phrases and even words. By tightening up the performance, you often can make a track shorter, and it still sounds natural. You'll be surprised how cutting out tiny amounts really adds up to significant change without hurting the performance. Don't try cutting out a full second when just hunting down three small thirds of a second will do the same job with virtually no impact on presentation.

When you need to slow down your take, simply add silence at appropriate times to lengthen the track. Again, add tiny bits here and there instead of putting in huge gaps that sound unnatural.

Plosives

Use microphone techniques to eliminate popped Ps and Ts in the first place. Try miking from the side and, of course, use a good pop filter. However, if a popped consonant gets by, you can use a special form of compression to reduce the noise a bit. See the following "Sibilance" section for details.

Often, you can edit the pop right out. Popped plosives are easy to spot because they stick out at the front of a word when you zoom in a bit, as in Figure 12.19. Many times you can delete them without even affecting the word; just be careful not to turn "purple" into "urple."

Sibilance

Once again, microphone technique (try side miking) and the right microphone and preamps for your particular voice are the front-line choices in the battle to overcome sizzling esses. If your *S* sounds still stick out a bit, try a little EQ to reduce minor sibilance. Remove 2–4dB between 5 and 8kHz. That's where those esses hide out. You might need to adjust this somewhat lower for an alto and higher for a soprano. Note, though, that this overall EQ fix may make a recording sound a bit dull. To combat this, apply the EQ to only those really harsh *S* sounds by making smaller selections and EQing them and not the entire file.

Another nice tool is a de-esser. This special software combines a compressor and EQ. Basically, the compressor kicks in *only* when the sibilant frequencies (or loud plosives) are present, reducing them significantly. When there's no sibilance present, the de-esser lays low and doesn't affect the sound. This same technique can reduce plosives as well. The *Sound Forge* software and other applications include some preset settings for reducing both plosives and sibilance effectively. There are also many third-party de-esser plug-ins. In Figure 12.20, the top half of the software deals with plosives, and the bottom half reduces sibilance.

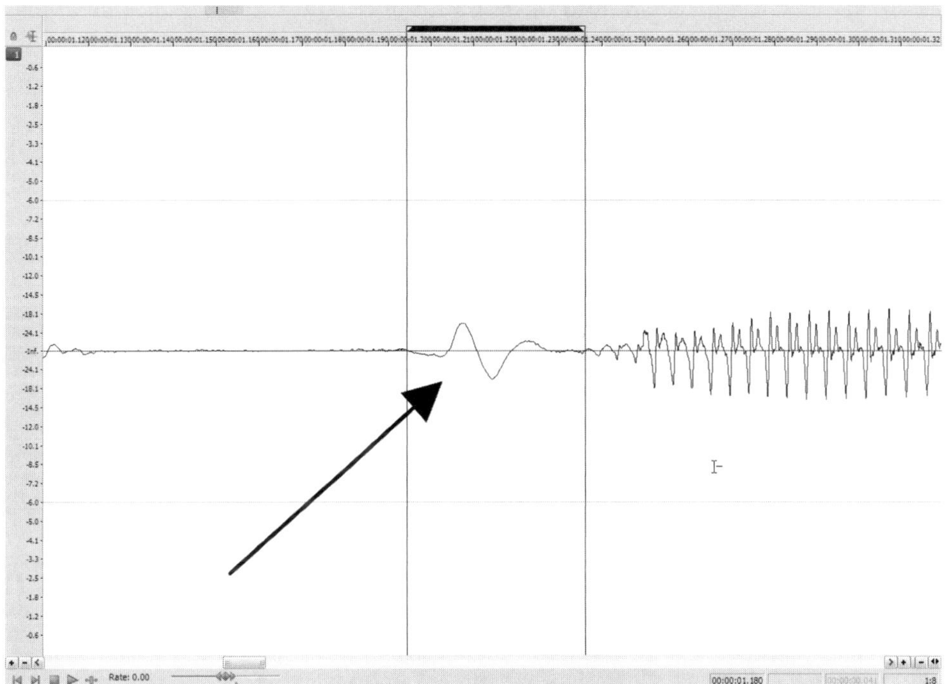

Figure 12.19 Popped P.

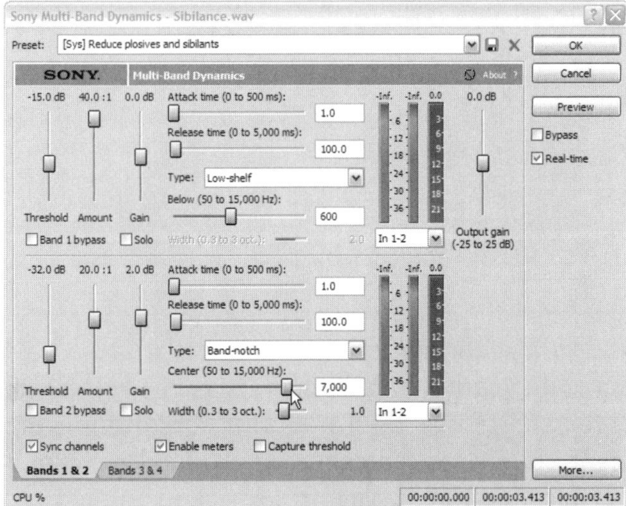

Figure 12.20 Plosives and sibilance.

Clipping

If you've broken the big no-no and let your recordings exceed the dreaded digital zero, they will sound distorted—clipped. Although you can reduce the volume of a clipped waveform to under zero, it will still sound distorted. Aside from rerecording the clipped part, there's little you can do. The iZotope RX noise reduction plug-in mentioned earlier and the clip restoration utility built in to *Sound Forge 9* may help with a short clipped spot, but not with a large section. *Audition* also has several clip restoration features that might save you—or not. So don't record past digital zero! Ever. Got it? You sure? Well, okay then. Let's move on.

Sweetening: Adding Some Pizzazz!

So far we've talked about using sound editing tools and techniques to fix mistakes. Now let's look at advanced post-production ways to sweeten your tracks.

Telephone Sound

Make your voice sound like it was recorded over a telephone with this EQ trick. Apply a graphic EQ and boost around 1kHz a little, and then cut all the other frequency bands around it. Cut everything below 400 and "above" 5,000. Your EQ will look similar to Figure 12.21, and what you hear will be that telltale thin telephone sound. This can also pass for police/fire and AM radio.

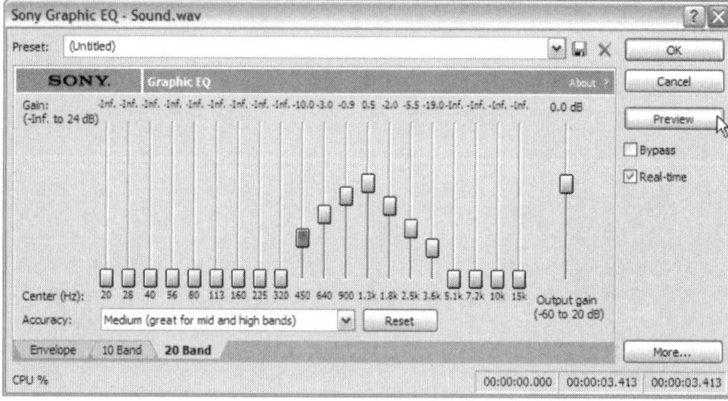

Figure 12.21 Telephone sound.

Caverns and Hallways and Bathrooms, Oh My

Large spaces and small, live rooms have distinctive sounds that are easy to re-create in software. Reverberation (reverb, for short) is a by-product of sound bouncing around a room. It's actually a series of closely spaced echoes that blend to form a room sound. Clap your hands sharply in a parking garage to hear reverb in action. (Harlan prefers to shout out, "Haaaaarrrr Laaaaaaan Ruuuuules" in parking garages in Chicago, and he suggests you try the same thing in your city.) Software reverbs such as the example in Figure 12.22 use sophisticated mathematical algorithms to re-create the sound of spaces. Simply select something that sounds good to your ears. Often the descriptions of the preset settings provide a clue, such as Cathedral, Small Hall, and so forth. Beware of really long reverbs, because things might start to sound a little mushy. Also, if you need to add reverb to your voice, make sure it's the last thing you do *after* you've finished editing. Otherwise, you'll have a hard time matching up edits.

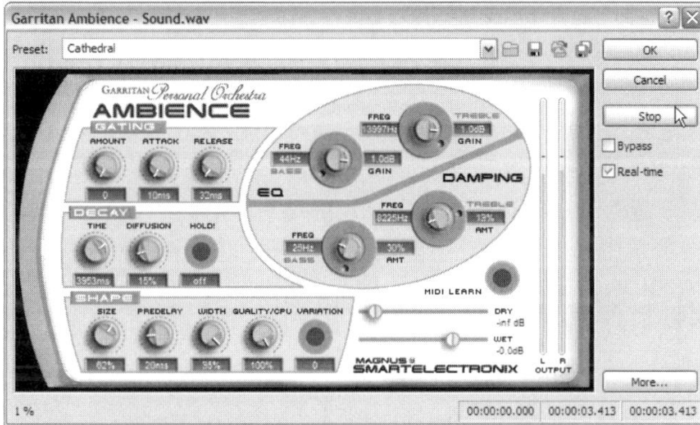

Figure 12.22 Reverb.

Echoes

When there are distinct repeats to your voice, it's called *echo,* and the tool called Delay works for this. Need to sound like a PA announcer at a large stadium? This'll do the trick. Delay repeats whatever you send to it after a specified time has elapsed. The settings determine how long before the delay starts, how many delays there will be, and how long it will take for the delay(s) to die away. A single repeat sounds like an echo in the mountains. Multiple repeats sound a little different. By feeding a little of the delayed sound back into the delay again, more echoes are created. The result is that twittering sound like John Lennon's vocals on the Beatles' "A Day in the Life."

Swirlies and Swishies

There are several effects that impart a dreamy, swirly, and swishing effect on your voice. Flanging, Chorusing, and Phasing are their names, and most audio editors include these effects. They're simply great fun to use and hear when appropriate, so take a sample file and apply one or more of these effects to it and listen. Like what you hear? Remember what you did, and use it when it makes creative sense.

Pitch Shifting

Turning males into females and vice versa is the realm of the pitch shifter (and some surgeons in Europe). Although obvious Chipmunks and Darth Vader extremes are possible, many subtle effects can be achieved as well. Pitch shift software is often musically based, so you'll see references to musical intervals (semitones, octaves, and so on). Just play around until you find what you're listening for. Be careful, though; extreme changes in pitch can sound unnatural.

Some pitch shifting tools (see Figure 12.23) let you maintain the length of the track when changing the pitch, while others only let you change the pitch, which speeds up or slows down the recording.

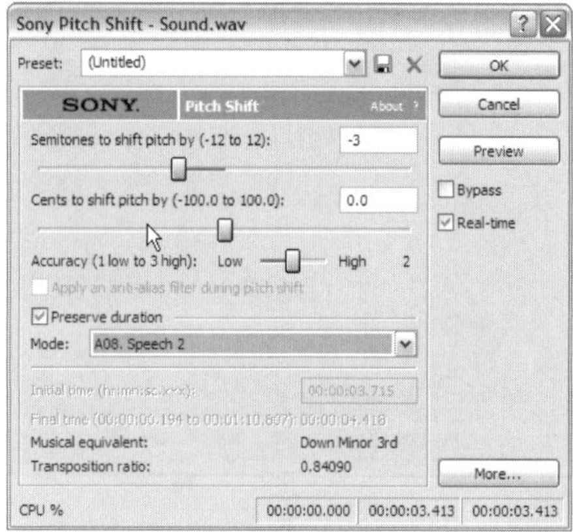

Figure 12.23 Pitch shift.

Harlan once produced a public service announcement in his home studio, and even though the voice performer he'd booked was a senior citizen and turned in a wonderful performance, Harlan's clients in New York felt he sounded "too young" when they heard the finished recording. Rather than rerecord (and pay) another performer, Harlan tweaked the same reading with the pitch controls in Adobe *Audition,* subtly slowing down the sound of the reading. After hearing the "new" track, his clients unanimously approved the "older" actor!

Adding Music and Sound Effects

Sometimes you may have opportunities to add other production elements, such as music and sound effects, to your recordings. No doubt, you'll add elements like these to tracks you record at home for your (or others') demos.

Music

There are two ways to use music: source and underscore. Source music emanates from within the scene, such as music coming from a radio. Underscore is the emotional music needed to enhance and accent the situation.

Where do you get the music you need? You cannot just grab a CD off the shelf and drop in a track or two from your favorite artist. You can hire a composer, but that can often cost more than your budget allows.

Happily, there is library music. This music is specifically created and licensed for use. Buyout licenses are cost effective because you pay only one fee, and then you can use the music nonexclusively whenever you want. Sources for music libraries include

- Digital Juice (http://www.digitaljuice.com)
- Fresh Music (http://www.freshmusic.com)
- Killer Tracks (http://www.killertracks.com)
- Music Bakery (http://www.musicbakery.com)
- VASST TrakPaks (http://www.vasst.com)

And you can compose your own music. Huh? We can hear you saying, "I'm no musician. I can't write my own music." Guess what? You *can* compose your own music with a little help from technology.

Both *ACID* software (see Figure 12.24) for the Windows environment and *GarageBand* for the Mac help you to create your own music scores quickly and easily. Both programs are easy to learn and fun to use. No musical skill is required, either. Both programs work similarly, letting you choose and combine music and sound "loops" to create your own original, royalty-free music. It's a snap to pick sounds, paint them on a grid, and make music. Adobe *Audition* handles loops as well.

And what are these loops? A music loop is a prerecorded—usually short—snippet of a musical performance that repeats continuously. Loops come as CD-quality sound files, usually in WAV format. A single loop might be a drum beat, a bass guitar riff, a piano part, or almost anything else. By selecting and arranging different musical loops, you create new songs. Purchased loops are royalty free, and the finished compositions you create from them belong to you.

The retail version of the *ACID* software includes a content CD with hundreds of loops to get you started. Adobe *Audition* also includes hundreds of loops free with its software. *GarageBand* is similarly decked out. Best of all, you can choose from a huge inventory of other music loops in a variety of styles, including rock, orchestral, hip-hop, techno, ethnic/world, electronica, ambient, and nearly everything in between and out on the extreme fringe. These are available from Sony Creative Software, Apple, and dozens of third-party vendors such as Hark Productions (http://www.harkproductions.com/loops/) and Big Fish Audio (http://www.bigfishaudio.com).

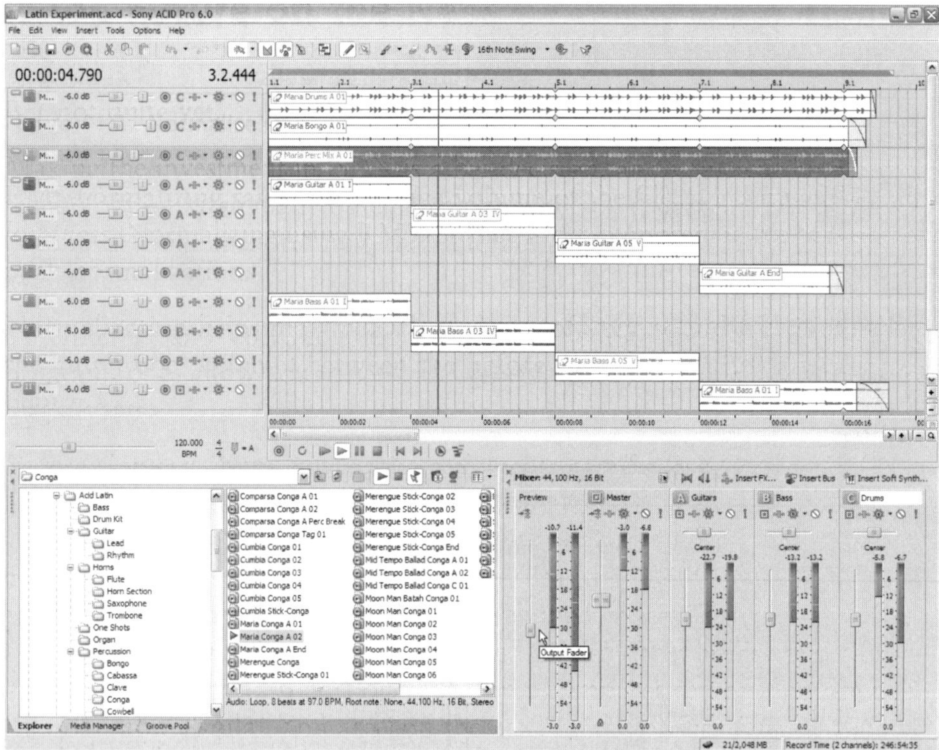

Figure 12.24 *ACID.*

If you think this might be a fun, creative way to enhance your voice productions, grab the *ACID Xpress* software *free* from ACIDplanet (http://www.acidplanet.com). GarageBand is included with the iLife suite, so Mac users may already have it, ready to roll.

Sound Effects

There are two primary kinds of sound effects. Hard effects correspond to the action in the scene, such as a door slam when a character exits. Ambient sound effects, or backgrounds, provide a general overall soundscape, such as playground sounds at a busy park.

You can buy sound effects on CDs and online. Several companies produce CDs jam-packed with almost any sound you can imagine. If you will be using sound effects frequently, investing in a few quality SFX libraries is a sound idea, so to speak. On the other hand, if you only need an occasional effect from time to time, consider purchasing effects on the Web as needed or getting them from a free site (listed a bit later).

Remember that paying the fee to the sound effect owner for a CD library or a downloaded sound means you can legally use it in your productions. If you steal an effect, you might be hearing the sound of the prison door slamming or at least a bank account emptying to pay for your legal defense!

Check out these sound effects library resources:

- Digital Juice (http://www.digitaljuice.com)
- The Hollywood Edge (http://www.hollywoodedge.com)
- Sounddogs.com (http://www.sounddogs.com)
- Sound Ideas of America (http://www.soundideas.com)

Two Web-based providers include

- Sonomic (http://www.sonomic.com)
- SoundSnap (http://www.soundsnap.com)

SoundSnap has free sound effects. You can also create your own. Bring props into your studio and record what you need right there. Or grab a long microphone cable or even a portable recorder and have fun capturing the sounds of your world. As an alternative, use your mouth to emulate the effects you need. Mouth sounds are great for cartoon effects and even a few dramatic ones. Later, you can use your audio software to manipulate these sounds while stretching (another bad, but intentional, pun) your creativity and budget.

Mixing in Music and Sound Effects

Adding sound effects and music to your voice work with your audio software is relatively easy. After finishing the voice track, select the sound effects and music you need, and get them on your computer hard drive. How you add them to your recordings might vary depending on the audio editing software you use.

For example, with *Sound Forge* you must embed the effects and music in the voice file. Here's how. Open the sound effect you need to insert in a separate window, select it, and copy it to the Clipboard. Switch to your finished voice track, and position the cursor where you want to add the effect. Click Paste to add the sound effect. To add music or sound effects that occur at the same time as the voice track, use Paste Special, Mix. This method lets you adjust the volume of the effect or music in relation to the original voice.

Frankly, this is not the easiest way to work. If you're going to do a lot of production like this, invest in multitrack audio software such as Adobe *Audition* or Sony *Vegas Pro*.

Extracting Audio from CD Sometimes the sound effects or music you need is on an audio CD. Both *Sound Forge* and *Audition* include a handy utility for extracting tracks. Go to File, Extract Audio from CD, select the track in the dialog box, choose a name and location for the WAV file, and then let the software do the work for you. With the music or sound effect in WAV format, you can add it to your project easily. Mac users can just use iTunes for this task.

Multitracking

The majority of this book has talked about using a stereo or mono audio recording and editing program for your work. We mentioned multitrack software in passing, but now it's time to revisit the concept. Multitrack audio software, as its name implies, lets you keep many audio tracks (voice, sound effects, and music) separate and then mix them together later. This means you can play several character parts in a scene or simply talk to and answer yourself. You can bring in other performers for dialog spots, too. And you can add sound effects and music and really build interesting finished audio productions.

Multitracking is the mainstay of music recording. All the parts that comprise a popular song are recorded and kept separate from the other element in the music. Sometimes the musicians might play together; other times they don't. Vocals, in particular, are almost always added after the basic background tracks are recorded. Keeping the elements separate gives the producer much better control over the finished recording.

Think of a collage, and the whole concept becomes clear. Picture the individual sounds as bits of paper and the multitrack software as the canvas and glue that holds them all together.

How does that apply to you? Imagine that you want to create a radio commercial.

Scene: Busy supermarket.

Three voices: Husband, wife, and announcer.

Using multitrack software, you record the husband on one track, the wife on another, and the announcer on a third. Using a sound effects CD, you add a supermarket background loop to a fourth track. Finally, you select some interesting music and put it on the fifth track. With this setup you can control the individual volume level of each element. For example, the supermarket background sound could start out quite loud and then get softer when the actors start to speak. The music could fade in around the middle of the spot, as the announcer begins to speak and the store background sounds fade out, and then swell up as the spot ends.

Multitrack software lets you record, edit, sweeten, and deliver a final audio mix or many versions of the mix. (Sony *Vegas* is shown in Figure 12.25.) Meanwhile, you still have all the individual separate sound elements available for remixing, changing, and editing. If you want, you can record all your separate sound elements using an audio editor such as the *Sound Forge* software and then switch to the multitrack to build and mix the final piece (see Figure 12.26). This is the precise method that Adobe *Audition* and *GarageBand* use, combining a mono/stereo recorder/editor with multitrack functionality.

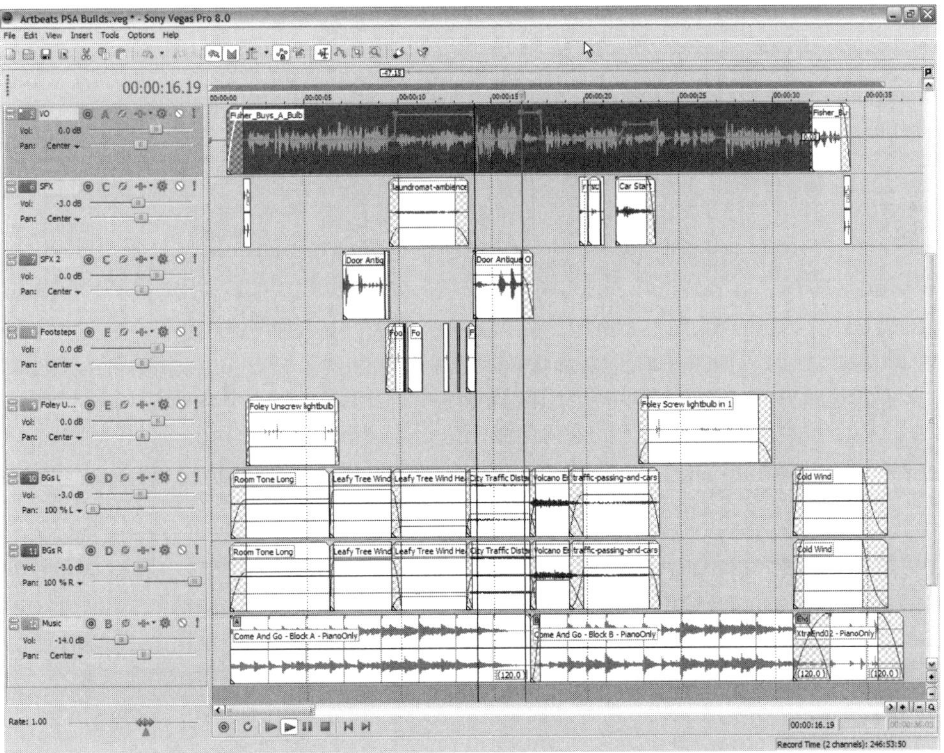

Figure 12.25 Multitracking.

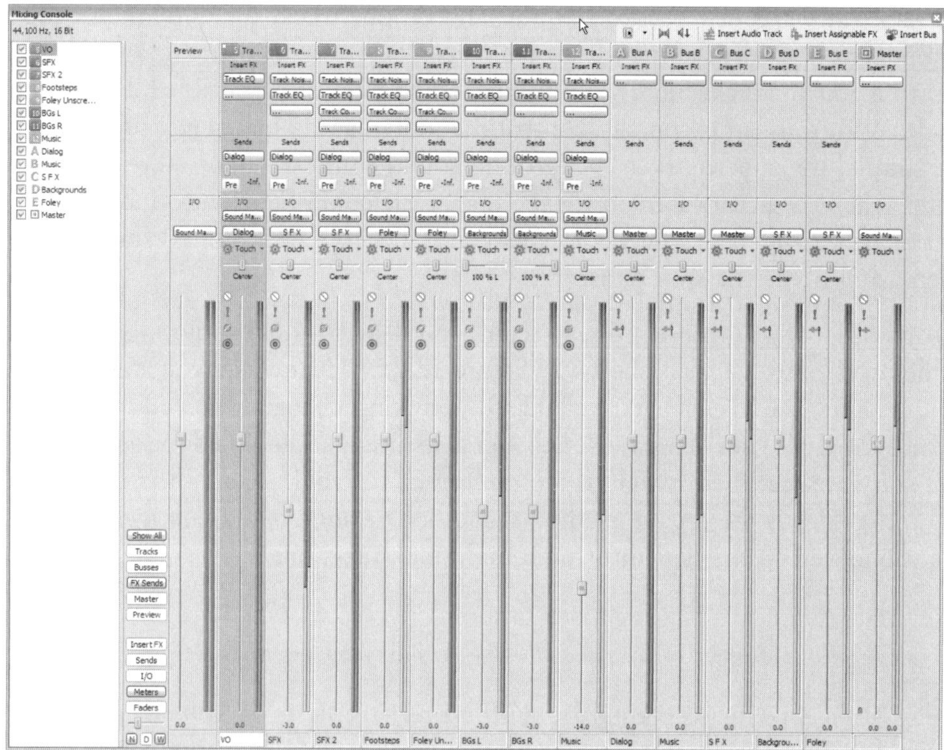

Figure 12.26 Mixer.

Multitrack software is usually nondestructive, which means any edits you make do not physically affect the sound files. The software keeps track of all your changes and applies them in real time. In other words, when you're finished, you must take an extra step to render the completed piece to the file format(s) you need (WAV, MP3, or AIFF). The render step (aka export, bounce-to-disc, etc.) compiles all the individual sound clips into a single mixed stereo or mono file. The great thing is that even if you make a mistake, you can go back and remix without losing any of your original audio.

Multitrack software is also ideal for putting together your demo. After you get all your spots into your computer, use the software to edit, rearrange, and mix a killer demo sequence. Then you can render it as a final mixed WAV file suitable for burning CDs or make MP3s for your Web site or your agent's.

On-Hold Secrets Many VOs find recording on-hold phone messages to be a nice income-producing source of work. Many produce these messages complete with music using their home studios. Here are a few secrets for finishing those projects. Obviously, the voice is the most important part of the mix; it must be clear, consistent, and fully intelligible. The music and sound effects, though also important, are secondary. Start with the music level 12dB below the voice track and adjust as needed. On the voice track, EQ out everything higher than 5kHz and lower than 300Hz, and add a slight bump (2–4dB) at 2kHz. Equalize the music track the same way, except do a 2–4dB cut at 2kHz. That carves out a hole for the voice to sit in. Last, compress the whole mix. Try a 4:1 or higher ratio with fast to medium attack and slow release.

CD: Burn Baby Burn

CDs use a laser to burn information onto a die-coated plastic disc. You can make two different kinds of CDs in a CD-R/CD-RW/DVD writer: audio and data. Many computers today have DVD burners that also can make CDs. Rarely, if ever, would you make a DVD for a client or an audition.

Burning an audio CD creates a disc that can play on virtually any home or car CD player. However, a data CD, or CD-ROM, contains only digital data, much like a hard drive. Data CDs do not work on audio CD players, only computers. Make sure you clearly tell your client whether the CD is audio or data. Harlan and Jeffrey can both recount several panicky calls from clients who didn't realize the data disc they'd requested wouldn't play on a CD player.

Some producers might want an audio CD, while others might prefer just the data CD with the finished WAV file on it. An advantage of the latter is that the producer can drag and drop your voice recording right into the software he uses to create the finished program.

There are several software utilities for burning both data and audio CDs. Chances are one shipped with your computer if it was equipped with a CD-R/CD-RW writer. Popular choices include Easy CD Creator (http://www.roxio.com), Nero (http://www.nero.com), and RecordNow (http://www.sonic.com). The software is typically easy to use. You simply drag and drop the files you want to the program, slip a blank CD-R into the drive, and click on Record. Slightly more advanced and more expensive versions of CD burner software allow you to create a mixed-mode or CD-extra that can contain both data and audio on the same disc.

The *Audition, Sound Forge,* and *Vegas* applications include burning CDs as part of their functions. Using one of these applications means you don't have to buy another software product, and that saves times and money.

By the way, always use blank CD-Rs for making CDs, not CD-RWs. The RW variety will not play on many playback-only CD players—you know, like the one in your agent's car.

Always burn your CDs in what's called disc at once (DAO) mode. This essentially burns and closes the disc in one operation. If you use track at once mode, you can add more tracks over time, but until you close the disc, it won't play anywhere except on your computer. To reduce errors and prevent otherwise ruined discs (called coasters), record at lower speeds. Just because you *can* burn at 24 times the normal rate doesn't mean you *should.*

To burn an audio CD, make sure your files are 16 bit, 44.1kHz stereo. If you followed our advice and recorded in mono, you'll have to convert the file to stereo before burning an audio CD. If you're making a data CD, you don't have to convert to stereo. In the *Sound Forge* application, choose Process, Channel Converter and then choose the preset Mono to Stereo, 100% Faders option. The program will convert your mono file to a "stereo" file. It won't be *real* stereo; it's what's called dual mono—equal sound in both channels. The file will still sound monaural, but the file format will conform to what the CD burner needs.

If you recorded at higher bit depths and sampling rates, you'll also need to use your audio editing software's bit depth converter and resample options to create CD-compatible files. When converting the bit depth, say from 24 to 16 bits, you'll want to apply some dither. Without moving to absolute geek central, let's just say that dither makes the conversion sound better. Dither adds a little noise to the file to mask the effects of quantization noise that result when you lower the bit depth. Okay, we said we wouldn't go there. Sorry, we just got carried away—you know, in kind of a dither. (*My, oh my. Now you've got even me in a dither. I'm speechless. —Prunella*)

What about Video Production?

The techniques of editing video are similar to working with audio. Video work requires some additional hardware, specialized software, and a relatively robust computer. You might want to compile your video demo reel of your onscreen/onstage work yourself and save a big studio bill. Perhaps make some interesting, educational, informative video for places like YouTube to add to your fame (or notoriety). We actually made our own training DVD called "Voice-Over Success: What You Must Know to Compete in Today's Very Different VO Marketplace" (http://www.audiosmartactors.com).

Also, you can be a hero to your whole family by taking all those old 8- and super-millimeter films, home videos languishing in the sock drawer, editing out the boring parts—usually 99 percent of the footage—and making DVDs for everybody. Video is fun to work with and deserves, of course, its own book.

Windows-based video editing software like Sony's *Vegas Pro 8* (see Figure 12.27) or its lighter sibling, *Vegas Movie Studio;* Adobe's *Premier Pro;* and Mac-based solutions like *iMovie* or *Final Cut Pro* are easy to learn—especially now that you're conversant with advanced audio editing, fixing, and sweetening techniques.

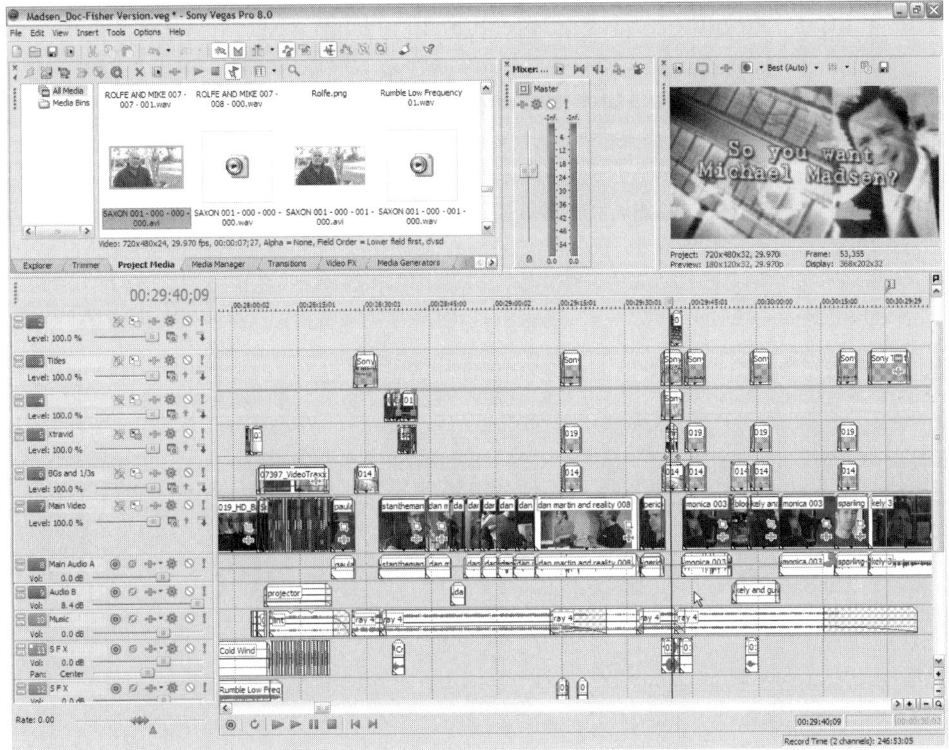

Figure 12.27 *Vegas Pro 8.*

(Screenshot from "So You Want Michael Madsen?" Courtesy of Xristos Productions.)

We promised that we'd stay as nontechnical throughout this book as possible, so we're stopping right now.

Really.

If you get hooked on audio editing and production, you may want to read the bible of audio engineers, *Modern Recording Techniques,* now in its 6th edition. This is not light reading, but it's fascinating to people like, well, you know who. Meanwhile, you now have some strong advanced production techniques to experiment with and implement and lovely new terms to kick around at cocktail parties, adding immensely to your aura. Remember back in Chapter 1, "The New Paradigm—A Home Studio Is a Required Tool of the Trade," when we told you we'd teach you just enough to "talk the talk" and demystify the nomenclature? Well, right now you can answer the question, "Would you prefer a soft or hard knee attack?" You know the difference between decibels and dirigibles and don't need to go to the beach to cast your eyes on lovely waveforms.

Along the way, if you get stumped, check out http://www.audiosmartactors.com or drop either of us an e-mail. If your question is really technical, Harlan will take a long hard look at your query and then with a characteristic smirk forward the question to Jeffrey and make himself another Bombay Gin Martini, very dry with two bleu cheese olives.

In Conclusion . . .

There isn't one.

Really.

There's only flux.

No, not that sticky paste geeks (like Jeffrey) use when they solder together capacitors and resistors and whatever. No, we mean a *state of flux*, and that has been the centerpiece of the first and now the second edition of our book.

As quickly as one of us wrote what we thought was a defining statement on a particular piece of gear or way of working, an e-mail or ad in an audio magazine would turn our carefully constructed prose on its collective ears. This daunting dilemma is the curse and challenge of writing about any ever-changing technology or industry, and audio recording at home or on the road is no exception.

So we acknowledge that whatever we recommended today may very well be passé tomorrow morning, but we're steadfast in heeding moviemaker Samuel Goldwyn's advice, "Never make forecasts, especially about the future." Pretty good consul from a guy savvy enough to legally change his name back in 1918 from Goldfish!

Of course, much of the basic equipment, software, and techniques won't change radically for at least a few more years; we'll still be using microphones, recording devices, and the Internet. But there will always be some degree of change to contend with, and although it's human nature to resist change, we encourage you to embrace new equipment and techniques whenever they make your work more productive and efficient. We both get excited about new ways to record at home or on the road, and we hope you will, too.

Luckily, the Internet lets us continue a dialogue with all our readers beyond these pages. We're happy to clarify or expand on anything we've written and always are anxious to tell you about the latest trends and gear. So feel free to e-mail either or both of us.

Harlan's address is harlan@harlanhogan.com, and Jeffrey's at jpf@jeffreypfisher.com.

We have also committed ourselves to maintaining our actor-friendly recording Web site, http://www.audiosmartactors.com. Here you'll find freshly updated information on new techniques, new trends, and new gear. That is, at least until we get a call from our publishers that it's time to start scribbling on the third edition!

—H2 & JPF

October 2008

A Glitzy, Glowing, Glimmering, Glamorous Glossary

Our oh-so-handy guide to arcane audio terminology for posturing, posing, pontificating pundits.

A-B. 1. Listening and comparing two or more music, sound effects, or voice-over takes. 2. Letters not appearing on any of Harlan's report cards.

Acoustics. 1. The art and science of controlling sound in a space. 2. Branches or twigs of a tree where the species Zenaida macroura (mourning doves) perch and make that ungodly cooing sound.

AES. 1. Audio Engineering Society. Meeting feature: Tuna sandwiches, fries, and cash bar. Membership includes personalized pocket protector. 2. American Egotistical Society. Meeting feature: All-you-can-stand buffet and open bar. Membership includes custom-fit earplugs for the networking meet-eat-greet portion of the program.

Ambience. 1. The audible sound of any room or environment, sometimes called room tone. 2. Fast-moving, siren-bedecked emergency vehicle.

Amplification. 1. The process that increases signal strength of an audio source, i.e., boosting the low-level signal from a mic to be loud enough to hear through a loudspeaker. 2. To re-explain/reiterate, as in, "What part of NO don't you understand?"

Analog. 1. Short for analogous. A fancy way of saying something is like something else. For example, electricity from a microphone is like (analogous/analog) the sound waves that strike it. Regular (non-computer) audio sounds are called analog versus digital audio when you get your computer involved. 2. To build a roaring fire, you'll need kindling, a match, an-a-log.

Analog-to-Digital (A/D) Converter. 1. A device that converts analog audio signal into digital data (1s and 0s) and back again (digital-to-analog converter). 2. The major component in an audio interface or sound card. 3. Adderall, Ritalin, and Dexedrine are often prescribed as attention deficit converters.

Assign. 1. To route or send an audio signal to one or more selected channels. 2. Graduation requirements Mr. Hogan consistently failed to complete, forcing him into a life as an itinerant actor trodding the boards, hat in hand. 3. Spiritual encounter; i.e., a burning bush indicating a necessary change in one's life—because you've screwed up and God *was* watching.

Attack. 1. The beginning of a sound. 2. Popular political advertising genre.

Attack Time. 1. When using a compressor to process audio signals, this is the time it takes for a reduction in gain (volume) to happen. 2. Decision to use popular political advertising genre.

Attenuate. 1. Reduce or lower the level (volume) of an audio signal. 2. Response to question, "What time did I dine last night?"

Balance. 1. The relative volume levels and placement of audio elements in a recording. 2. Lifestyle—wherein real people don't talk like this.

Balanced Line. 1. A cable with two conductors surrounded by a shield, in which each conductor is at equal impedance to ground. The cable's conductors are at opposite polarity, and the signal flows through both conductors. Balance lines help reject noise. 2. Conversation starter that includes even a feigned degree of interest in another person. i.e., "Say, isn't that a patch cord in your pocket? Tip, ring, sleeve? Wow! That's my favorite, too!"

Bass Trap. 1. An acoustic array that absorbs low-frequency sound waves in the studio. 2. A much-underestimated way to feed the family with fresh-caught, freshwater fish.

Bus. 1. Large vehicle used to spoil America's youth—Jeffrey, for example. He never had to march through waist-high snow, ford turgid torrents of ankle-deep water, or run in Forest Gump terror from tornado-infested winds on the way to school like Harlan did. This explains a lot. 2. A common wire connecting a group of signals—kind of the equivalent of USB only with audio gear. Did you know USB stands for universal serial bus? Yep!

Bus Master. 1. The Grand Poobah control of the audio zooming along the bus, this fader controls the output volume of all the signals on the bus master. 2. Jackie Gleason.

Buzz. 1. An unwanted edgy tone that sometimes accompanies audio, containing high harmonics of 60Hz. 2. Woody's antagonist in *Toy Story*.

Cans. 1. Slang for headphones. 2. Our pronunciation of that ritzy film festival we'll never get invited to.

Cardioid Microphone. 1. A microphone with a one-sided, heart-shaped directional pattern. Sound arriving at the rear of the microphone is much lower in volume. Therefore, these mics tend to reject more room noise and give a more in-your-face vocal sound. 2. The microphone most VOs use.

CD-R and CD-RW. 1. CD-Rs are recordable compact discs that can't be erased and reused, while CD-RWs are the opposite. 2. R2-D2's second cousins.

Cellular Buzz (GSM noise). 1. The sound that gets inadvertently recorded when you leave your cell phone on. 2. *See also* Angry Engineer. 3. *See also* Really Angry Client.

Complex Wave. 1. A sound wave containing more than one frequency or harmonics. 2. Hairstyles often involving extenders, curling irons, and weaves.

Compressor. 1. A signal processor that reduces the dynamic range of an audio gain using an automatic volume control. The result is that louder sounds are lowered to the level of softer sounds. This allows the whole file to be raised in volume. 2. Superfast Germanic automobiles zipping down the Autobahn.

Condenser Microphone. A microphone that uses variable capacitance to generate its electrical signal. Condensers require external power to operate. *See also* Phantom Power.

Connector. 1. Devices used to connect a cable and an electronic component or to connect two cables so that signals can flow from one to the other. 2. Yente, the matchmaker in *Fiddler on the Roof.*

DAT (R-DAT). 1. A digital audio tape recorder. 2. Popular New Jersey query, "Who R Dat dere?"

DAW. 1. Digital Audio Workstation, a combination of a computer, sound card, and editing software that lets us record, edit, mix, and deliver audio programs entirely in digital form. 2. Abbreviation for **D**igital **A**udio **W**orkstation. 3. Abbreviation for **D**aughters of the **A**merican **W**orkforce.

Decay. 1. The declining end of a sound or musical note over time. 2. Corollary result of failed flossing and botched brushing.

Decibel (dB). 1. Logarithmic scale for measuring audio level, with 0dB being the threshold of hearing and 120dB the threshold of pain. 2. Abbreviation for **D**ead **B**eat. *See also* Actor, Itinerant.

De-Esser. 1. An audio processing device that removes excessive sibilance (*s* and *sh* sounds) by detecting it and then reducing the sibilance volume automatically. A de-esser is, in essence, a frequency-controlled compressor. 2. Ice-removal techniques used by most major airlines.

Desk. 1. The British term for mixing console/mixing board. 2. The British are weird.

Destructive Editing. 1. Editing that permanently rewrites data on a hard drive so edits cannot be undone. 2. Terrifying technique of our own much feared Prunella Sykes.

Diffusion. 1. An even distribution of sound in a room. 2. Fusion that makes a difference.

Distortion. 1. Any unwanted change in the audio waveform. It may be accompanied by a nasty, raspy, or gritty sound quality. The appearance of frequencies in a device's output signal that were not in the input signal. Distortion is caused by recording at too high a level, improper mixer settings, components failing, or vacuum tubes distorting. (Distortion can be desirable for some instances, such as a distorted electric guitar in the heavy metal music Harlan drifts off to most evenings about 9:30.) 2. Another popular political advertising genre. 3. Lies! I'm tellin' ya! It's all lies!

Dry. 1. Recorded tracks that have not yet had signal processing applied to them. 2. Recorded tracks with no music or sound effects. 3. Ephraim, Wisconsin.

Dynamic Microphone. 1. A microphone that generates its own electricity when sound waves cause a moving coil to vibrate within a magnetic field. 2. She was slim, trim, and oh so powerful. One look, and Jeffrey knew this was one dynamic mic. Now, where could he hide her from Lisa?

Dynamic Range. 1. The range of recorded volume levels softest to loudest, i.e., the range of a whisper to a shout. 2. Although not as popular as the ubiquitous microwave, dynamic ranges are being embraced by many of the world's top chefs.

Echo. 1. The delayed and distinct repetition of a sound. If you shout "Hello" into a canyon, you'll hear hello, hello, hello, hello . . . repeating. 2. Little Sir's last name.

Echo Chamber. 1. The British name for a physical echo chamber consisting of a hard-surfaced room with a widely separated loudspeaker and microphone to create and record reverberation. The Brits call reverb "echo" and the Americans call reverb, uh, "reverb," and then we call echo "delay." Weird, eh?. 2. Electronic echo chambers can be hardware or software based. 3. The legendary movie sound effect, dubbed the *Wilhelm Scream,* was enhanced with echo chambers since first being heard in the 1951 B-movie *Distant Drums*. Since then, the scream has found its way into over 300 video games, commercials, and movies from *Star Wars* and *Raiders of the Lost Ark* to *Batman Returns* and *Toy Story*. Who says Hollywood isn't green? They have been recycling this for a long, long time.

Editing. 1. Originally, physically cutting and taping together magnetic tape to delete or rearrange audio. 2. Today, editing is done using computers without cutting tape or your fingers.

Effects. 1. Sound changing/enhancing effects like equalization, reverberation, echo/delay, flanging, chorusing, compression, de-essing, noise gate, etc. 2. See last.

Equalization (EQ). 1. You know those tone controls you fiddle with in your car to adjust the bass and treble? Yeah, well, that's the same as EQ, but tone control sounds so ... pedestrian, and it's hard to bill studio time for that. 2. The adjustment of frequency response to alter the tonal balance or to eliminate/reduce unwanted frequencies.

Expander. 1. A signal processing device or software that increases the dynamic range of audio through it. 2. Clever clothing invention introduced in 1959 by the Jaymar-Ruby company of Michigan City, Indiana. The Sansbelt comfort-fit waistband allowed gentlemen to subtly "adjust" one's trouser's waist size without anyone being the wiser.

Fade Out. 1. To gradually reduce the volume of the last several seconds of a recorded song, from full level down to silence, by slowly pulling down the master volume fader. 2. *See also* Career, Hogan.

Fader. 1. A rotating or sliding volume control used to adjust signal levels. 2. In da Bronx, you've got a Mudder and one of these.

Feedback. 1. That ear-piercing squealing sound heard when a microphone picks up its own amplified signal through a loudspeaker. 2. An even more ear-piercing sound when feedback involves your headphones. 3. Unsolicited critique of your performance.

Flutter. 1. A rapid, periodic variation in pitch usually caused by uneven tension between the tape reels in analog recording. 2. Jeffrey's heartbeat when he finds the latest edition of *Electronic Musician* magazine in his mailbox.

Frequency. 1. The number of cycles per second of a sound wave, measured in hertz (Hz). 2. Think of, and be depressed by, the corollary.

Gain. 1. Amplification or volume. 2. *See* Ill-Gotten. 3. *See also* Residual.

Gate (Noise Gate). 1. Software or hardware that turns off a signal when its amplitude falls below a preset level. 2. Device used to keep wannabees and fans at a distance from Mr. Fisher's and Mr. Hogan's mansions.

Ground Loops. 1. A hum result from having more than one grounding point in an electronic connection. 2. Bi-plane wannabees in the late 1920s who, though afraid to actually take off, still managed to entertain the crowd.

Harmonic(s). 1. An overtone whose frequency is a whole-number multiple of the fundamental frequency. For comparison, an octave is a doubling of frequency. 2. Once a very popular musical device due to its low cost and portability.

Headroom. 1. The safe zone (measured in decibels) between the average signal level and the maximum undistorted signal level. 2. Area (measured in inches) between forehead and ceiling.

Hertz (Hz). 1. Cycles per second, the unit of measurement of frequency. 2. Humans hear from 20Hz to 20,000Hz, with the higher numbers reduced with age. (*Right, H2?*) 3. Pretty much on a par with Avis. We prefer Enterprise because, you know, they pick us up—and usually we both need picking up.

Hot. 1. A high recording or playback level. 2. Equipment that is receiving power. 3. A "live" microphone, i.e., watch what you say. 4. Catherine Zeta-Jones, Jennifer Love Hewitt, Scarlett Johansson, Jessica Biel. 5. The two Ls, Lisa and Lesley, our wives. 6. Really.

Hum. 1. Low-pitched tone (usually around 60Hz) generated in audio circuits and cables by alternating current due to faulty grounding, poor shielding, and ground loops. 2. Way of re-creating music without the need for costly instruments or lyrics.

Input. 1. The signal going into an audio device, usually through a connector for a microphone or other signal source. 2. Advice and opinions, usually unsolicited. *See also* Feedback.

Insert Jacks. 1. Special jacks that allow you to insert effects, such as reverberation, directly into your audio from other (outboard) processing gear. 2. Dangerous technique to cheat in Texas Hold 'Em.

Leakage. 1. Unwanted audio bleeding onto a track, frequently due to headphones being too loud or loose fitting. 2. We refuse to do some sophomoric joke about Depends. Nope, not us.

LED Indicator. 1. A recording-level indicator using one or more Light Emitting Diodes. 2. Electronic device the EPA uses to find toxins in paint.

Level. The degree of intensity of an audio signal.

Limiter (Peak Limiter). 1. A signal processor whose output stays the same above a preset "never to be exceeded" input level. 2. Overbearing parent.

Line Level. 1. In balanced professional recording equipment, a signal whose level is approximately minus 4dBv. 2. Relative overall height of high-kicking dance troupe.

Loop. 1. In a software sampling program, repeating loops of audio can be combined to create music. 2. Encircled by the Chicago Transit Association's elevated trains.

Loudspeaker. 1. Device (transducer) that converts electrical energy (the signal) into acoustical energy (sound waves). 2. Jesse Jackson.

Low-Pass Filter. 1. A hardware or software filter that allows frequencies below a certain frequency through but stops frequencies above that same frequency. 2. The opposite is a high-pass filter. 3. Warning device required by the Interstate Commerce Commission on semi-trailer trucks.

Mask. 1. To hide, cover up, or make a sound inaudible by playing another sound along with it. 2. *See also* Jim Carrey.

Microphone (Mic). 1. Metal thing one speaks into as greenbacks emerge from the other end. 2. Metal thing that is a *transducer,* i.e., a device that converts an acoustical signal (sound) into an electrical signal. *See also* Loudspeaker. 3. Abbreviation is mic, pronounced as "Mike," Harlan and Lesley's Newfoundland-Lab mix.

MIDI. 1. Abbreviation for **M**usical **I**nstrument **D**igital **I**nterface. This is a common encoding language that allows synthesizers, drum machines, and computers to communicate with or control each other. 2. Popular leg-revealing dress style remembered fondly by gentlemen of a certain age.

Mixdown. 1. The process of playing one or more recorded tracks through a physical or virtual mixing console and combining them into one combined audio track. 2. Julia Child's technique for combining ingredients without spattering the ceiling.

Mixer (Mixing Board). 1. A hardware device or software program that mixes and combines audio signals and controls the relative levels of the signals. Many mixers also have equalization controls, pan pots, monitoring controls, solo functions, and channel assigns and can control how signals are sent to external devices. 2. Mixing console. 3. Control surface. 4. Stupid party whose aim it is to acquaint boring people with other equally boring people they have no desire to be acquainted with.

Monitor. 1. Fancy name for expensive loudspeaker. 2. Video display screen used with a computer. 3. Carnivorous lizards including the King Kong of reptiles, the Komodo Dragon. 4. U.S. ironclad warship.

Monitoring. 1. Listening to an audio signal with a monitor or headphones. 2. Civil War–era derogatory slang for sailors who drowned, referring to the 16 who died when the USS *Monitor* sank in a storm off Cape Hatteras in 1862.

Mono (Monophonic). 1. A single channel of audio with the same sound coming from all monitors or speakers. 2. The so-called kissing disease mononucleosis.

MP3. A lossy format that enables audio to be distributed on the Internet with short upload and download times compared to WAV or AIF files.

Muddy. 1. Unclear sounding; having excessive leakage, reverberation, or overhang. 2. The late McKinley Morganfield.

Multitrack. 1. Hardware or software that can separately record and play back one or more tracks. 2. Churchill Downs.

Mute. 1. To turn off an input or output signal on a mixing console. 2. Clown White–faced sorry-sad-sack, forever trapped in an invisible box.

Near-Field Monitoring. 1. Mixing audio by placing the speaker (monitors) very close to the listener, lessening the influence of the control rooms' acoustic sound. 2. Attempting a mix near Clark and Addison on game day.

Nondestructive Editing. 1. The reverse of destructive editing, i.e., a nondestructive edit can be undone. 2. Our own, constantly encouraging Karen Gill.

Off-Axis. 1. Performer who isn't directly in front of a directional microphone. 2. Device popular with executioners before Messier Guillotine's invention.

Omnidirectional Microphone. 1. A microphone that is sensitive to sounds arriving from all directions. 2. A microphone that has yet to find its true raison d'art; thus, it is unfocused and easily distracted by sounds arriving from all directions.

Outboard Equipment. 1. External gear or programs outboard of the mixing console. 2. Evinrude, Nissan, and Mercury are good examples.

Output. A connector in an audio device from which the signal comes and feeds successive devices.

Out-Take. 1. A take, or section of a take, that is to be removed or not used. 2. A take, or section of a take, that is then embarrassingly posted throughout the Internet. 3. Slang for carryout or, as the British say, takeaway. See, we told you the British are weird.

Overdub. 1. To record a new part on an unused audio track in synchronization with previously recorded tracks. 2. Too much of a good dubbing.

Pad. 1. A setting to reduce volume (attenuate) by a preset amount. 2. Beatnik slang for crib.

Pan Pot. 1. Abbreviation for **Pan**oramic **Pot**entiometer. How's that for cool phraseology? On mixing consoles, a pan pot control divides a signal between two or more channels in an adjustable ratio, such as the left and right channels of a stereo signal. 2. Partygoers' opinion of bad grass. 3. The chef's perennial decision dilemma: use the frying pan or the stock pot?

Patch. To connect one piece of audio equipment to another with a cable. *See also* Tape, Duct.

Patch Bay (Patch Panel). 1. Multiple jacks wired to various audio inputs and outputs, making it easy to interconnect various pieces of equipment from one place. 2. The easy way to interconnect all your outboard gear. 3. Uber-exclusive, secluded, and gated Caribbean retirement community.

Patch Cord. 1. A short cable with plugs on both ends, used to route audio in the patch panel. 2. Decorative eyewear accessory, favored by members of the Members-Only Patch Bay Yacht Club.

Peak. 1. On a graph of a sound wave or signal, the highest point in the waveform's amplitude. 2. Harlan's career—20 years ago.

Phantom Power. 1. DC voltage (usually 48 volts) used to power condenser microphones. 2. Unexplainable and inexplicable fan base that demands constant revivals of the interminable Andrew Lloyd Webber musical.

Phase. 1. The degree of progression in the cycle of a sound wave. (A complete cycle is 360 degrees.) 2. Adolescence.

Phase Cancellation. 1. The elimination of certain frequencies in a signal, when that signal is combined with its (slightly delayed) duplicate. 2. Graduation. 3. Leaving the familial homestead. 4. Parental cessation of support. 5. Student loan repayment begins.

Phone Patch. Remote recording session conducted via Plain Old Telephone Service (POTS), ISDN (Integrated Services Digital Network), or VoIP (Voice over Internet Protocol).

Phone Plug (Phono Plug). 1. A cylindrical plug (usually 1/4-inch diameter). 2. An unbalanced phone plug's tip carries the hot signal and the sleeve (the tube portion) the shield or ground. 3. A balanced phone plug has a tip for the signal hot signal, a ring for the return signal, and a sleeve for the shield or ground (Tip-Ring-Sleeve or TRS). 4. An RCA or S/PDIF phone plug has a central pin for the hot signal and a ring of pressure-fit tabs for the shield or ground. 5. Unsolicited commercials on your telephone—cell spam.

Pitch. 1. Late-night infomercials that seem to solve all the world's problems in three easy payments. 2. The relative lowness or highness of a sound; its fundamental frequency.

Plug-In. 1. Software audio effects that you install in your computer. 2. The very first step in audio production.

Polar Pattern. 1. The directional pickup pattern of a microphone, such as omnidirectional, bidirectional, unidirectional, cardioid, super cardioid, and hypercardioid. (Note:

Hypercardioidism can often be controlled through the use of drugs like Ridilin.) 2. Alarming result of global warming. An emerging pattern of migration is being noted by scientists, as most North Pole animals are catching busses to the nearest zoo.

Pop. 1. A thump/explosive sound heard in a voice-over's track. Pop occurs when the user says words with "p," "t," or "b" so that a turbulent puff of air is forced from the mouth and strikes the microphone diaphragm. 2. A noise heard when a mic is plugged into a monitored channel or when a switch is flipped. 3. Overly familiar term of endearment for voice talent of a certain age, i.e., "Pop's dozing in the Green Room. Shall I wake him up?"

Pop Filter. 1. A screen placed on a microphone grille that attenuates or filters out pop disturbances before they strike the microphone diaphragm. Usually made of open-cell plastic foam, silk, or metal, a pop filter reduces pop and wind noise. 2. Okay, the down-and-dirty truth is that this thing keeps saliva off the delicate and expensive-to-replace microphone diaphragm. However, pop filter sounds better than spit filter in mixed company. 3. Bouncer at a trendy nightclub who refuses entry to men of Harlan's age.

Preamplifier (Preamp). 1. In an audio system, the first stage of amplification that boosts a mic-level signal to line level. A preamp is a standalone device or a circuit in a mixer. 2. Similar to a prenuptial agreement—slang for taking more than 50% of marital assets. "Man, I preamplified him!"

Prefader/Postfader Switch. A switch that selects a signal either ahead of the channel fader (prefader) or following the fader (postfader).

Proximity Effect. 1. The increase in bass when speaking very closely into a directional microphone. 2. Another loser movie from M. Night Shyamalan.

Punch In/Out. 1. In recording, this is the ability to insert a new track into a previously recorded one. 2. What people with real jobs have to do at the beginning and end of their shift.

Rack. 1. A 19-inch-wide wooden or metal cabinet used to hold audio equipment. 2. Antlers. 3. Not even thinking that. Really, we're not.

Radio Frequency Interference (RFI/RF). 1. Noise (often distant radio stations) picked up by audio cables or equipment.

Ribbon Microphone. A dynamic type of microphone using a long metallic diaphragm (ribbon) suspended in a magnetic field.

Ride Gain. 1. To turn down the volume of a microphone when the source gets louder, and to turn up the volume when the source gets quieter. 2. Tonto's second cousin twice-removed's mount.

Sampling. 1. Recording sound into the computer. The audio signal is converted into digital data representing the signal waveform, and the data is stored in memory chips, tape, or disc for later playback. 2. Indulging in an entire box of Whitman's finest.

Scratch Track. 1. Rough VO: recording usually done by a nonprofessional for client approval. 2. What the DJ does in a hip-hop group. 3. A sure way to get a spanking back in the 78 and 45 rpm record days according to Mr. Hogan.

See Also. *See also* See Also.

Sensitivity. 1. The output of a microphone in volts at certain sound pressure levels. 2. Mrs. Fisher and Mrs. Hogan—in solidarity—claim we don't know anything about this, so we defer to their collective wisdom.

Shock Mount. 1. A suspension system that isolates a microphone from its stand. 2. Black stallion ridden by Abraham "Brom Bones" Van Brunt in *The Legend of Sleepy Hollow.*

Sibilance. 1. Harsh and shrill "S" sounds in the 5- to 10kHz range. 2. Brothers and sisters you wouldn't deign to even speak to if you weren't somehow—through a cruel trick of nature—related to them.

Signal-To-Noise Ratio (S/N). The ratio (in decibels) between signal and noise. An audio component with a high S/N has very little background noise, but a component with a low S/N is noisy.

Slap, Slapback. 1. An echo following the original sound by about 50 to 200 milliseconds, sometimes with multiple repetitions. 2. A Three Stooges staple.

Slate. 1. At the beginning of a recording, the engineer announces the name or number of the take. 2. The most expensive roof one could possibly imagine over one's head, and one that the lovely Lesley Hogan wants Mr. Hogan to install instead of that tar-paper thing they have at the moment, as soon as the royalties from this book come a-rollin' in.

Sound Card. *See* Analog-to-Digital Converter.

Speaker. *See* Loudspeaker/Monitor.

Standing Wave. 1. The buildup of certain frequencies in a space due to the acoustic reflection between opposite room surfaces. 2. Appreciative gesture given by an audience to a performer who doesn't quite deserve a standing ovation.

Take. 1. A recorded performance. Usually, many takes are done, and a whole take or the best parts of several takes are assembled into a "hero" take. 2. Amount received by actor.

Talkback. 1. Essentially an intercom in the mixing console for the engineer and producer to talk to the voice actors in the studio. 2. *See also* Phase and Phase Cancellation.

Transient. 1. A short signal with a rapid attack and decay, such as a drum stroke, cymbal hit, or acoustic-guitar pluck. 2. Hotel frequented by actors, musicians, and former ad executives.

Tweeter. 1. A high-frequency loudspeaker. 2. Sylvester's nemesis.

Unity Gain. 1. A steady state signal with no increase or decrease in strength at the output of an amplifier or device compared to the signal strength at the input.2. Increase in weight observed throughout the populace of Northwestern Minnesota during February.

Valve. British term for vacuum tube. They just get weirder and weirder, don't they?

Virtual Track. 1. The computer's equivalent of a tape track on a multitrack tape recorder. A key component of mixing. 2. *Second Life*'s ever-popular, always jammed, Jameson Straights Racecourse—admission 17.00 Linden dollars.

VU Meter. Abbreviation for **V**olume **U**nits. The VU meter shows relative volumes of signals.

Waveform. 1. The graphic representation of audio. 2. Movement of one's hands to acknowledge others. Popular examples include the enthusiastic "YO wave" and the restrained Queen of England's "I'm moving my hand back and forth but ignoring your existence, you commoner you, wave." We don't need to mention how weird that is.

Woofer. 1. A low-frequency loudspeaker. 2. Ally, the Hogans' Border Collie/Chow mix.

Workstation. 1. A system of MIDI- or computer-related equipment that helps you compose and record music. Usually, this system is small enough to fit on a desktop or equipment stand. *See also* Digital Audio Workstation. 2. Popular daytimer AM in the outskirts of Lansing, Illinois, reputed to be owned by **W**oodrow **O**rren **R**obert **K**ensington the third, Lansing's leading land baron and sponsor of the Lan-Oak Park Fourth of July fireworks.

XLR. 1. Oldies station in Graham, Georgia, where Harlan did his first DJ gig. When his Chicago-accented double-u in WXLR sounded to management like *doubyaw XLR,* they obligingly removed the offending consonant. 2. A tube-shaped 3-pin balanced professional audio connector.

Y-Adapter. 1. A cable that combines two audio signals into one or separates one into two. 2. That nagging question, while deciding whether to take home the Tabby or the Maine Coon kitten, from Orphans of the Storm Animal Shelter.

Essential Resources Guide

ACOUSTIC/SOUNDBOOTH SOLUTIONS

Acoustics First (http://www.acousticsfirst.com)

Auralex Acoustics (http://www.auralex.com)

Marketek (http://www.markertek.com)

RealTraps (http://www.realtraps.com)

sE Electronics (http://www.seelectronics.com)

SM Pro Audio (http://www.smproaudio.com)

Sonex (http://www.sonex.com)

VocalBooth.com (http://www.vocalbooth.com)

VoiceOver Essentials (http://www.voiceoveressentials.com)

WhisperRoom Inc. (http://www.whisperroom.com)

AUDIO INTERFACES

CEntrance (http://www.centrance.com)

Edirol (http://www.edirol.com)

Focusrite (http://www.focusrite.com)

Lexicon (http://www.lexiconpro.com)

M-Audio (http://www.m-audio.com)

PreSonus (http://www.presonus.com)

Sound Devices (http://www.sounddevices.com)

AUDIO SOFTWARE

Adobe (http://www.adobe.com)

Apple (http://www.apple.com)

Bias (http://www.bias-inc.com)

Cakewalk (http://www.cakewalk.com)

Digidesign (http://www.digidesign.com)

GoldWave Inc. (http://www.goldwave.com)

iZotope (http://www.izotope.com)

Mackie (http://www.mackie.com)

Magix (http://www.samplitude.com)

n-Track Studio (http://www.ntrack.com)

Sony (http://www.sonycreativesoftware.com)

Steinberg (http://www.steinberg.net)

Universal Audio (http://www.uaudio.com/)

Voxengo (http://www.voxengo.com)

AUTHOR WEB SITES

http://www.audiosmartactors.com

http://www.jeffreypfisher.com

http://www.harlanhogan.com

BOOKS

Fisher, Jeffrey P. *Instant Sound Forge* (San Francisco, CMP Books, 2004).

———. *Profiting from Your Music and Sound Project Studio* (New York: Allworth Press, 2001).

———. *Ruthless Self-Promotion in the Music Industry*, 2nd Edition (New York: Artist-Pro, 2004).

Hogan, Harlan. *VO: Tales and Techniques of a Voice-Over Actor* (New York: Allworth Press, 2002).

Levinson, Jay Conrad and Seth Godin. *The Guerrilla Marketing Handbook* (New York: Houghton Mifflin, 1995).

CAREER

ActorTrack (http://www.holdonlog.com)

Commercial Voices.com (http://www.commercialvoices.com)

Disc Makers (http://www.discmakers.com)

E-Learning Voices.com (http://www.e-learningvoices.com/)

Evatone (http://www.eva-tone.com)

iStockphoto (http://www.istockphoto.com)

Modern Postcard (http://www.modernpostcard.com)

PrintingForLess.com (http://www.printingforless.com)

VerticalResponse (http://www.verticalresponse.com)

Voice123 (http://www.voice123.com)

Voicebank.net (http://www.voicebank.net)

VoiceHunter.com (http://www.voicehunter.com)

Voices.com (http://www.voices.com)

COMPUTER

Contour Design (http://www.contourdesign.com)

Frontier Design (http://www.frontierdesign.com)

Keyspan (http://www.keyspan.com)

Nero (http://www.nero.com)

Roxio (http://www.roxio.com)

XRackPro (http://www.xrackpro.com)

DVD/CD

Voice-Over Success: What You Must Know to Compete in Today's Very Different VO Marketplace DVD with Jeffrey P. Fisher and Harlan Hogan (http://www.vasst.com)

Advanced Voice-Over Success Career Strategies CD by Harlan Hogan (http://voiceoveressentials.com)

HEADPHONES

Rolls Corporation (http://www.rolls.com)

Sennheiser (http://www.sennheiser.com)

Sony (http://www.sonystyle.com)

INTERNET

Addr.com (http://www.addr.com)

CoffeeCup (http://www.coffeecup.com/)

GoDaddy.com (http://www.godaddy.com)

HostIndex (http://www.hostindex.com)

Pair Networks (http://www.pair.com)

VeriSign (http://www.networksolutions.com)

ISDN, INTERNET, AND PHONE PATCH

Audio TX (http://www.audiotx.com)

CircuitWerkes (http://www.broadcastboxes.com)

Comrex Corporation (http://www.comrex.com)

EDnet (http://www.ednet.net)

JK Audio (http://www.jkaudio.com)

SoundStreak (http://www.soundstreak.com)

Source-Connect (http://www.source-elements.com/Source-Connect)

Telos Systems (http://www.telos-systems.com)

MICROPHONE/RECORDING ACCESSORIES

AKG (http://www.akg.com)

Atlas Sound (http://www.atlassound.com)

Avantone Pro-Shield (http://www.avantelectronics.com)

Entertainer's Secret (http://www.entertainers-secret.com)

Mighty Bright (http://www.mightybright.com)

Mogami (http://www.mogamicable.com)

On-Stage Stands (http://www.onstagestands.com)

Popless Voice Screens (http://www.popfilter.com)

Stedman (http://www.stedmancorp.com)

MICROPHONES

AKG (http://www.akg.com)

Audio-Technica (http://www.audio-technica.com)

Avant Electronics (http://www.avantelectronics.com)

Blue Microphones (http://www.bluemic.com)

Cascade (http://www.cascademicrophones.com)

Electro-Voice (http://www.electrovoice.com)

Heil (http://www.heilsound.com)

Lawson (http://www.lawsonmicrophones.com)

MXL / Marshall Electronics (http://www.mxlmics.com)

Neumann (http://www.neumann.com)

RØDE Microphones (http://www.rodemic.com)

Sennheiser (http://www.sennheiser.com)

Shure (http://www.shure.com)

MIXERS

Alesis (http://www.alesis.com)

Behringer (http://www.behringer.com)

Mackie (http://www.mackie.com)

MONITORS/SPEAKERS

Alesis (http://www.alesis.com)

Behringer (http://www.behringer.com)

Event (http://www.event1.com)

KRK Systems (http://www.krksys.com)

M-Audio (http://www.m-audio.com)

Mackie (http://www.mackie.com)

MUSIC

Digital Juice (http://www.digitaljuice.com)

Fresh Music (http://www.freshmusic.com)

Killer Tracks (http://www.killertracks.com)

Music Bakery (http://www.musicbakery.com)

VASST TrakPaks (http://www.vasst.com)

PERIODICALS

Advertising Age (http://www.adage.com)

Adweek Magazine (http://www.adweek.com)

Electronic Musician (http://www.emusician.com)

Hollywood Reporter (http://www.hollywoodreporter.com)

PerformInk (http://www.performink.com)

Variety (http://www.variety.com)

Voice Over Resource Guide (http://www.voiceoverresourceguide.com)

PREAMPS

ART (http://www.artproaudio.com)

Avalon (http://www.avalondesign.com)

Focusrite (http://www.focusrite.com)

Grace Design (http://www.gracedesign.com)

John Hardy M1 (http://www.johnhardyco.com)

PreSonus (http://www.presonus.com)

Studio Projects (http://www.studioprojectsusa.com)

Universal Audio (http://www.uaudio.com)

RECORDING EQUIPMENT AND SUPPLIES

American Musical Supply (http://www.americanmusical.com)

B & H Photo & Electronics Inc. (http://www.bhphotovideo.com)

Full Compass (http://www.fullcompass.com)

Markertek.com (http://www.markertek.com)

Musician's Friend (http://www.musiciansfriend.com)

Sweetwater (http://www.sweetwater.com)

VoiceOver Essentials (http://www.voiceoveressentials.com)

SOUND EFFECTS

Digital Juice (http://www.digitaljuice.com)

The Hollywood Edge (http://www.hollywoodedge.com)

Sonomic (http://www.sonomic.com)

Sound Ideas of America (http://www.soundideas.com)

Sounddogs.com (http://www.sounddogs.com)

SoundSnap (http://www.soundsnap.com)

Index

A

B

C

D

G

H

I

J–K

L

Q–R

S

T

X–Z

COURSE TECHNOLOGY
CENGAGE Learning™
Professional • Technical • Reference

SHARPEN YOUR SKILLS, RELEASE YOUR SOUND
with these learning resources from Course Technology PTR

The Studio Business Book, Third Edition
ISBN: 1-59200-747-3 ■ **$34.99**

The Tour Book:
How to Get Your Music on the Road
ISBN: 1-59863-371-6 ■ **$29.99**

Cash Tracks: Compose, Produce, and Sell Your Original Soundtrack Music and Jingles
ISBN: 1-59200-741-4 ■ **$24.99**

The Mastering Engineer's Handbook, Second Edition:
The Audio Mastering Handbook
ISBN: 1-59863-449-6 ■ **$34.99**

The Art of Mixing:
A Visual Guide to Recording, Engineering, and Production, Second Edition
ISBN: 1-93114-045-6 ■ **$49.99**

Live Sound Reinforcement, Bestseller Edition:
A Comprehensive Guide to P.A. and Music Reinforcement Systems and Technology
ISBN: 1-59200-691-4 ■ **$49.99**

Ruthless Self-Promotion in the Music Industry, Second Edition
ISBN: 1-59200-745-7 ■ **$24.99**

Course Technology PTR also publishes a complete offering of books, interactive CD-ROMs, and DVDs on music technology applications.

With various levels of instruction on leading software—

Pro Tools ■ SONAR ■ Home Studio ■ Cubase SX/SL ■ Nuendo ■ ACID
Sound Forge ■ Reason ■ Ableton Live ■ Logic ■ Digital Performer
GarageBand ■ Traktor DJ Studio ■ Soundtrack ■ and many more—

you are sure to find what you're looking for.

Visit our Web site for more information and **FREE** sample chapters.
To order, call **1.800.648.7450** or order online at **www.courseptr.com**

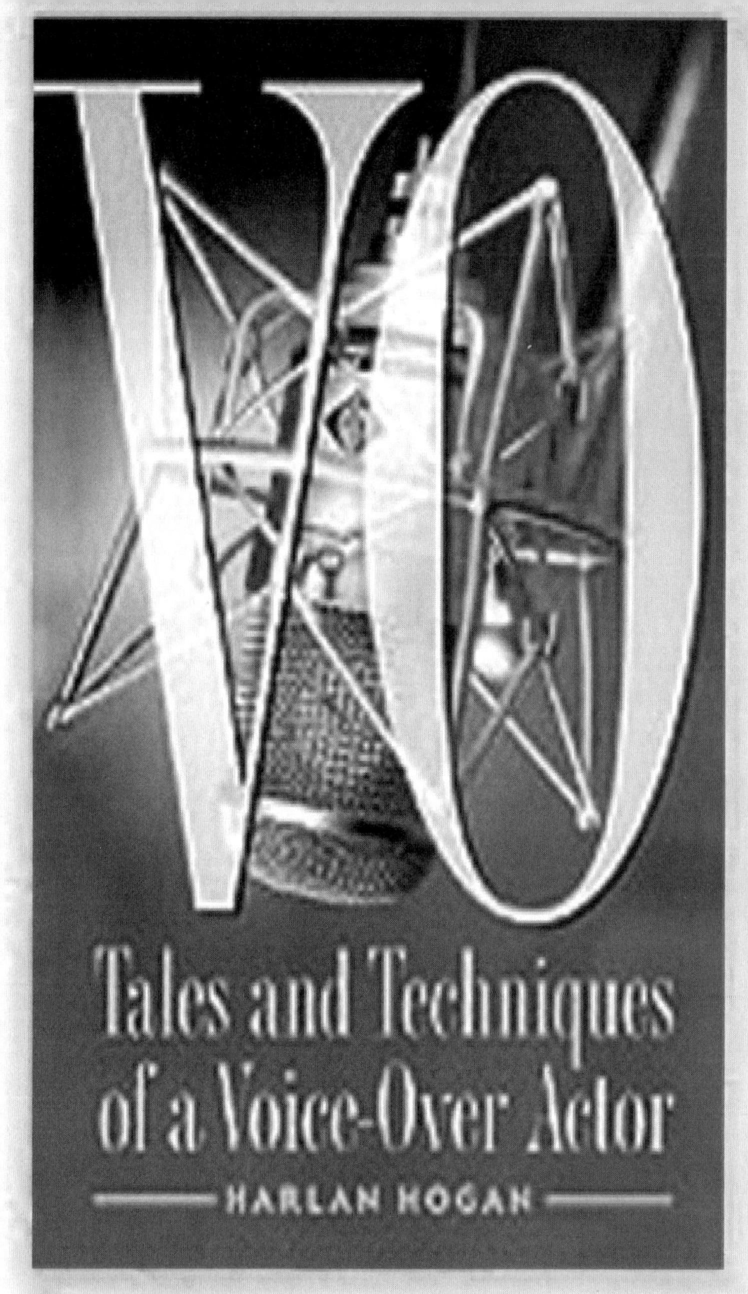

VO: Tales and Techniques of a Voice-Over Act

One of the country's top voice-over talents shares his secr
to success in this insider's guide to the voice-over industr

ISBN 1-58115-249-3 ■ $19.95